Greg Growden is one of Australia's leading sports journalists. For more than three decades he was a senior sportswriter with *The Sydney Morning Herald*. He spent many summers sitting next to Bill O'Reilly, covering Sheffield Shield and Test cricket for the *SMH*, before becoming in 1986 the newspaper's chief rugby union writer.

He was the *SMH* and *Sun-Herald*'s chief rugby union correspondent between 1987 and 2012, but has always retained a strong cricket interest.

Between 2012 and 2018, he left the *SMH* to become the Australian rugby correspondent for ESPN. In February, 2019, he returned to the *SMH* as a sporting columnist.

This is his fourth cricket-related book.

OTHER BOOKS BY GREG GROWDEN

The Wallabies' World Cup! (with Spiro Zavos, Simon Poidevin and Evan Whitton)
A Wayward Genius: The Fleetwood-Smith Story
With the Wallabies
Gold, Mud and Guts: The Incredible Tom Richards – Footballer, War Hero, Olympian
Rugby Union for Dummies
The Snowy Baker Story
My Sporting Hero (editor)
It's Not Just a Bloody Game! Timeless Rugby Union Stories
Jack Fingleton: The Man Who Stood Up to Bradman
Inside the Wallabies: The Real Story – the Players, the Politics, the Games from 1908 to Today
More Important than Life or Death: Inside the Best of Australian Sport (co-editor with Peter FitzSimons)
Wallaby Warrior: The World War I War Diaries of [Tom Richards] Australia's only British Lion (editor)
Bowled by a Bullet: The Tragic Life of Claude Tozer
The Wrong 'Un: The Brad Hogg Story (with Brad Hogg)
The Wallabies at War

CRICKETERS AT WAR

GREG GROWDEN

ABC BOOKS

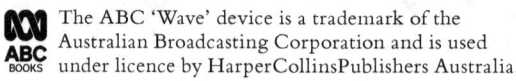 The ABC 'Wave' device is a trademark of the Australian Broadcasting Corporation and is used under licence by HarperCollinsPublishers Australia.

First published in Australia in 2019
by HarperCollins*Publishers* Australia Pty Limited
ABN 36 009 913 517
harpercollins.com.au

Copyright © Greg Growden and Associates Pty Limited 2019

The right of Greg Growden to be identified as the author of this work has been asserted by him in accordance with the *Copyright Amendment (Moral Rights) Act 2000*.

This work is copyright. Apart from any use as permitted under the *Copyright Act 1968*, no part may be reproduced, copied, scanned, stored in a retrieval system, recorded, or transmitted, in any form or by any means, without the prior written permission of the publisher.

HarperCollins*Publishers*
Level 13, 201 Elizabeth Street, Sydney NSW 2000, Australia
Unit D1, 63 Apollo Drive, Rosedale, Auckland 0632, New Zealand
A 53, Sector 57, Noida, UP, India
1 London Bridge Street, London, SE1 9GF, United Kingdom
Bay Adelaide Centre, East Tower, 22 Adelaide Street West, 41st floor, Toronto, Ontario M5H 4E3, Canada
195 Broadway, New York NY 10007, USA

A catalogue record for this book is available from the National Library of Australia

ISBN 978 0 7333 3992 9 (pbk)
ISBN 978 1 4607 1114 9 (ebook)

Cover design by Hazel Lam, HarperCollins Design Studio
Cover images: Cricketer Keith Miller, 1950 / photographer Max Dupain courtesy Mitchell Library, State Library of New South Wales (FL1712516); Poster courtesy AWM (ARTV05206)
Typeset in Bembo Std by Kirby Jones
Index by Garry Cousins Indexing

CONTENTS

Introduction   1

PART ONE — BOER WAR
1   J.J. Ferris   11

PART TWO — FIRST WORLD WAR
2   International and Suburban Murder   27
3   No Trace   47
4   C.E.W. Bean and That Photo …   57
5   Whereabouts Unknown   65
6   The Big 'What If'   77
7   Cricket's VC   87
8   Tibby   96
9   The AIF Team   112

PART THREE — SECOND WORLD WAR
10   Barney, Ross and the Greatest Ever   141
11   Our Country's Keepers   164
12   Women at War   181
13   For Club and Country   200
14   Bradman and Beyond   209
15   The Secret War   228
16   The Australian Services Team   240
17   The Most Testing of Tours   256
18   The Aftermath   281

PART FOUR — VIETNAM WAR
19   Tony Dell   293

Epilogue   305
Bibliography   310
Index   318

INTRODUCTION

For many, it is not just their favourite cricket quotation. It is their favourite quote of all, helped along in being uttered by their favourite sportsman.

The quote bobs up somewhere every year.

Ron Barassi, among AFL football's most important individuals, was recently asked who his sporting hero was. Easy. Keith Ross Miller.

'I remember talking to him, many years after the Second World War, and asking him about the pressure of playing cricket at the top level,' said Barassi, another who knew all about pressure as a successful player and coach. 'Keith replied: "Pressure, mate. In cricket? You've got to be kidding. Pressure is turning around and seeing a Messerschmitt flying up your arse!"'

Miller often used that Messerschmitt line in newspaper, radio and television interviews. There were slightly different versions. The most common was: 'Pressure? Pressure is having a Messerschmitt up your arse!' When he died in 2004, the Messerschmitt quote was used in virtually every Miller tribute. For one of Australia's most admired cricketers, it became his catch-cry.

While placing the life of an often over-inflated elite sportsman into some sort of perspective, the quotation also reminded all of Miller's and numerous other cricketers' intense links with war.

Miller is one of Australian cricket's most charismatic characters. The aura remains. It wasn't just his vast sporting skills, which included not just his immense all-round cricketing abilities but also his prowess as an Australian Rules footballer, that made him such an attractive figure. It was the way he embraced life. There was always a touch of the Australian larrikin about him. He loved a drink. He loved a party. He loved his mates. He had no qualms appearing just before the start of play wearing a dinner suit, somewhat muddled by a long night of revelling — but as soon as he was required he would be ready for the contest. He attracted glamour. Princess Margaret swooned every time he was in the vicinity. The Princess pursued him.

Miller's wartime experience enhanced that persona. He was a dashing, debonair and accident-prone Second World War fighter pilot who was occasionally let loose over Europe. A warrior who had a touch of the mug lair, Miller was often in trouble with officialdom as he couldn't avoid the occasional near miss, through a sometimes reckless approach to piloting a plane. Miller abhorred hypocrisy, authority, and especially incompetents who cunningly used their position of power to avoid responsibility. The English class system particularly irritated him.

In 1945, Miller and a mate were on their way back to an English air base following several days of leave. As they walked along the tight village track, an RAF official sedan drew up next to them. A pompous British twit called from the back seat: 'Officers, take your hands out of your pockets immediately!'

Miller peered inside. 'Get stuffed.'

The vehicle took off. His mate was quivering, as he knew the twit was 'at least a vice-marshal, judging from the gold braid around the peak of his cap'.

Miller replied: 'Yes … and a shiny arse, I'll bet.'

But those war years deeply affected Miller. He would get emotional whenever talking about lost colleagues, who included countless close friends who had displayed incredible courage. He had little interest in talking about his own exploits. He instead did all he could to praise others' wartime exploits. He wasn't alone in being scarred by the experience.

Countless Australian cricketers were shaken to the core by their involvement in battle. The Great War, Second World War and Vietnam War ruined many flourishing cricketing careers, but also enhanced some. Some found themselves entangled in a relentless recruitment propaganda campaign. Others were portrayed as national heroes — being used to reinforce the message that if they're defending the country then why not you? Some were abused by the system. Cricket authorities at the beginning of both world conflicts debated over whether they should be completely committed to the war effort, or be providing an alternative for those who weren't serving. Whether to continue playing cricket or not during wartime became an emotional argument. Friendships, alliances were affected. Religion, patriotic beliefs, allegiance to the Empire all played a part, and often created divides.

The majority were sucked in by the nationalistic push, as portrayed by J.C. Davis, the editor of Sydney's weekly sporting newspaper, *The Referee*, in a piece glorying 'great sportsmen who died while on active service'. Davis's article began: 'The national call to arms sounded in August, 1914. The men were volunteers from the first to the final contingent. The early contingents, marching through Sydney, and down what is now known as Haig Avenue, to the troopships at Woolloomooloo Bay, were the finest body of men I ever saw. Tall, six-footers to a man, one thought. Square-shouldered, deep-chested, well-groomed. They marched like gods of war.'

Many became ghosts, though, even if Davis stressed that those men involved in the first wave at Gallipoli on 25 April 1915 were 'brothers-in-arms, as they were brothers in sport ... they leapt from the boats with the instincts of free men, hardened by their field sports'.

Not all of those hardened by their field sports came back.

Australia lost many important, vibrant sportsmen, in particular cricketers, on the battlefield. In the Great War, 15 Australian first-class players were killed, including one Test representative —

Tibby Cotter. Others, like Norman Callaway, would have almost certainly represented Australia if they had survived the war. Overall, counting all nations, 12 Test cricketers and more than 250 first-class players perished.

In the Second World War, it was a similar Australian equation: 12 first-class players, including one Test representative — Ross Gregory. This time, overall, nine Test players and more than 150 first-class players were killed.

Among the male and female cricketing ranks sent to battle were fearless frontline soldiers, leaders of distinction, those who suffered badly in prisoner-of-war camps in Europe and Asia. Many experienced years of torture, but rose above it all to provide support to comrades worse off than them. Others were involved in secret, dangerous missions deep behind enemy lines. Some defied constant pain by refusing to have limbs amputated because their dream was of returning to the cricket fields as soon as this nightmare ended, and they achieved that dream. There were shirkers, reprobates, deserters, conmen, those who used the system. Some simply disappeared, their bodies never found, one even murdered, while the deaths of several notable Australian cricketers were mysterious, even sinister. Those who survived often wouldn't talk about it, and some cricket careers were later badly affected by mental breakdowns caused by frontline stress. All were unable to forget the war. There were mighty fighter pilots, courageous men willing to charge any trench, fearless stretcher-bearers, commanders and workers. Some took on the enemy alone. The cricketing ranks had them all.

It also affected those who didn't make it to the frontline. Closely ranked with Miller as Australia's most popular postwar cricketer is Doug Walters. He was another who seemed to be one of us. A knockabout from the bush who played cricket with abandon — an aggressive, adventurous middle-order batsman and efficient medium-pace bowler renowned for breaking dangerous partnerships — he loved a drink and a durry. He had first made his name in November 1962 as a 16-year-old who had been beckoned from a dairy farm near Dungog as a late NSW Colts replacement to play Queensland Colts. In his first serious cricket appearance, Walters's feat generated headlines.

Playing on the SCG No 2 ground, Walters pulled one short delivery over the high back wall, across Driver Avenue and into nearby Kippax Lake. *Sydney Morning Herald* journalist Jim Webster, sniffing a good story, sprinted off in pursuit of the ball. Webster found the battered four-stitcher on the side of the lake.

'I took it back to the ground. They gave it a bit of a clean and continued playing with it,' Webster said in an interview with the author. The *SMH* headline the next morning was 'Sixer ends up in lake'.

Walters scored an unbeaten 140, accompanied by another bush cricketer, John Watkins, who finished with 94 following a 172-run seventh-wicket partnership. This was the same John Watkins who suffered through the most dreadful of one-off Tests a decade later when he couldn't land his leg-spinners on the SCG pitch. He sprayed the ball all ways in his six overs, which included three wides. Umpire Tom Brooks admitted he was lenient 'and could have called him for more than I did'.

The decidedly more accurate Walters was playing first-class cricket for NSW just eight days after his 17th birthday, and when 19 made a Test century on debut against Mike Smith's 1965–66 England team at the Gabba, followed by a second ton in the next Test.

The following year there was a major disruption. His birthdate number came out of the barrel. He was conscripted into the army for two years' National Service. Walters was suddenly a nasho — facing the serious prospect of heading to Vietnam.

His Test cricket career had to be put on hold. He tried to get out of the draft, as being a nasho would mean missing the 1966–67 Australian tour of South Africa. He appeared before the army doctor, who asked him if he had any ailments.

Walters explained he had suffered from mumps, hepatitis and chicken pox, and believed he had flat feet.

As explained in *The Doug Walters Story*, the 75-year-old doctor drew breath, peered over his thick glasses and said: 'I've seen every game at the Sydney Cricket Ground since 1901. You're fit enough for me.' Walters walked out the door, classified medically fit and was 'in the Army'.

The calling-up of Walters among other 20-year-olds appeared suspicious amid the growing backlash towards anything involving Vietnam — Walters was among Australia's most popular young sportsmen, and it was assumed his call-up could lure others to sign up.

Adding to the suspicion that specific notable young identities had been targeted was that Normie Rowe, the country's singing heart-throb, was also on the list. The authorities relentlessly promoted the fact that Walters and Rowe — among the most recognisable faces in the nation — were now in the armed forces. Their photographs decked out in army gear or at camp or in training were constantly splashed in newspapers, or in television news footage. It all appeared a bit staged, but reinforced the fact stressed by the government and military that, while cricket was important, Australia's armed forces were even more so.

Walters took it all very seriously and refused to complain about how he was treated, even though admitting to finding out many years later that there were countless people born on exactly the same day as him who weren't called up.

He made it known when joining up that he didn't want preferential treatment. 'I just want to be like all the other fellows going in. If I get to Vietnam, well, I will go — there'll be no trouble,' Walters told *The Sun*.

Walters was involved in National Service from April 1966 to April 1968, flitting between camps at Wagga Wagga, Singleton and Holsworthy, near Liverpool in NSW. While at Holsworthy, he was a batman to future deputy prime minister Tim Fischer, who thought it ridiculous 'a farmer from Boree Creek is being brought a cup of tea by someone in the Australian XI'. This was interspersed with jungle training in Rockhampton. Walters saved up sufficient leave time to enable him to play enough cricket during those two years to keep his eye in.

But, like Miller, he looked down on those who, intoxicated by power, lost their bearings. While in Wagga, a strutting platoon leader made his life horrible, explaining that he would not be getting any preferential treatment because he was a Test player, and would instead force him to do every dreadful job around the camp. The strutter later became aide-de-camp to NSW Governor and Victoria Cross winner Sir Roden Cutler.

Walters scored a century at the SCG some years later, and Sir Roden, a sports enthusiast, headed to the dressing rooms to congratulate him. They gladly greeted each other. Behind Sir Roden, Walters could see the Wagga pest, who thrust his hand towards Walters.

According to his biographer Ashley Mallett, Walters ignored it, telling the aide-de-camp to 'get stuffed'.

Some days later, Sir Roden told Walters he'd sacked him.

Walters was discharged before being required to go to Vietnam, and instead of experiencing a gruesome, futile war was able to re-establish himself in the Australian team. But it was a close call. At the end of his term, an officer called him into his office to convince him to sign for another six months and so head to Vietnam. The officer argued that serving in Vietnam would be better for his image than being part of the Australian Ashes tour of England in 1968.

Walters declined the offer, stating that, unlike the army, the Australian Board of Control[1] was guaranteeing a return overseas ticket. Eleven days after leaving the army, Walters was on his way to England with Bill Lawry, Ian Chappell and co.

Then there is Walters's Test teammate Tony Dell. This gigantic Queensland pace bowler wasn't so lucky. Before playing his first Test for Australia, accompanying Walters on the field at the SCG to take on Ray Illingworth's feisty England outfit in 1971, Dell had served for ten months in Vietnam. Many cricket followers were unaware of Dell's Vietnam involvement, including that he was involved in several dreadful frontline experiences.

---

1 The Australian Board of Control for International Cricket became the Australian Cricket Board in 1973, and from 2003 has been Cricket Australia.

He witnessed war at its most brutal. He also wasn't encouraged on return to discuss what had happened in battle. It was recommended to him not to talk about his Vietnam experiences. That didn't help. He had to bottle it all up. 'It was as if I had gone to the shops … and suddenly returned,' Dell said.

To this day, war is a constant, hovering dark cloud for Dell. The nightmares don't go away, and how he copes with that is inspiring.

As *Cricketers at War* details, Dell is the latest in a long line of notable Australian cricketers who have fought hard to not let their wartime involvement get the better of them. War is hell. But they are doing whatever they can to counter it.

Their life stories, which include some who did not rise to the top levels of the game but were important figures at either club or district level, involve every emotion. Some are sad. Some funny. Some frightening. Some silly. Some show boundless courage and belief. Some sound as if they have been made up. Some are too crazy to have been made up. Some will astound. Others display the importance of camaraderie, and mental and physical resolve. All deserve to be publicly told — often for the first time.

There remains one important constant: the human spirit can conquer all.

PART ONE

BOER WAR

CHAPTER 1

J.J. FERRIS

Tucked away in a snippets column on page 13 of a newspaper on the other side of the world was an unusual but revealing item.

The paragraph in *The Singapore Free Press and Mercantile Advertiser* on 10 January 1901 read: 'The circumstances of the death of Mr J.J. Ferris, the famous Australian bowler and subsequently member of the Gloucestershire Eleven, were peculiar. He had come to Durban, from the "front" on furlough, and boarded a tramcar. He appeared to be in good health and was observed to be reading a newspaper, when he suddenly fell as though in a fit. Mr Ferris was removed to Hospital in an unconscious condition and never rallied. He had been serving in Brabant's Horse.'[1]

In those times newspapers played it straight, not questioning how someone had died.

The mention of 'peculiar' circumstances suggested there was more to Ferris's passing than suddenly collapsing on a tram. Had this impoverished individual been poisoned? Had he taken the drastic step of deciding to kill himself? Or had he suffered a stroke?

The official line was that Ferris had died of enteric fever (typhoid) — a line taken up by numerous newspapers and still used today to explain his early demise, at age 33. Others said simply

---
1   Brabant's Horse was a light horse regiment, headed by Major-General Sir Edward Brabant, which included South African colonials, British, Canadians and Australians.

this special sportsman 'had died suddenly', which in newspaper parlance has long been a way of hinting someone had committed suicide. Still, enteric fever doesn't usually see someone suddenly collapse on a tram but instead suffer a slow bed-ridden death.

All very strange. Then again, J.J. Ferris's life had for some time been peculiar. His was a case of a flourishing life that had fallen away dramatically. An idol had become idle. Going from top to bottom in a few years could have easily prompted drastic action in his final days during the Second Boer War. As Max Bonnell explains in his exemplary biography on Ferris, serious questions remain about what exactly happened to Australian cricket's first major wartime victim. Why it needs to be probed is that John James Ferris remains one of this country's most intriguing cricketers, one of only five Australians to have played Test cricket for more than one country.[2]

In his prime, Ferris was rated international cricket's best left-handed medium-pace bowler and notable finger spinner. His combination with Charlie Turner was among the most devastating Australia had ever fielded. He was unpredictable, mixing up pace with an ability to spin it both ways. His action was something else. England cricketing royalty C.B. Fry described it as 'complex'.

A strange, one-of-a-kind action, which involved repeated swinging of his arms, clearly worked, as Ferris finished with 61 Test wickets at 12.70 and 812 first-class wickets at 17.54.

His origins were also one of a kind. No other international cricketer could boast they were born at a water police station. His father, Thomas, was a Sydney water policeman, based in Phillip Street near Circular Quay. The eighth of 11 children, J.J. was born on 21 May 1867 at the family home, part of a sprawling police station that included a courtroom and numerous gaol cells. Father Thomas, a well-known sub-inspector, was a hard, demanding prosecutor in the busy courtroom next door, which catered for a

---

2 The other four are Billy Midwinter, Billy Murdoch, Sammy Woods and Albert Trott, all of whom like Ferris played Test cricket for Australia and England. The South African-born Kepler Wessels played for Australia and then South Africa in the 1980s and '90s.

long line of miscreants who made the Quay area one of the most violent spots in the colony. When J.J. was ten, his father had a fit at home, muttered a few words, and died shortly after of 'heart failure'.

In spite of his mother bringing up her children alone, J.J. was schooled at Fort Street Model School and then St Kilda House in Woolloomooloo. It was there that Ferris discovered the joys of competitive cricket. After school he joined the Eastern Suburbs club and then Belvidere, where in his first five senior matches he took 32 wickets. Soon the NSW and Australian selectors were hovering around this stout figure with a dapper moustache who was described in the Sydney press as 'quiet and unassuming'. In town in late 1886 was Alfred Shaw's touring England team, and with NSW missing three leading players — Tom Garrett, Ted Evans and Sammy Jones — Ferris opened the bowling at the SCG while still a teenager. He excelled in both innings, with 4/50 and 3/49 respectively. Charlie Turner and Ferris finished with all 20 England wickets between them in the six-wicket victory.

This was the beginning of a four-year period where Ferris and Turner, a quicker bowler than his partner, who upset countless batsmen with an accurate off-cutter, took charge of the Australian cricket scene. While Turner became known as 'Terror' Turner, Ferris had the nickname of 'The Tricky'. In two months, the pair were fully fledged Test players, taking 17 of the 20 England wickets in their first international, again at the SCG. Fred Spofforth, bowling first change, took a solitary wicket in the second innings.

The following season, Ferris was as adept in England, revelling in the overloaded itinerary — playing all of the 40 tour matches, he finished with 220 wickets. In the first-class matches, Ferris bowled 8321 balls for 199 wickets at 14.74.

He was back in England two years later with the Australian side led by Billy Murdoch and managed by Harry Boyle, which had its flaws, including a backup wicketkeeper, Kenny Burn, who admitted several days into the sea cruise that he had never been behind the stumps before. Not surprisingly, the team struggled, but Turner and Ferris remained prominent.

Ferris's interest in Australian cricket had begun to wane and, eager to become a professional, he was easily enticed by an offer from W.G. Grace to join the England county club Gloucestershire. The other lure was the strong possibility of appearing for England. He left with the good will of the NSW Cricket Association (NSWCA), which presented him with a gold chronometer at a presentation in the SCG Members Stand. Former NSW captain Joe Coates told the gathering 'the names of Turner and Ferris have become household words'.

It did not take long for Ferris to receive an offer to play for England, and he headed to South Africa in 1891–92, where on the way over he finished second in the ship's skipping competition. Now he was England's standout on a difficult and exasperating tour in which the team constantly criss-crossed a desolate country, playing endless matches against opponents of varying ability. One trip involved a five-day coach ride. Accommodation was rudimentary. One night Ferris shared a room in a farmhouse with fellow Australian Billy Murdoch. There was only one bed, and Murdoch tested it out. The mattress collapsed, and Murdoch's head 'became stuck in the ironwork'. 'It was quite a work of art to pop him out again, and it was an even greater work of art to prop up the bed in such a way that we could use it,' Ferris said in an interview with *The Cricket Field*.

Despite the many touring trials and tribulations, Ferris somehow kept his composure, taking more than 230 tour wickets, while being the star bowler with 13/91 in the one-off international against South Africa at Newlands in Cape Town. These admirable figures would have been better if an England fielder had been more competent. While Ferris was bowling, one-time Kent batsman Victor Barton twice missed shots that rolled between his legs, and dropped at least one easy catch. Ferris's effort remains a record for the most wickets taken by a player in their first England Test.

Then it all dried up.

It was assumed that in the following season back in England, Ferris, now qualified to play county cricket, would be the spearhead of Gloucestershire's campaign. Instead he took a mere 46 county wickets at 28. As *Wisden Cricketers' Almanack* put it, Gloucestershire's 'repeated failures ... caused great disappointment among the supporters of the club'. Ferris's first county cricket season was 'singularly unsuccessful'. He took the most wickets of any of the county's bowlers but 'was terribly expensive'.

He could not replicate what he had done in two tours with Australian teams in England, prompting critics to state he was nothing without 'The Terror' at the other end.

Ferris's bowling continued to deteriorate over the next few seasons. He no longer mystified batsmen. Many blamed over-bowling on the South African tour for him losing his way. As E.H.M. Baillie wrote in *The Sporting Globe* after that trip, 'Ferris completely lost his bowling ability and was practically useless in this department of the game. On the other hand, he developed his batting.'

In 1895 there was no alternative but to return to Australia, as his five-year term with Gloucestershire was over, and there was absolutely no interest from anyone to take him on. Ferris was a demoralised soul when he arrived in Melbourne on the RMS *Oceania*, especially with *Wisden* giving him a blunt send-off, describing his time with Gloucestershire as 'an utter failure'. In his final season with the county, he 'lost his pace, his spin, his action, and everything'.

Back in Australia, distressed to be labelled a flop, Ferris bobbed up here, there and everywhere. He was sighted watching a minor Melbourne club match. He then inquired if NSW wanted to pick him. He was passed by, because the state selectors had not seen him for years. He travelled Victoria and Tasmania with a private cricket team. He appeared for South Australia against Victoria at the Melbourne Cricket Ground in February 1896, out first ball and bowling only one over. He then moved to Sydney in hope of regular employment. That was difficult, and soon Ferris, restricted to club cricket, was broke. In 1897 he appeared for Burwood, but according to *The Cumberland Argus and Fruitgrowers' Advocate* 'was not the Ferris of old, and much relished by the batsmen'.

Ferris was given one last chance. NSW was short of players for a December trip to Melbourne. He was used as an opening batsman, scoring four and seven, and a second change bowler, taking two middle-order wickets as part of a losing outfit. The following week in Adelaide, his bowling was not required, but as a lower-order batsman he was NSW's top scorer with a first innings half-century. Then it was back to club cricket. With no trade to fall back upon, and his athletic skills waning, he kept moving, even spending some time in a lonely hotel room in the Sydney suburb of Rockdale.

He again believed heading overseas may provide a solution. He knew of numerous Australians heading to South Africa and reaping its riches, especially in the gold and diamond fields near Johannesburg. Intrigued by what he had witnessed while with the England touring party, he thought this new frontier would provide broader employment options. After all, his name still meant something in South Africa, and if everything else failed maybe he could eke out some sort of living playing cricket.

However, when Ferris arrived in Cape Town in February 1899, he discovered a country distracted and divided by looming conflict. The ever-expanding British Empire for some time had had its gaze firmly fixed on Southern Africa, especially its gold and diamond riches.

These rampant imperialists also wanted to be in charge of the southern cape region, so they could control the rich sea trade routes to India. The Boers were similarly belligerent, realising the country's rural qualities. Infuriated by the British intrusion, in particular its abolition of native slavery, thousands of Boers embarked on The Great Trek, heading east from Cape Town and then northwards to resettle in what they assumed would be lush pastures. The Boers, who had relied on slavery for cheap labour, established two republics — the Orange Free State and the South African Republic (known as the Transvaal Republic). This led to the First Boer War in 1880–81, when Britain attempted to annex the Transvaal. The Boers reacted, outfought the British, and won. The independence of the two republics was restored, but each side remained extremely wary of the other's motives.

The discovery of diamonds in Kimberley in 1866 saw the Orange Free State become the number one destination for thousands of immigrants — including numerous British — wanting to strike it rich. A gold-strike in the Witwatersrand mountain ridge led to thousands of uitlanders (foreigners) swarm the Transvaal in search of immediate wealth. The once-poor Transvaal was now among the richest regions in the world. The British attempted to intervene in the Orange Free State and Transvaal by demanding voting rights for the uitlanders, but the Boers continued to stand up to them.

In October 1899 the Boers went onto the front foot, issuing an ultimatum that, within 48 hours, the British had to withdraw all troops from the two provinces. The ultimatum was ignored, prompting Boer commandos to launch raids on British troops in the Cape and Natal on 11 October 1899. The Second Boer War had begun.

Although numerous newspapers claimed Ferris had gone to South Africa to fight for the Empire, that was not the case. When he left Australia there was growing tension but no certainty a war would erupt.

Nonetheless, it didn't take long for Ferris to sign up with the South African Light Horse in late 1899. Apart from defending the Empire, it provided him with a much-needed wage.

There is little detail about what Ferris did with the Light Horse, which was under the command of Colonel Julian 'Bingo' Byng, a fearless leader Mentioned in Despatches five times. Australia learnt in February 1900 that Ferris was now a soldier through a brief paragraph in the *Western Mail* in Perth. It read: 'The London Sportsman states that J.J. Ferris, the Australian cricketer, who also played for Gloucestershire for two or three seasons, is in Natal with Gen. Buller's force. He is a trooper in Col. Byng's South African Light Horse.'

After a few months Ferris transferred to Brabant's Horse, which was comprised of mounted volunteers. But he became agitated when it was suggested he had joined the Boers. A New Zealand magazine, *The Free Lance*, wrote that Ferris had been upset by a report in the *Auckland Weekly News* which said: 'Mr Percy MacMillan, formerly of Whangarei, tells me he was surprised and shocked to meet Mr Ferris, the famous cricketer, once of NSW, and later of Gloucestershire, in the Boer ranks and fighting against England. An Aucklander who is serving in Brabant's Horse, has sent the item back with a request that it may be positively contradicted. He says: "Ferris belongs to K Squad, 2nd Brabant's Horse, and is fighting for England, not against her." He is very wild about this untruthful par and says for two pings would have [the newspaper's publisher] Wilson and Horton up for libel.'

Around October 1900, Ferris was discharged for unknown reasons. His biographer, Bonnell, suggests it was for dubious reasons, citing a document he had discovered which stated that an application had been made for the Queen's South Africa Medal for Ferris. 'But in the last column of the document, under "Remarks" are the words: "Discharged. Ignominy",' Bonnell writes. 'All we know for certain is that his service ended badly, probably on or about 15 October 1900, and that by the middle of November, he had returned to civilian life in Durban.'

It was clear civilian life was tough, as he died penniless. After collapsing on the tram, in the words of *The Natal Mercury*, 'where he suddenly fell, as though in a fit', Ferris was taken to Addington Hospital 'in an unconscious condition, and he never rallied'.

It was only the intervention of a Melbourne businessman in Durban at the time of his death that stopped Ferris from being buried in a pauper's grave. Even though a Catholic, he was buried in the local Church of England cemetery.

Ferris wasn't entirely forgotten. Vic Richardson's 1935–36 Australian team and one-time Test cricketer and now travelling scribe, Arthur Mailey, placed a wreath on his grave. 'The Terror' never quite got over his partner's sad demise. During the Fifth 'Bodyline' Test in Sydney in February 1933, a *Sydney Morning Herald* reporter found Turner in the Member's Bar. 'Turner now lives at Manly, but every Test, apart from other matches, sees him at the Cricket Ground,' the *SMH* said. 'He was there for the present Test. Anyone who knew him would have observed him perform a solemn rite to the memory of his old partner. "I must have a drink with Jack Ferris," he said, as he had said many a time before, and so he went to the end of the bar and there drank in silence to the memory of the man he knew and loved more than 30 years ago.'

The Boer War experiences of the other notable Australian cricketing identity on the veldt at the time are far more comprehensively chronicled. The Boer War attracted its fair share of transients, mercenaries, deviants, fortune-hunters and thrill-seekers. It lured numerous literary figures, including Rudyard Kipling, Banjo Paterson, Dr Arthur Conan Doyle, Richard Harding Davis, Edgar Wallace and Winston Churchill, many of whom worked as newspaper correspondents. Countless writers rushed to Southern Africa, realising the news and self-promotional value of observing the Empire showing its might. Adding to the allure was that the scuffle was expected to be over in a few weeks. After all, it was skilled soldiers up against backward farmers. Colourful, brave-heart writing was inevitable.

The first Australian correspondent to arrive in South Africa was the Melbourne *Argus*'s Donald Macdonald. At the time, Macdonald was one of the country's most versatile, authoritative and trendsetting journalists, having transformed the way cricket and VFL football was covered in Australia.

As 'Observer' for *The Argus*, Macdonald covered Test cricket for many decades, and over a 40-year period repeatedly travelled overseas with Australian sides. Unlike numerous sporting writers of his time, who would provide a dull, ball-by-ball report, Macdonald provided insight, colour and comment, as well as being evocative. Macdonald thought the traditional cricket writing style was 'a lifeless way of doing things', instead believing it important to give 'a clear idea of how the match was played without tiresome detail'. He was prolific, and could write on any subject, making him *The Argus*'s number one scribe — and the country's most authoritative cricket correspondent.

He was a Ferris fan. At the start of the 1888 season, Macdonald wrote that he was praying a struggling Victoria team would at last improve its act and that someone of note would appear at their trial matches. 'There is always hope of finding a Turner or Ferris, if not a Murdoch in such a match.' Two years later, Macdonald wrote: 'Turner and Ferris were an almost necessary pair to any Australian team which is to be successful.'

This tall, skinny Victorian farmer's son was as fascinated by nature, agriculture and military matters as he was by cricket, which made him the obvious choice to head to South Africa in October 1899. Macdonald arrived in Cape Town on 21 October — the same day 3000 soldiers under Major-General John French attempted to clear 800 Boers from Elandslaagte (Elands Dale) station on the trainline to the Transvaal. The British won the early skirmishes, but the Boers rallied, succeeding in getting the enemy to withdraw to Ladysmith, where they surrounded them on all sides. For 118 days the British troops were stuck in Ladysmith, with Macdonald arriving at the last minute to experience the siege. He described himself as 'an Australian novice', ignorant of war, but after some months he had experienced many of the ills of battle, including endless shell-fire, and had almost died from various fevers. It proved an infuriating time as, while he wrote countless extensive reports from Ladysmith, they went nowhere — due to the siege, the articles could not be telegrammed back to Melbourne. Eventually his despatches got through — on the same boat which brought a desperately ill Macdonald home after the siege ended in late February 1900. His efforts were not wasted, however, as a country which vigorously celebrated the end of the Ladysmith siege, when General Buller finally broke through the Boer positions, delighted in his reports when printed some months later in *The Argus*. They were collected in book form, titled *How We Kept the Flag Flying*, and it became a bestseller in Australia and England, making Macdonald a recognised Boer War authority.

In the book were cricket references, including a match involving the Imperial Light Horse organised to while away the boredom, 'in accordance with the traditions of other campaigns, for whenever British armies are in a really serious fix they bluff it on the national affection for sport'.

When the siege went into its 101st day, 'one of the enemy on Bulwan, who was evidently familiar with England's national game, called up the signallers at Caesar's Camp, and flashed the curt message, "101 not out" ... The Manchesters were equal to the little pleasantry, and replied "Ladysmith still batting".'

The Australian devotion to sport puzzled the Boers, as it has puzzled many others. 'What is the use of shelling them?' said a weary Boer artilleryman. 'They just go on playing cricket.' 'It was the Armada and the game of bowls all over again.' The cricket lasted only a short while.

'No sooner had we acknowledged their cricket message than Long Tom[3] opened on our naval 12 pounders at Caesar's Hill, and his first shot just missed the gun-trail and threw about half-a-ton of earth over the shell-backs. "They've put on a new bowler," remarked the gunnery lieutenant.'

In *How We Kept the Flag Flying*, Macdonald struggled to comprehend the Boer — 'a strange mixture of Christian fervour and pure brutality. On the one day he is a stern Sabbatarian; on the next he will relax sufficiently to schambok[4] an offending Kaffir to death without a qualm. As a fighter, he prefers to see the back rather than the face of his enemy.'

The surrounds also made his homesick. 'For its best shelter during this trying time, Ladysmith was indebted to Australia. Standing on a point above the town one noticed squares of trees that far overtop the camel thorn, syringa, umtola and carob bean which grow locally. They were Australian gums, most of them filled with the swinging-cot nests of the weaver bird and sheltering also hundreds of the volunteer tents.'

Macdonald was playing his illness down. He was desperately ill with dysentery, losing three-and-a-half stone in weight. On several occasions he was close to death, but he was able to get back to

---

3 Long Tom was a gun used by the Boers.
4 An African leather whip.

Australia to 'recuperate in a more genial climate'. His last few days in South Africa were in 'comfortable quarters' near the Newlands cricket ground, in the shadow of Cape Town's Table Mountain. 'A pleasanter spot in which to rest and recruit, after the horrors of the Ladysmith siege, could not well be found in all Africa.'

It didn't take too long to bounce back. Several weeks after returning, he drew a capacity crowd to the Melbourne Town Hall to hear him speak on his African adventures, before embarking on a year-long lecture tour through Australia, New Zealand and Great Britain. Then back to the typewriter. While giving away football writing, as wet, cold weather while covering the game at windswept Melbourne grounds had led to numerous illnesses, he kept up his cricket fascination. He repeatedly wrote about The Don, describing Bradman in 1930 as 'the young wonder of the Australian Eleven'. He constantly backed Bradman during his numerous feuds with the Australian Board of Control. He got it wrong, though, when he thought the Board would leave Bradman alone after the 1930 England tour, instead fining him £50 for writing a book.

'Bradman is all the more a marvel in that he seems to have faced every cricket crisis with a boyish abandon, yet to have displayed a clever man's capacity for capitalising his gifts to sound business advantage, and in doing so to have broken some of the boarding-school rules and maxims with which the Board of Control almost managed to make its team ridiculous,' Macdonald wrote.

'In addition to recovering the Ashes, he just about saved the enterprise from a monetary peril in a disastrous summer for English cricketing finances. Bradman was a money-maker as well as a run maker — the board is not likely to repeat the initial error of trying to kill its own publicity.'

In October 1932 Macdonald came to Bradman's defence when the Board of Control would not allow The Don to write newspaper articles about the upcoming Test series, because, unlike teammate Jack Fingleton, he was not a 'professional' journalist. 'Whether you call Bradman a professional or an athlete is really beside the point,' Macdonald wrote. 'What we ought to do is to give him every help to go on with this one big thing as long as he is capable of doing it.'

A month later, Macdonald died of emphysema, aged 73, prompting heartfelt tributes from countless cricketing identities, including England team manager and MCC luminary Pelham 'Plum' Warner. Warner said Macdonald 'wrote upon cricket as few others have done ... his death grieves me very much'. Macdonald, according to Melbourne Cricket Club secretary and former Test cricketer Hugh Trumble, was 'loved by those with whom he came in contact'. Few Australian cricket writers have been so idolised — the only one to compare was Ray Robinson many decades later.

Macdonald's war links were not forgotten. The secretary of the South African Soldiers' Association of Victoria, T.E. Stapleton, told *The Argus*: 'The few comrades of this association who helped to keep the flag flying with Mr Macdonald were deeply sorrowful when hearing of the demise of their illustrious Boer War colleague.'

PART TWO
FIRST WORLD WAR

CHAPTER 2

INTERNATIONAL AND SUBURBAN MURDER

The Great War cut deep into Australian society. It devastated families. It killed many of its best, most vibrant. It incited inflamed beliefs. It provoked rampant nationalism. It led to reckless behaviour, exposing Australia's racist underbelly, sectarian differences and industrial conflicts. It divided the nation with two vicious conscription debates. It led to courageous people being cruelly labelled cowards. Many cowards, who hid well away from the battle lines, became public heroes through ineptly leading others to unnecessary and often tortuous deaths.

Some looked upon it as a great adventure. For all, it was anarchic. Humans revealed their worst characteristics. Virtually all who served never got over what they experienced.

It deeply affected what people wanted to do when they needed to relax. Many Australians relied on sporting activities and competition to keep them motivated. Sport was at the core of this young nation. But even that was shaken.

The Great War forced rugby union, the private school game, to close down in Australia between late 1914 and 1918 while hockey, amateur athletics, tennis, rowing, swimming and amateur and country Australian Rules football were curtailed. Rugby league consolidated itself during the war years, wisely taking over many of the ground leases left through the absence of rugby union, as well as snaring the code's best players. Boxing and horseracing thrived — in dire times, people relied on gladiators and gambling as a diversion.

All sporting organisations debated whether it was frivolous to continue playing when the nation was overwhelmed by more pressing matters. Decisions varied — often depending on the sport's political and religious allegiances. League, with its solid working-class Irish Catholic base, had a core who refused to defend the British. They believed it was imperative that Sydney football fields remain occupied. Still, many from the league ranks willingly served. There were endless contradictions.

It was soon evident Australia's summer game could not continue. Cricketing links with the British Empire were overpowering. The game's main officials were often Anglican or Presbyterian with deep Masonic links and intense patriotic beliefs. They often looked upon their real home as England rather than Australia — more a colonial offshoot they were trying to tame. Countless leading cricketers were convinced they were dual citizens, British and Australian, with their parents or grandparents deriving from Britain. They treated trips to England as pilgrimages, and several were determined to end their careers there.

For some time, the Australian Board of Control for International Cricket was hopeful of overseas ventures continuing, including a five-Test tour of South Africa starting in November 1914. To revive hope, it publicly announced a 13-man touring party to be led by Warwick Armstrong.[5]

However, the South African Cricket Association in early August sent its Australian counterparts a cable calling for the tour to be pushed back due to the anticipated outbreak of war. A few

---

5   The selected Australian squad was Armstrong (capt), Warren Bardsley (vc), Charlie Macartney, Eric Barbour, Charles Kelleway, Tommy Andrews, Gerry Hazlitt, Frank Baring, Jack Ryder, Barlow Carkeek, Edgar Mayne, A.G. 'Johnnie' Moyes and Bill Whitty. Some weeks later Roy Park replaced Barbour and Bert Folkard replaced Hazlitt. Clem Hill, Victor Trumper, Vernon Ransford, Dr Herbert Hordern and Jack Massie all made themselves unavailable.

days later, Australia was officially at war. There was no option but for the tour to be abandoned.

At a meeting of the Board in October 1914, there remained blind hope the war could be over by Christmas, leading to inquiries about a 1916 Australian team heading to England and the West Indies. Yet the Board's secretary, Syd Smith, soon realised there was no point pursuing such fanciful dreams. In the Board's 1914–15 annual report, Smith wrote: 'Sport must take a secondary place when the interests of the Empire are at stake.'

At state level, however, there was resistance. While rugby union became rampant recruiting agents for the AIF, there was vigorous debate within the NSWCA over whether competition at grade level should continue. Not all were eager for recruitment to be the country's number one priority.

In September 1914 the Association, at its delegate meeting, was read a letter from former state captain Austin Diamond calling for 'all cricketers in this state, excepting those at present under the cadet system, to volunteer for [military] training'. The Association 'expressed its hearty sympathy with the principles suggested in Mr Diamond's letter that all cricketers will, if needed, take part in the defence of the Empire'.[6]

The Association was also distracted by another concern. Public support of cricket, which for several years had been sidetracked by endless bickering involving players and administrators, had dropped off dramatically. Spectators had grown tired of the feuding.

The Australian Board of Control had been involved in a series of bitter disputes with Australia's leading players, who were disenchanted with how they were being treated by the game's new leaders. The Board's aim was to take over as the prime controlling body and extinguish the power of the Melbourne

---

6   Yorkshire-born Diamond, who captained NSW 14 times as well as leading an unofficial Australian team to Canada and the United States in 1913, persistently supported the war. He attempted to organise military training for NSW cricketers, including enrolling them in special units. He was involved in the establishment of the Sportsmen's Unit, where the aim was to 'train together, sail together, fight together'. Diamond served on the Western Front, suffering from gas poisoning on The Somme in 1918. In December that year he was back playing for NSW.

Cricket Club, which had been the local game's prime promoter, including organising tours to Australia by English teams. It looked upon itself as Australia's version of the Marylebone Cricket Club (MCC), but with the added benefit of giving the country's leading players a substantial say in the running of the game. The 1899 Australian captain, Joe Darling, emphasised how powerful it had become when he said after that tour the Melbourne club was regarded in England as 'the Marylebone of Australia'. The Board was determined to put these militant players and the Melbourne club in their place. But Melbourne kept up the fight. In 1906 it received written undertakings from 11 frontline NSW players, many of whom were opposed to the new Board, that they would play for the club if it could entice an England team to tour Australia the next season. This led to the NSWCA suspending ten of the 11 players.[7] For some time Australian cricket was deeply divided between the Board, and its allies in the NSW and Victorian associations, and the Melbourne club, which had support from South Australia, the SCG (which was constantly bickering with the NSWCA) and the country's best players. There were occasional moments of harmony, but it remained volatile.

Australia collapsed during the 1911–12 Ashes tour, losing 4–1 to England. It was clear the country's main cricketers had been distracted by the Board wanting to diminish their power, including no longer allowing them to choose the manager for overseas tours. The dispute also revolved around who controlled and accessed the revenue from those tours. It culminated in the 'Big Six' cricket dispute of 1912, in which Test selectors Clem Hill and Peter McAlister came to blows at a Sydney meeting, and the country's six leading players — Armstrong, Vernon Ransford, Victor Trumper, Tibby Cotter, Hanson Carter and Hill himself — refused to tour England for the 1912 Triangular Tournament between England, Australia and South Africa. A

---

7   The NSW players were Monty Noble, Victor Trumper, Reg Duff, Tibby Cotter, Hanson Carter, the Reverend E.F. Mick Waddy, George Garnsey, Jack O'Connor, Austin Diamond, Jim Mackay and A.J. Bert Hopkins. Waddy was spared as he had written to the Melbourne club to cancel the agreement.

weakened team headed by Syd Gregory enjoyed only sporadic success, while upsetting their hosts with uncouth drunken behaviour and foul language.

After postponing Sheffield Shield cricket in July 1915 and calling on the NSW Premier to erect recruitment posters in 'prominent places' at various cricket grounds, several NSWCA club delegates opposed stopping grade competition. The NSWCA originally decided to continue grade cricket, as it didn't think it would 'interfere' with enlistment. If it did, the NSWCA would stop the competition immediately. It argued that grounds had to be maintained and caretakers had to be paid: 'We can't all go to war, and we feel we should cater for those whose obligations compel them to remain here. We think it be far better to encourage men to play cricket than to drive them to find amusement elsewhere, perhaps in hotels or Billiards saloons.'

This prompted a vigorous debate. A.W. Jones from the Western Suburbs club argued that 'carrying on our grade fixtures at this period is nothing less than criminal'.

C.B. Cochrane boomed: 'The proper colours for the young players at the present is khaki … Why, last season I felt ashamed to be seen carrying a bat.'

Redfern's C.G. McMillan believed the NSWCA had to 'study the economic situation', adding, 'If we suspended the competition, we are going to throw a lot of people on the labor market. Cricket keeps a lot of people employed.'

Glebe's William Bardsley, father of Test batsman Warren Bardsley, said: 'I may be a British heathen. I can't see any harm in playing cricket. We don't show anyone loyalty in walking the streets having wet towels round our heads. Cricket is going to do more good than harm. Look at Mr Kelleway.[8] [Playing cricket] will stand him in good stead when he gets to the front. What are players to do if they do not play cricket?'

The NSWCA heavies stood firm. While secretary Syd Smith said in September 1915 that it wasn't proper 'for the Association

---

8   Charles Kelleway, a notable Test allrounder, joined up in September 1915.

to do anything … that might cause the younger players to play cricket instead of doing their duty to their country', chairman J.H. Clayton was adamant:

'Our national life depends on our national service. We must all do something.

'The game has done a great deal of good for our soldiers. What does Mr Ashmead Bartlett say: "that only a race of athletes could have scaled the cliffs of Gallipoli".

'We should all serve. Why leave the matter to our conscience? The time is coming. The war is going to make a great deal of difference to Australia. We should show no respect to men who won't do their duty.'

Clayton got his wish. The NSWCA committee agreed unanimously that 'matches not be played'. In Melbourne, the pennant competition was discontinued but clubs could play 'friendly' matches. The general tone was provided by Melbourne Cricket Club president Mr Justice Cussen, who said at the 1915 annual general meeting that 'cricket and sport generally had been thrown into comparative insignificance owing to the crisis'. VCA chairman Ernie Beans was meanwhile obsessed with 'draft-dodging cricketers'.

In Melbourne, the complaint that some notable cricketers had opted against enlisting became an emotional issue. Some were labelled cowards. After all, numerous politicians, including Attorney-General Billy Hughes, were applying pressure. Hughes declared: 'As you have played the game in the past, so we ask you to play the greater game now. You are wanted in the trenches now far more than you were ever needed in the football and cricket fields.'

There was originally great excitement that Victoria, after a string of poor seasons, won the Sheffield Shield in 1914–15, skilfully led by the overbearing Armstrong, ably supported by Jack Ryder and Roy Park.

The VCA was in raptures, explaining in its annual report that it was 'a glorious season for Victorian cricket; and but for the gloom that has been cast on the civilized world in consequence of the devastating war ... the dominant note of this report would be one of joy and general satisfaction'.

This tone infuriated those at the weekly *Australian Statesman and Mining Standard*, which ran an editorial titled 'Cricket and Shirking'.

The editorial thundered that, while there had been a lot of fuss over footballers not being patriotic, they were more noble compared to the state's cricketers. The Victorian cricketers were 'altogether unheroic' compared to those of the other states. While in the first 15 months of war 11 NSW players and six South Australian players had enlisted, only one Victorian — T.J. (Jimmy) Matthews — had 'come to the defence of their country':

'The state of affairs here shown constitutes an enormous disgrace to Victorian cricket and Victorian cricketers; but not only is the Association not ashamed of itself, it has even the audacity in its annual report to indulge in an amount of cock-crowing over the fact that last season the State obtained possession of the Sheffield Shield.'

As NSW was weakened by leading bowlers having already left for the front, making it easier for Victoria to win the Shield, 'it would have been in much better taste for the Association to have said as little as possible about a matter that reflects so little credit upon it'.

'When the country is at war, its only heroes are those who serve it, not those who, in ministering to the pleasure of its idle and disloyal, minister to their own vanity and give proof of their own lack of patriotism.'

Those who played were 'enemies of their country'.

The editorial was written by Ernest Oliphant, a reputable author, journalist and Elizabethan scholar. The VCA responded in its next annual report by stating that, up to 31 August 1916, 2854 registered cricketers from Victoria had enlisted. Some clubs had even disbanded as they had lost so many players.

The South Australian Cricket Association decided late in 1915 not to hold a pennant competition for district matches. Fixtures could go ahead but only on a club-to-club basis. The following year some South Australian delegates wanted cricket to continue, but were shouted down.

As for the national Board of Control, the scheduled 1915 meeting 'lapsed through want of a quorum'.

Leading first-class cricketers from England, Scotland, Ireland, Australia, New Zealand and South Africa were fighting at the front. In all, more than 490 first-class players, including 15 Australians and 12 Test representatives, were killed. The first to perish was Cambridge University allrounder Lieutenant Archer Windsor-Clive, who was killed by a German shell in France on 25 August 1914. By the end of 1914, 27 first-class cricketers had died.

Among the first major Australian cricketers to enlist was the exceptional Robert John Allwright (Jack) Massie, who developed into the most admired of soldiers. His courageous wartime feats were not exactly a shock, as the tall, elegant son of aggressive Test opening batsman Hugh Massie was extraordinary at any sporting pursuit he attempted. Jack was a quality rower and rifle shooter, and state title-holder for the 120-yard hurdles. He won the 1913 NSW heavyweight boxing title, and, as a pugnacious rugby forward with Sydney University and NSW, was selected the same year to tour New Zealand with the Australian team, though he withdrew due to university studies.

Ditto the Australian cricket team for the aborted 1914–15 South African tour. Massie was in the original squad but pulled out after graduating with first-class honours and the University Medal in civil engineering. He believed it was time to begin a professional career. Australian cricket authorities were captivated by him. At 193 centimetres, he was imposing, and he was able to extract dangerous bounce and pace with his angular left-arm bowling. Between 1910 and 1914, he took 99 wickets for NSW at the impressive average of 18.42, including seven five-wicket hauls and four ten-wicket hauls. With Sydney University he took 166 wickets at 13.79.

Countless opponents raved about him, including another who was picked for the 1914–15 South African tour but instead became a notable cricket journalist, author and ABC commentator — A.G. 'Johnnie' Moyes. Moyes fervently believed Massie was the greatest cricketer never to have played for Australia.[9]

Renowned Test cricketer and writer Frank Iredale believed that if Massie were to concentrate on his cricket, 'Lord's and the Oval will be slaughter grounds for him'. Charlie Macartney thought the same, believing Massie had the potential to be one of Australia's greatest players.

There was no delay in Massie's enlistment, joining up on 17 August 1914, less than a fortnight after Britain had officially declared war on Germany. After being commissioned as a 2nd Lieutenant in the 4th Battalion, and several weeks' training, he sailed to Egypt in early October, a voyage on which he discovered he had been appointed Assistant Adjutant to a long-time colleague, Captain Iven Mackay. Mackay was a former Sydney University cricketer and had taught Massie rugby and rowing at the prestigious Sydney private school Shore, where he was a physics teacher.

Writing to his father, Massie explained that after stopping off in the Western Australian town of Albany — 'a pretty little place but very sleepy' — there had been drama on board: 'All our batmen have been excluded from our quarters. Some of them starting using the officers' baths and made a general mess. They were warned, but in spite of that they were all booted out next day.'

Massie was part of the first landing at Gallipoli before dawn on 25 April 1915, and was immediately under siege. On the second day, his unit was involved in a daring advance towards the Turkish

---

9   Moyes had an exemplary military career. Wounded several times during the Great War, Major Moyes commanded the 48th Battalion on the Western Front in 1918. The future newspaper news editor who became a household name through his ABC cricketing broadcasts in the 1950–60s received the Military Cross for his leadership at Passchendaele and Polygon Wood. In 1919 back in Australia, he suffered badly with double pneumonia and pleurisy. He told *The Referee*'s J.C. Davis that in hospital, doctors took 'gallons of poisonous gas from my chest'. In the Second World War, Moyes served as Commander of the 7th Australian Garrison, which was involved with internal security. A close confidante of Don Bradman, Moyes wrote 15 cricket books before he died in 1963.

line, where one of his superiors was shot down. That didn't deter Massie, who fearlessly helped his officer back to safety. He was constantly in danger, once wounding himself when in a trench he accidentally dropped a 'jam-tin bomb', and another time lucky not to be killed when one of his own, believing he was a Turkish intruder, lunged at him with a bayonet.

Letters written by Massie which are now in the Australian War Memorial archives give an insight into his frontline experience. On 4 May 1915 he scribbled a quick note to his mother: 'We've been in the trenches now for 10 days without a spell. The men were very down for a few days as just as we dug in on place we were shifted to another place and had to re-dig all over again.'

'I've got a landing here after a bit of a scrap and now hanging on making our position stronger. The Turks have not appeared in very great force against us but they keep on sniping all day and at first we had a lot of casualties on this account. They do not like the bayonet and one only has to suggest it and they are off like rabbits.'

Five days later he wrote home: 'Nobody ducks for a shell or a bullet. They all know that the one you don't hear coming is going to hurt. The Turks do waste a hell of a lot of ammunition.'

In June he admitted 'one of our own bombs burst just in front of me and peppered me a bit on the legs and arms (right). One piece hit me in the abdomen but stopped in the abdomen wall and did not penetrate. I went to the hospital ship, but was discharged.'

In August he was seriously injured when, reputedly, shot in the shoulder blade by the Turkish leader, Kemal Atatürk, during the Battle of Lone Pine. Massie, who had the reputation on Gallipoli for being among the most accurate thrower of jam-tin bombs into the Turkish trenches, had been sent by Colonel Macnaghten to relieve Mackay, who had been injured but refused to leave his post. Massie was beside Mackay when, bending over to pick up a wounded body off the floor of the trench, Massie was shot. He frantically clutched his shoulder as blood flooded his fingers.

Apart from a shrapnel wound in his left shoulder, he suffered a splintered shoulder blade, broken ribs and a punctured lung.

Due to Massie's extensive wounds he had to be transported to Alexandria and then England, spending two-and-a-half months in a London hospital. From his Alexandria hospital bed, he wrote to his Aunty Tatty that the doctors 'were not quite satisfied with the look of the wound … so they operated on it and explored a bit'. 'They found that the bullet knocked me about a good bit but after which it got foul of my left shoulder blade and pulled it about a bit before coming out. The wound was not clean, but is doing very well now. I cannot use my left arm at present.'

A week later, he told his parents his 'left hand was quite useless', but his spirits had been revived by the hospital orderlies providing him with 'excellent chocolates'. The fruit on offer was 'not bad'.

It was finally decided a soldier listed by the AIF as 'dangerously ill' would return to Australia to recuperate, granted four months' leave in the hope he would fully recover. In January 1916 he was Mentioned in Despatches, and the following month was awarded the French Croix de Guerre for his services at Gallipoli.

When informed of the Croix de Guerre, Massie was embarrassed, writing to his Aunty Tatty: 'I must say I am a bit mystified as to how it came about. Probably the French President said that he wanted to decorate some Australians and asked for recommendations and my name went in for some unknown reason.'

He could have easily spent the rest of the war years back in Sydney. But that was never his intention, leaving Sydney in May 1916 as second in command of the 33rd Battalion. To while away the time on the *Marathon*, Massie gave boxing lessons which 'most of the officers attended'. 'Some are quite keen, but all very ladylike in their methods.'

Arriving in France in late 1916, Massie went on to display brilliant leadership that warranted him being Mentioned in Despatches a second time, before being attached to the divisional HQ.

Despite his extensive injuries, he was talked into returning to the cricket field. Future England team manager Plum Warner invited him to play at Lord's in August 1917 for a combined Australia/South Africa Services team against a British Army and Navy line-up. Whenever possible, cricket matches were played in England and away from the front as a way of lifting spirits.

In front of 5000 spectators, including Admiral Sir John Jellicoe, who had commanded the Grand Fleet at the Battle of Jutland in 1916, the colonials were vastly superior, boasting numerous quality performers, including Kelleway, Macartney, Eric Barbour (who captained the team), Carl Willis and Cyril Docker. Navy and Army, skippered by Warner, weren't mugs, boasting Patsy Hendren, Percy Fender and Ernest Tyldesley, but struggled on a damp wicket. For some, it was the first time they had held a bat or ball in years.

Massie ignored concerns about his mangled left arm, opening the bowling with Macartney. He bowled virtually the whole innings, taking 2/39 off 14.3 overs as England battled to reach 106. He scored six batting No 10, but the game had already been well won by Barbour scoring a century. *The Times* noted what might have been, explaining that the locals were always going to struggle because 'of course, C.G. Macartney and T.J. Matthews are Test Match bowlers'. 'But for the war Major Massie would before this have earned the same distinction,' *The Times* noted.

The following day Massie wrote home, explaining: 'Plum won the toss and batted. He should have sent us in really, but did not do so. It was a bowler's wicket and there was a nice head wind and I could not use either. I am no bowler now, I am afraid, so I will have to go in for batting instead. As a matter of fact I am no batsman either, but may make something of myself. My arm was a good bit better than it was last time although I did not bowl so well. After the match I went to dine with Plum and we went on to see "Round the Map" at the Alhambra. It was not a good show at all. I don't think I have ever seen a show with less in it.'

That was Massie's last serious cricketing appearance, as he was struck down again in 1918 when at a training camp well away from the frontline. Shrapnel from a German bomb dropped from an aeroplane damaged his left foot, right forearm, left buttock and face. When hearing of Massie's extensive injuries, Johnnie Moyes wrote to *The Referee*'s J.C Davis: 'Thus Australia loses her best bowler.'

There was another Mention in Despatches in May 1918, and the following month he received the Distinguished Service Order. He was promoted to lieutenant colonel after excelling at Senior Officers' School.

Even after the armistice, Massie's duties weren't over. Due to his vast sporting and organisational skills he was appointed to the AIF Sports Control Board to run sporting tournaments for the Australian troops stranded in Europe, who had to be kept occupied until transport was organised to get them home.

Once home, Massie enjoyed a flourishing postwar business career and, off a short run-up, continued to take wickets for the Sydney University Veterans cricket side. For the NSWCA he wrote an authoritative booklet on how to be a menacing bowler — it all revolved around attacking the batsman.

Massie suffered further tragedy during the Second World War when his son John was killed in New Guinea in 1943. His wife Phyllis died shortly afterwards. In February 1966 Massie himself died, of cancer.

Massie wasn't the only NSW cricketer who failed to extensively prolong his first-class career after the war. His long-time friend Claude Tozer was another who didn't fulfil his potential, but the reason was more macabre.

Tozer and Massie had long been mates, and met up on the Western Front at Boulogne. They had known each other since teenagers when colleagues in the Shore first XI — Tozer the compact star batsman, Massie the imposing star bowler. They were first XI teammates at Sydney University, sitting side by side in the official 1913–14 premiership-winning team photo. They made their NSW debuts together against the touring South African team at the SCG in February 1911.

After graduating from Sydney University with a medical degree in 1914, Tozer waited until 12 May 1915 before heading to Victoria Barracks, near the SCG, to join up. As the Gallipoli campaign — just a few weeks old — was at a furious stalemate, and more Australian troops were required, pressure was applied on Tozer to enlist. Newspapers were constantly booming that capable doctors were desperately needed on the frontline.

The Sydney University Cricket Club made a point of letting everyone know it was fervently behind the war effort. Every member of the first XI, and the 12th man, joined up. Many were subsequently awarded military distinctions, with 12 University cricketers decorated for courage. The 1916 University annual report recorded that of those who played for the club from 1910 to 1915, 'nearly three-fourths are at present on active service'. More than 500 students from Tozer and Massie's school went to the front. By the end of the war, the University had 11 cricketers killed in action.

Tozer, assigned to the First Field Ambulance, left Sydney on 16 June aboard the No 1 Australian Hospital Ship — TSS *Karoola* — for Alexandria and Gallipoli. His was a harsh war with serious ramifications.

By early August he was at Anzac Cove, and within weeks the rumour had hit Sydney that, after just a few days in battle, Tozer had been killed at Lone Pine, shot while treating a wounded soldier. Several NSW newspapers stated his death as fact, which led to flags at Sydney University being flown at half-mast. A minute's silence was held at numerous grounds.

Some weeks later, army authorities reported back to the Tozer family that their son was actually alive. Witnesses had been 'speaking to him on the Peninsula about August 10 or 11 after the charge at Lone Pine. He was then well. Tall, young, medium complexion, no moustache, fresh looking.'

But the family relief was relatively brief, as they soon discovered that, even though evacuated from Gallipoli, he was gravely ill with typhoid in Cairo. Then they found out he was in Marseilles and on his way to the Western Front.

In July 1916, Tozer was close to death again after being bombarded by the German artillery at Pozières. He was hospitalised after a shell exploded near him, leading to widespread injuries. His head had been cut apart by shrapnel, with a substantial piece passing into the right temporal lobe of his brain, lodging under the skull.

Doctors opted against operating, believing it was too dangerous. Instead 12 weeks' recuperation in England was recommended. He was also suffering from trench fever, a disease transmitted by body lice. Tozer tried to keep his spirits up, writing from Wandsworth Hospital to his (Sydney Church of England Grammar) school magazine *The Torch Bearer* that 'the bit of steel in my head should keep me out [of] mischief for some time'.

He was back in France the following year, where, after another bout of trench fever, he was promoted to major. His leadership abilities were also rewarded, earning a DSO when he ignored his own safety to care for other soldiers.

The citation described Tozer's bravery on the Western Front. It read: 'At Hooge Tunnel, east of Ypres during the operation on 19–23 October 1917, this officer displayed most conspicuous courage and devotion to duty in dressing wounded in the open under fire and in visiting and organising the forward relief of bearers as far as the Regimental Aid Post. The position and line of evacuation was under constant shell-fire and the labour was extreme and unceasing. His complete disregard of danger in this performance of his duty and his unremitting personal attention both to the wounded passing through his station and to the requirements of the posts under his charge are worthy of very high praise.'

He spent the rest of the war as a chief medical officer at the No 3 Australian Hospital in Abbeville in the Somme, tending to the wounded, especially during the Battle of Amiens. It wasn't entirely hands-on, as Tozer had ample cricketing opportunities away from the frontline, playing 19 matches for the 3rd Australian General Hospital in 1918, losing only one. He was their best batsman, compiling 405 runs at 135, including one century.

Tozer returned home in December 1918. While presenting a stoic exterior, inside he was a mess. Like thousands of other returned servicemen, Tozer suffered badly from shell-shock which clearly affected his thinking. He would constantly wake up in the middle of the night with cold shivers, the sounds of war crashing through his already aching head. Constantly complaining of headaches and distressed that so many of his colleagues, including 134 ex-Shore students, had been killed, Tozer tried to bring some decorum to his life by starting up a medical practice on Sydney's plush North Shore.

His most pressing assignment was marrying his fiancée, Sydney socialite Kathleen Crossman, who had patiently waited for almost four years for him to come back from the front. A wedding date was set for late June 1919. Plans were well in place when suddenly, at the end of May, his fiancée fell ill. She had been complaining of sore tonsils, constant hot spells, vomiting and lack of energy. Taken to a private North Sydney hospital, she did not improve, and, on 12 June 1919, died. She was only 26.

Tozer was devastated, burying himself in his medical practice as a way of overcoming his intense grief. He also attempted to resurrect his cricketing career, joining the nearby Gordon club at Chatswood Oval, and returning to the NSW team, skippered by Monty Noble, for their trip to Brisbane in late November 1919, where he scored a second-innings century. NSW appearances then became intermittent as he focused on his Chatswood medical practice.

He soon had a large list of patients, including a well-dressed gentleman who appeared in his surgery one evening and explained how worried he was about his wife's unstable mental state. His name was Harold Mort, and he pleaded with Dr Tozer to make a house visit in the hope of settling down his wife, Dorothy, whose family had mental issues, including her father, who one night took to the rest of the family with an axe before trying to cut his own throat. (He died some years later by throwing himself off a third-floor landing in Auckland.)

The Morts were high achievers. The figurehead of the family was Thomas Sutcliffe Mort, of Goldsbrough Mort fame and a major figure in Australian trade and industry. It was a family not attuned to coping with deranged, unsociable behaviour, such as from Mrs Dorothy Mort née Woodfull. Numerous local doctors in the Lindfield area where the Morts lived turned Harold away, saying a patient constantly depressed and withdrawn was too hard to handle. They were more cough and cold experts.

The next closest GP was Tozer, on Boundary Street, Chatswood, who, although not well versed in treating clients with mental issues, believed his war work might help. He told Harold that, although no psychiatrist, he would try to help, and he visited Dorothy at the family home. The consultation took an unexpected turn.

When Dorothy met Tozer for the first time, she looked upon him as her escape route. She was besotted by his courteous, caring nature. 'I loved him immediately I saw him,' she said. 'He was so handsome and big and splendid that I thought how wonderful a son would be of his.'

Within a week of their first meeting in June 1920, they were writing letters to each other. Still stung by losing his fiancée, Tozer was taken aback with how his patient openly flirted with him. Though Dorothy, with a hawk-like face and dour expression, was no beauty, he was flattered.

It took some time before the relationship became physical, with Tozer telling his mother after the first meeting, 'I don't know why God made these neurotic women.' But, after several more visits, Tozer was sufficiently charmed to provide enough clues in his letters to indicate this was far more than the customary doctor–patient relationship.

It turned into a tangled web, especially when his cricketing life became complicated. After excellent innings at grade and state level, he was a candidate for the Australian team against the 1920–21 touring England side. Overlooked for the first Test team, the softener was that he had been appointed NSW captain to play Queensland. He had been given the hint he would appear in one of the later Tests.

He realised he had better rein in his personal affairs. Concerned Dorothy had become over-possessive during their six-month relationship, and worried about the inevitable scandal if the press or her husband found out, he knew he had to end it.

Two days before the start of the Australia–England Test series, Tozer and his lover met at her Lindfield house. She listened in disbelief. He said he was about to get engaged to another woman. She didn't know whether it was the truth or not.

As Dorothy appeared relatively calm, Tozer agreed to meet her the following afternoon to say their farewells. But that was delayed several days due to his heavy workload.

He also had to attend the Sydney Test.

Tozer had not picked up the warning signs that Dorothy had been deeply distressed. After he had left, she had headed straight for the city. After selling a diamond brooch to a Castlereagh Street jeweller, she went to the Cowles and Dunn gunsmith shop and bought a revolver with cash. She told the shop owner, William Cowles, that she wanted it as a present for her husband in India. It was a lie. Cowles showed her how to load, aim and shoot the revolver.

Her final call was to a Pitt Street chemist to buy laudanum, supposedly for her son's earache. She was warned as she left the shop: 'You must not drink this, Mrs Mort.'

'Why, will it kill me?'

'Yes, it would. You have a sufficient amount there to poison everyone in the house.'

On 21 December, Tozer arrived at the Morts' house around 11.30am. He was in a buoyant mood, reading that morning that he had been picked as NSW captain. He realised that Test status was hovering, because the numbers were in his favour. After all, he had now tallied 3395 runs in grade cricket, including nine centuries and 15 half-centuries, at an average of 52.23 — twice being the leading grade run-scorer. His first-class figures were also admirable — 514 runs at 46.72.

He was let in by the Morts' maid, Florence Fizelle (the younger sister of renowned Australian artist Rah Fizelle). Florence escorted Tozer to Dorothy's bedroom.

Ten minutes later, she heard two revolver shots and rushed back to the bedroom, the door of which was ajar. Crossing the corridor to the drawing room door, she found it locked. Banging on the door, she yelled: 'Whatever is the matter? Can I come in?'

'No, everything is all right,' Dorothy replied after a few seconds.

By that time Tozer was dead. Dorothy had directed him to her drawing room and told him to sit on the Chesterfield couch. While he was distracted, she grabbed the revolver from the mantelpiece and placed it inside her dress. She sat next to him, explaining she wanted to give him a gift so he could always remember her. It was a photograph of her. On the back she had written: 'Claude Tozer. From the woman you swore you loved and above all other, and said was the biggest incentive for good in your life. From the woman you swore you said you loved and had made the mother of your child.'

As she handed him the photograph, she moved her hand until it was behind his head, and with the concealed revolver shot a bullet into the back of his skull. She shot him a second time in the head, and then blasted him in the chest.

She tried to kill herself, shooting herself in the left breast, and took a dose of laudanum. Neither worked. Then for several hours she rested her head in Tozer's lap, seeking forgiveness.

The next day in *The Sydney Morning Herald* side by side were the headlines: 'Dr Tozer Dead. Woman Injured. Lindfield Tragedy' and 'Brilliant Batting. Australia Leads. Armstrong's great innings'.

Armstrong had overpowered the England bowling attack by scoring 158, an exceptional innings considering he had had some serious family news of his own — his brother-in-law had a few hours earlier been dragged underneath a Sydney tram, suffering serious injuries.

On the final day of the Test, players wore black armbands in Tozer's honour, while the SCG flags remained at half-mast in honour of the murdered cricketer.

The following week, Dorothy Mort was charged with murder and, after a heavily publicised court case, was confined under the 'Lunacy Act' of 1898 to the State Reformatory for Women at Long Bay Gaol 'until the Governor's Pleasure is known'.[10]

Just a few years after congregating at Victor Trumper's gravesite, the Sydney cricketing fraternity again assembled about 100 metres away to witness Tozer's burial in the family plot at Waverley Cemetery. Among the most emotional mourners were Austin Diamond and Jack Massie.

---

10 Dorothy Mort remained in Long Bay until 1929. She outlived Harold, who died in 1950 after a long illness. She died in July 1966 of cerebral thrombosis and myocardial degeneration.

CHAPTER 3

NO TRACE

More than 10 per cent of the 747 Australian soldiers killed at Gallipoli on 25 April 1915 were never found. They are recorded as 'no trace'. They were either never discovered or their bodies never identified.

Among them was the first Australian first-class cricketer to perish at the Great War — Charles James Backman, a 31-year-old Adelaide boilermaker's assistant.

Around dawn, Sergeant Backman, from C Company, 10th Battalion, plunged into freezing water, clambered his way to shore, and scampered across the beach and towards the cliffs. How long he survived, where exactly he was killed, and what happened to his body, like many others that confusing day, is a mystery. Some soldier reports say that Backman was struck down by a Turkish bullet on the beach and had 'crawled away into the bushes'. Others thought he advanced into the hills towards Baby 700 and was butchered by bullets. Some thought he just went missing. The army authorities had no clues about the whereabouts of Sergeant Backman, which led to his family suffering months of grief.

The army also had no idea, or even interest, that he was a sportsman of note. He never pushed it, because he was a cheeky knockabout who didn't believe in talking up his own credentials, even if it included confronting the MCC touring team at

Adelaide Oval less than four years earlier. His working-class mates at the Islington Boiler Shop, who knew him as good old 'Rappie', would never let him get away with having a big head anyway.

He hailed from a family of Swedish origin, the eldest of 12 children. His father was known as Kasper Bachman, but after five or six children the family changed its name to Backman.

Charles joined the South Australian Railways, shortly after causing a public nuisance. When 15, he had appeared before the Hindmarsh Magistrates' Court for 'shouting and yelling'. At the time of the Boer War, a Union Jack flag had been hoisted at a friend's house, which led to Backman and co singing patriotic songs, aimed at upsetting a neighbour, whom they mistakenly thought was South African.

Backman's lawyer argued that rather than causing a ruckus they were guilty of 'singing out of tune'. Backman and his two friends were each fined five shillings.

This slight must have convinced Backman to concentrate more on his cricketing talents, and with various Adelaide clubs he became a reliable batsman — one season topping the Adelaide and Suburban competition batting average. He also was a competent medium-pace bowler. South Australian Junior selection followed, then promotion to the Adelaide grade competition with West Torrens and then Adelaide.

When the 1911–12 MCC team arrived in Australia, their first fixture was against South Australia, who were short of players. After three late withdrawals, Backman was beckoned. Even though the South Australian team was led by the combative Clem Hill, it was completely overshadowed by the visitors. They had endless quality players, including Jack Hobbs, Wilfred Rhodes, Frank Woolley, Sydney Barnes, Frank Foster, George Gunn and Johnny Douglas. The South Australian match was a no-contest, with the MCC winning by an innings and 194 runs after Warner, Foster and Gunn each scored first innings centuries.

But Backman wasn't disgraced. With 3/53 off 16 overs, he was South Australia's highest wicket-taker. *The Advertiser* noted that Backman had been 'put on as a change bowler, as he was recognised chiefly as a batsman'. He could also 'claim the credit of being the first bowler to dismiss Warner on the present tour'. His batting was less impressive — 16 and a duck batting at No 8.

In spite of lobbying in *The Advertiser* by several letter-writers who believed Backman had been poorly treated, as there were worse players in the team, that was the end of his first-class cricketing career. He was overlooked for South Australia's three remaining matches that season.

The following seasons, Backman's grade scores drifted off, and when war was declared he needed no prodding to enlist with several of his workmates, joining on 19 August 1914. In October he was on his way to Egypt on the *Ascanius*, with the only mishap occurring when just out of Colombo it collided with the *Shropshire*. Fellow troops said Backman was 'out in a flash' onto the main deck trying to help anyone in trouble.

Once in Egypt and when told they were heading to a faraway peninsula, he continued to keep charge of his men. After hitting the beach that Anzac Day morning, there was soon confusion over what happened next to Sergeant Backman.

In his Australian Red Cross Wounded and Missing Enquiry Bureau file are conflicting reports. Private Gillett informed them that 'this man was killed on the beach at Anzac on the 1st day of the landing. I was told this by several of my pals who was there and saw Blackman [sic] killed.'

Private Cade said: 'On April 25th 1915 at the Dardanelles landing, it was generally reported that Sgt Backman (not Blackman as in List) was wounded in the advance at the landing on April 25th and crawled away into the bushes. The ground was lost the next day.'

For months no one would admit he was dead. The army would only confirm he had been reported wounded and missing in action. Even in August 1915 his war papers declared he 'was seen wounded' on 25 April. 'Nothing since has been heard of him and he is now reptd Wounded and Missing.' In February 1916 family connections were told by a defence official that: 'So far as the records show he may still be alive.' It was not until May 1916 the official line in the records was changed to 'killed in action'.

This official meandering prompted a string of emotional letters from members of the Backman family to the Minister of Defence seeking answers. On 4 August 1915 his sister wrote: 'Could you give me any information concerning my brother ... We have not had a line from him. His last letter dating April 20 1915 an there has been eight letters what we have seen stating he is killed. I could give you to names of these men if you wish it they are in the fighting line. My dear mother is nearly out of her mind with grief so I thought by writing you could let me know something as I fear there is something wrong but we thought it the Military's place first to let us know if anything is wrong hoping to hear as soon as possible.'

The following day another letter, where she adds: 'I can tell you of men we have met returned soldiers that met him there and tell us that my brother was in the hospitable in the next bed to one of these men they tell us that he wounded in the leg an was crawling to the trenches an his own men called halt an he never stopted as they shot in the back now. I think any thing like that we ought to have heard before now an another letter I have just got from the hospitable an states that Backman is in the hospitable with him now. I think it awful not to know before this is this letter was July 4 1915. I hope to hear as soon as possible whether it is true or false.'

In August 1916, his sister again pleaded to the Ministry to give the family 'some setlment', particularly as several returned soldiers had told them Charles had been killed. They had also received an identification disc. His sister wrote: 'If he was not killed where did his disc come from. It is over twelve months since we had a line from him do you think my mother can stand the strain much longer I think it a terrible shame to think she is kept like this so long without military news witch ought to be first to let us know not like as only letters as soldiers to tell us.'

Further letters were sent off in October 1916 telling the authorities that 'waiting for news' was 'awful ... it will kill my mother'. 'I think it awful no news whether he dead or alive an I ask why did you stop his pay and send us his disc home could you send and tell me if it right to stop his money ... Your silence will drive us mad after all these months ... Call it a disgrace.'

There also were dramas retrieving Charles's belongings from the front. His mother, Annie, wrote in March 1917: 'I heard he won a trophy on Christmas Day 1914. I would be very glad to get his things.' That prompted a response, as shortly afterwards a parcel arrived at their Adelaide home. Inside were their son's scarf, body belt, two handkerchiefs, 11 books, photos, semaphore cards, postcards, cigarette cards, 24 coins and another disc. But no trophy.

A short time later, *The Advertiser* recorded Backman's death. Adding to the family uncertainty was that Charles's younger brother, Edward John, had also enlisted, and for a time had disappeared. In France in 1918 he was fined five shillings for drunkenness, and six days' pay when found guilty of going absent without leave. Due to a foot problem, he was then hospitalised. But at least he got home.

Some relief, but the ordeal did not end there for Mrs Backman. In financial trouble, she sought assistance from the Commonwealth Government in 1920. The reply was brutal, stating that, even though her incapacitated husband had just died, the application was rejected because 'other members of family should contribute to applicant's support'.

The announcement of the second Australian first-class cricketer to die was more immediate, but also involved heartache for the family due to the stupidity of those in charge. Alan Marshal was one of the first Australians to make a name for himself in the English county ranks. At 188 centimetres, he shadowed all, using his height for big middle-of-the-order hitting and intense medium-fast pace bowling. A photograph exists of Marshal in a strikingly similar pose to that of Victor Trumper in the famous photograph by George Beldam, with Trumper in full stride leaping down the pitch. Not a complete surprise as the Marshal photograph was also by Beldam.

It was taken while Marshal was at the Surrey club, which he joined in 1905 after growing up in Queensland. Marshal was born in Warwick in 1883, moving to the Queensland capital when four. He learnt the game at South Brisbane State School and later at Brisbane Grammar. In April 1904 he made the Queensland team, playing 11 games for his state, as well as playing a season with the Paddington club in Sydney before furthering his career in England. He qualified through residency to play for Surrey, where he became one of their favourite players. His aggressive batting drew in the crowds and with it rich accolades as he tallied more than 1000 runs per season for the county between 1907 and 1909.

Among his admirers was England wicketkeeper Dick Lilley, who described him as 'a fine all-round player, and as a batsman he reminds me in style and method of Australia's great batsman, Victor Trumper'. W.G. Grace agreed with the Trumper comparison, saying of Marshal: 'Since he arrived in England he has come on wonderfully, and is now one of the most promising allround young cricketers we have had for years.'

Wisden named him as one of their Five Cricketers of the Year in 1909, with editor Sydney Pardon explaining that when he established himself in the Surrey first XI he 'revealed himself as a driver rarely equalled for sheer speed since the days of C.J. Thornton and Bonnor'.

'Some of his hits in the matches against Middlesex and Kent at The Oval, in August, were, I think, beyond the capacity of any other batsman now playing in first-class cricket. His fame will no doubt rest chiefly on his batting, but in every way he is a thorough cricketer.

'There is no finer fieldsman to be found — he is about the safest catch in England — and though there has perhaps been a tendency to exaggerate his merits as a bowler, he commands a good variety of pace with plenty of spin. Taken altogether he is one of the most interesting figures in the cricket field, and if he should go on as he has begun there will be no limit to his success.'

Then it all went sour.

In 1910, Surrey terminated his contract, even though he scored more than 1000 runs during the previous season, admittedly at a lower average than in 1908. It had more to do with off-field misdemeanours. He was suspended for several matches following an 'incident' when Surrey played Derbyshire at Chesterfield. What exactly happened is uncertain, Surrey refusing to release details. Some years later it was revealed that Marshal and teammates were heading to the team hotel, kicking a ball among themselves on a street. A police constable believed they were causing mischief and Marshal refused to give the officer his name. He told the over-officious constable where he could 'stick our names'. The players were taken to the local police station. Even though the chief constable let them off, Surrey wasn't impressed. On its committee were several autocratic businessmen who abhorred professional cricketers like Marshal. They wanted to revert to an all-amateur line-up. This gave them the chance to get rid of the upstart Brisbanite, especially as there had been a further 'unfortunate affair' involving Marshal during Surrey's match against the touring 1909 Australian team. Again, details of what Marshal was supposed to have done were kept within the confines of the committee room. But he was now persona non grata.

Surrey terminated his contract after only six matches in 1910. He had no option but to return to Australia, and the Queensland line-up. The possibility of making the Australian Test team was not beyond him, especially when he scored a second innings century opening for an Australian XI against the South African XI at the Gabba in December 1910. This was classic Marshal, scoring his century in just over two hours, including 13 boundaries. The *Brisbane Courier* described his driving as 'brilliant'. *The Referee* said his innings 'evoked much enthusiasm'.

However, his 'cards had been marked' by English authorities, who had relayed to their Australian counterparts the troubles they had had with this great but wayward competitor. He continued playing until December 1913, his last first-class innings an unbeaten 66 against a New Zealand XI at the Gabba. He finished with the admirable career figures of 5177 runs at 27.98 and 119 wickets at 22.84.

When enlisting in Brisbane on 19 October 1914, he put down his 'trade or calling' as 'Cricketer'. From the start he struggled with authority. In November 1914 Marshal was docked pay for twice being absent from parade or rollcall at the Broadmeadow Military Camp. Later, in Egypt he was absent from parade for two days running.

What happened after that is scanty, except that for a short time he was at Gallipoli, where he was struck down with enteric fever — the same illness blamed for J.J. Ferris's death. Evacuated to Malta, he did not recover. He died at Imtarfa Military Hospital on 23 July 1915 and was buried at Pieta Military Cemetery.

Then there was confusion.

Within a month, the Marshal family received a cablegram indicating their son had died. But they thought it may have been a case of mistaken identity, as the cablegram said the person was Alan Marshall. His widowed mother wrote an angry letter, asking why she had 'received no notice of my son's illness and that I did not receive the cable until a week after his death'. 'And I also wish to draw your attention to the fact that my son's name is Alan Marshal. A name that ought to be well known as he was famous both in England and Australia as a brilliant cricketer. In the cable received they say A Marshall died of enteric fever. How am I to know if this is my son or not. I know there were two other A Marshalls in the division. My son's name is spelt with one L. Marshal.'

Mrs Marshal didn't have to wait long for the fateful confirmation that a talent described by *Wisden* as 'a cricketer of unfulfilled promise' was gone.

A person of 'unfulfilled promise' who survived Gallipoli but died shortly after was the versatile Tasmanian batsman Stan McKenzie, who knew all about ill fortune well before he joined the Australian Army Medical Corps. Like the Backman and Marshal families, the McKenzies endured unnecessary stress due to ineptitude. McKenzie hailed from one of Launceston's most respectable families, with his father, Harry, the warden of the local Marine Board. Matthew Stanley McKenzie, who soon demanded that all call him 'Stan', made the Tasmanian cricket side as a stylish early-order batsman, showing his potential when, like Backman, he played against the 1912 England team. The visitors were granted two games in Tasmania — Launceston and Hobart.

As Tasmania was lowly regarded in Australian cricket circles, the MCC didn't take the games seriously. Several senior players, such as Jack Hobbs and George Gunn, remained on the mainland. Hobbs was no fan of unnecessary sea-travel. Instead he and Gunn spent four days on a Victorian farm shooting rabbits.

In Launceston, 21-year-old bank clerk McKenzie top-scored in Tasmania's first innings of 217 with 59, and was one of the few to pass 20 in the second. It took England three days to win the game, prompting a frantic overnight trip to get to Hobart for the start of the next game the following morning. As bleary-eyed as McKenzie was, he opened the batting and, like his partner, lasted only a few balls and failed to score a run. He did little better in the second innings with 29, and the team could not avoid the humiliation of a loss to England by an innings and 95 runs.

Tasmania respected McKenzie more as a footballer, rating him 'the most brilliant centre man of recent years'. He was among the first selected in Northern Tasmania representative sides.

In 1914 McKenzie was lured to the powerful Carlton Football Club in Melbourne. Still, he picked the wrong moment to have a slightly off preliminary final performance against South Melbourne. For the grand final McKenzie was dropped, and he missed out on being a premiership winner as Carlton won the flag by six points. He never played football — or cricket — again.

He enlisted in Hobart in November 1914 as a medical orderly in the 1st Australian Imperial Force. For several months, McKenzie tended the wounded on the Gallipoli Peninsula, and was among the last to be evacuated. He went to Mudros, but then on the trip to Alexandria became gravely ill with appendicitis. He died on board the hospital ship *Gloucester Castle* on 8 December 1915 while it was berthed in Alexandria Harbour. He was buried the following day at the Chatby Military and War Memorial Cemetery in Alexandria.

Five months later the family was still awaiting official word as to their son's death. His father wrote the first of several scathing letters to the army in May 1916. Addressing himself to the Officer in Charge of Base Records in Melbourne, Mr McKenzie wrote: 'I wrote you 9–2–1916 and have been waiting a reply re the personal effects of deceased. Will you kindly send them along at your earliest convenience. It seems very strange if this boy died that we can get no information as to his death, where he was buried, even his brother who is still fighting and has been since the first shot was fired (barring the period he was wounded)[11] cannot get any news. You may quite understand how his mother looks at the business. It seems very cruel to say the least when no one replys [sic]. If there is any charge for the information, we will endeavour to pay, when we know what is the charge.'

To add to the indignity, when eventually the family received their son's 1914–15 Star medal, except that it was inscribed to Private M.S. McKenzie. The family was adamant Stan had been promoted to sergeant. Mr McKenzie wrote to Captain N. Mackintosh explaining the error and asking: 'What will I do with it?'

No reply.

A month later, he wrote again to Mackintosh. It was straight to the point. 'You have not replied to mine of the 23rd August. Kindly do so and prevent further trouble.'

Then followed a bureaucratic spat as the authorities determined whether he was a private or a sergeant. Eventually it was agreed he had been promoted — especially as his war paybook, retrieved by the family, called him that rank about a dozen times. It is unknown whether the family received a new, updated medal.

At least they eventually received their son's belongings. Holding pride of place in the parcel were his false teeth.

---

11   His younger brother, George McKenzie, was awarded the Distinguished Conduct Medal for conspicuous gallantry in rescuing a comrade under fire at Gaba Tepe in May 1915.

CHAPTER 4

C.E.W. BEAN AND THAT PHOTO ...

As the Anzac troops prepared for their only masterstroke of a flawed and traumatic Gallipoli campaign — a brilliantly conceived and executed evacuation — Australia's intrepid official war correspondent, C.E.W. Bean, walked among them. Major Thomas Blamey had lent Bean his camera, and he took a variety of shots of his final days on Gallipoli, one of which is now a cricketing classic.

It shows a group of Light Horse soldiers playing an impromptu game, supposedly to distract the Turks into believing they were there for the long haul. The Turks were unaware this was a diversion. The Anzac soldiers would soon all be gone from the Gallipoli killing fields without suffering any more casualties. It was a masterful display of deception and planning.

Shell Green, at the southern end of Anzac Cove, was chosen as the venue for the cricket match, on 17 December 1915, as it was one of the few level areas on the peninsula. Twenty-two yards of relatively flat ground were paced out, and stumps, bat and ball were found. The wicket was hard, so there was a chance to get some bounce and lift.

But this one-time cotton field had a serious drawback: it was one of the most heavily bombed areas during the Gallipoli campaign. This didn't deter our cricketing soldiers.

In the photograph, the right-handed batsman lunges forward, playing an on-drive past a soldier perched close to the pitch. The bowler, balding and appearing somewhat aged, is taking it all seriously, having taken off his coat to give himself more chance of providing a troubling delivery on this barren, dry track. The coat appears to have been dropped at deep mid-on. Six fielders wait for a catch while some soldiers watch, one at backward square leg sprawled on the ground, others with their back to the play. There's no wicketkeeper — instead there appears to be a pile of equipment acting as a backstop.

The batsman, who had organised the game and lured Bean to the spot, had a strong link to another sporting code. He was also well connected. George Macleay Macarthur-Onslow was the great grandson of John Macarthur, the hot-blooded pioneer of the Australian wool industry, and white settlement, of the new colony.

Born at Camden Park near Sydney, George was educated at Rugby School in England — which claims to be where William Webb Ellis started the rugby code in 1823 by picking the ball up during a soccer game and running with it. While the Webb Ellis tale is more fantasy than fact, Rugby School to this day indignantly protects its claim to being the birthplace of the game. When Macarthur-Onslow returned to Sydney, he joined the New South Wales Mounted Rifles. Then, as a 40-year-old, Major Macarthur-Onslow took command of the Australian Imperial Force 7th Light Horse while it was a dismounted unit at Gallipoli.

The aim of this mock cricket game, apart from bamboozling the Turks, was to keep his men entertained. Macarthur-Onslow understood the importance of being in charge of a contented, well balanced group of men.

That night, Bean wrote in his diary: 'I took some final photos today ... A little further on I found 1 Light Horse playing cricket on Shell Green (Major Onslow batting) while shells were flying far overhead. I got a picture of Padre Dexter sowing wattle in cemeteries.'

Major General Granville Ryrie, who was at the time a federal parliamentarian, wrote to his wife: 'We had a game of cricket on Shell Green on Sunday just to let them see we were quite unconcerned ... and when shells whistled by we pretended to field them.'

Bean was naturally drawn to the game. Since a child he had been a cricketing obsessive. Born in Bathurst, NSW, but educated in England, he was fascinated by the navy and cricket. An early photograph of the three Bean boys — Montague, Charles and John — shows Charles holding a cricket ball, while John has a cricket bat over his left shoulder. Another family photograph has Charles in full cricket regalia, brandishing an old, well-worn bat. While not a prominent player, he was always enthusiastic, making the second XI at Clifton College, near Bristol, as an allrounder. He could do a bit of everything but knew his shortcomings.

'If I could only manage to field really well I should feel quite at home. But I must practise fielding hard to be good.'

He missed out on his school colours because he was too edgy in the field.

'I dreaded missing catches, and consequently missed one in the match against Liverpool. W.G. Grace's son, Charles Butler Grace, got the colours instead,' Bean said.

The passion remained, though, and was revived in 1912, when, as *The Sydney Morning Herald*'s London correspondent, he covered the Triangular Tournament, in which Syd Gregory's Australian team played England and South Africa.

Cricket references regularly appeared in his war writings. In one of his first pieces from Gallipoli, he wrote to the *SMH* on 5 July 1915 of the courage of the Australian soldiers as they headed up the cliffs in the opening days of the campaign.

For some time there was confusion whether the soldiers 'on the skyline' were Turks or Australians. 'These men are Australians,' wrote Bean in his *SMH* report, 'and whilst we were looking for them on the nearer ridge and especially on that shoulder rising from the beach on the right, they were right back there on the further hills. I can't say what a load that has lifted off one's mind. One has known that relief and elation before — I can't help thinking of it — when one has seen a hard-fought match pulled off for Australia on the Sydney Cricket Ground.

Only there is behind it this certainty — this victory this time has big consequences — they will not be finished with a single publication in the evening papers.'

The following year on the Western Front, he was impressed with the Australian soldiers' willingness to confront all. At Pozières, the Australian 'bombers from the word "go" took no heed of their lives'. 'They went into it as Australians go into a game,' Bean wrote in the *Swan Hill Guardian and Lake Boga Advocate*. 'In the pale early night they stood up straight near the edge of that circular trench, and hurled bombs into it as a man throws a cricket ball. Wherever a German showed, someone had a rifle to his shoulders, and immediately shot him. Then down would go the rifle, and bomb after bomb would be hurled straight into a likely corner as a fielder throws down a wicket.'

He described in the *Morning Bulletin* (Rockhampton) that, after 'a bomb fight, lasting many hours in the German trenches, in which our men fought like cricketers, standing to their full height in the open and throwing for all they were worth', portions of the German trenches were taken.

At Lagnicourt, 'our field guns began to bang like so many well driven cricket bats overhead'.

At Bapaume, 'we were looking down into a great grassy drain, 30 feet deep and as wide as a cricket pitch is long'.

Here Bean was impressed with the lackadaisical manner of 'the digger'.

'The Australian has a distinct manner in action — everyone notices it. He does not alter his ordinary style of walking, or even of standing, or of sitting around and yarning, unless there is pretty urgent need for doing so. He strolled through the streets of that exploding town as if he were walking to catch a Sydney ferry boat. You saw him coming towards you out of the smoke, chatting in couples, as he might saunter to the Cricket Ground.'

Most importantly, with army recruitment, 'just as in picking a cricket or a football team to represent Australia, the inclusion of a man who does not have the necessary qualities, however splendid his physical qualification may be, is apt to do more harm than good'.

Cricket also appears in the early volumes of his official history. In *The Story of Anzac*, he describes how at Lone Pine, when the first wave of Australian attackers reached the enemy's trenches, there occurred 'an unforeseen check': 'Instead of disappearing into the trench, they could be seen standing along it a crowd not unlike that lining the rope round a cricket field.' In *The Official History of Australia in the war of 1914–18*, Volume III *The AIF in France 1916*, he described how, at the Battle of Fromelles, the Germans were 'tossing stick-bombs from the shelter of the trench, while the Australians, up on the parapet, flung their missiles like cricketers throwing at a wicket'.

There are several other Gallipoli cricket photos from the day that famous shot was taken. The State Library of Victoria has a hand-coloured photograph taken from behind the stumps the same afternoon. It shows a knobbly-kneed left-handed batsman about to face a delivery, with a wicketkeeper hovering near the stumps. Soldiers, some in khaki, others in white top, await at point, cover, wide mid-off and short midwicket. Just over mid-off are five soldiers watching the action. Everyone is either wearing a slouch hat or a military cap. Except for the head-gear, you could almost imagine this was being staged not on a horrific killing field but on a gentle beach or hinterland somewhere in Australia.

Shortly after, the area was deserted. That night, Bean left for Imbros on board a boat captained by Henry Edgar Grace, son of W.G. Grace and older brother of that same William Butler Grace who had 'got the colours' when Bean had dropped a catch at Clifton College.

As Bean wrote in his diary the following day: 'So I have left old Anzac. In a way I was really fond of the place. I have certainly had some quite enjoyable times there in my old dugout, yarning to friends or going round the lines. I can't pretend that I ever liked shells or attacks but one came to put up with them much as one does with toothache.'

During the 1932–33 Bodyline series, when Bean was involved in writing the fourth volume of Australia's official Great War history, he wrote letters to Australian and British newspapers to complain that cricket had lost its way. His concerns were issued early in the series, following the first Test in Sydney, highlighted by Stan McCabe's unbeaten 187 in the first innings and Harold Larwood's ten-wicket haul — five in each innings — to ensure a ten-wicket England triumph. Although England captain Douglas Jardine's prime Bodyline target — Don Bradman — did not play in this Test, as he was 'completely run down', other Australian players, including McCabe, Jack Fingleton and Bill Ponsford, were constantly pounded in the body by rising deliveries from several opposing bowlers, notably Larwood and Bill Voce.

On the final day of the Test, the *SMH* ran an editorial which appeared to defend England's inflammatory bowling tactics.

'The Larwood–Voce combination is now plainly a danger which the Australian opening batsmen will have to find means to combat,' the editorial said. 'It is puerile to complain of the Englishmen's "shock bowling" as something unfair. We have seen Voce force both Bradman and Ponsford across the wicket to "avoid being hit" (as their action made it seem) by a ball which knocked out the middle or leg stump. As for the bumping ball, have Australians no memory? Are Jones, Cotter, McDonald and Gregory[12] so soon forgotten? Did they never make the ball fly high at the batsman here and in England?'

Bean was unimpressed with the editorial's tone.

He began his letter to the editor with: 'As a lifelong lover of cricket may I, with all respect, urge certain considerations opposed to the view expressed in your leading article today?

'Surely the fact that some Australian fast bowlers have occasionally sent down balls that flew past the batsman's head is not to be urged as a justification for the authorities of cricket permitting this form of attack to become a main feature of the game.

---

12 The editorial is referring to former Australian Test speedsters Ernie Jones, Tibby Cotter, Ted McDonald and Jack Gregory. Voce had bowled to Bradman in an earlier tour game.

'From their boyhood millions of cricketers have learnt to regard bowling at the body as a mean trick, not to be used on pain of losing one's school colours or being ruled out of order in decent club cricket. If some great bowlers in the past have occasionally broken this unwritten rule, it has been generally felt that they offended against the ethics of cricket, and their captains would have done well to check them. It may have been on the basis of that bad practice that these new tactics have been built up, but the fact that a small breach of the ethics of cricket develops into a greater breach is no reason why the greater breach should not be prevented.'

If cricketing administrators allowed this to continue, he argued, then 'the threat of bodily harm to a player may be used as a means of winning the game'. 'We shall have batteries of fast bowlers produced, whose main object will be bowling at the body. It is only a matter of time and we shall have a leading player killed. The game will have an element of the prize fight, and in the spectators we may expect, what we have actually seen, not less excitement, but an undercurrent of angry feeling, which previously has been absent from cricket, and is repugnant to the whole spirit of the game.'

During the third Test there was crowd unrest, and diplomatic links between the two countries were frayed after Australian captain Bill Woodfull and wicketkeeper Bert Oldfield were hit by Larwood with sickening blows. It remains Australian cricket's most volatile moment.

Bean was asked by the *SMH* to comment, and he wrote: 'Though amply warned both in England and here, the MCC authority lacked the wisdom to foresee the trouble for which it was inevitably steering when it gave its tacit approval to an obvious breach of the old ethical standards of cricket, through "body bowling". As a consequence it has landed international cricket in the most serious mess in the history of the game. This result was foreseen before the MCC team left England. The singularly unpleasant atmosphere which, for the first time, has surrounded a series of these splendid games is not due to lack of sportsmanship among the spectators — on the contrary. It was inevitable from the moment when the controllers of the game authorised, by their attitude, the importation into it of the principles of the prize fight.

'Surely, we may hope that they will now recognise that cricket as a medium of international goodwill is dead, unless this mistake can be rectified. Should not the Australian Board of Control consider the sending to the British authorities of a dignified, reasoned protest, setting forth the results of the new practice, and asking for suitable amendments of the laws of cricket? The alternative — that we should ourselves produce a batter of super "body-bowlers" who will reduce that method to an absurdity by ruining the game, is not to be thought of. If our request for an amendment is not granted, we could decline to send or receive another team until agreement is reached.'

Cricket remained one of Bean's overriding passions until he died in 1968 — three days after England won the fifth Test of the Ashes series at The Oval.

He didn't boast about it, but Bean was privately enthused that he took such an important historical cricketing shot just before the Australian troops headed to the Western Front. For him it emphasised the pluck and daring of the troops he deeply admired.

CHAPTER 5

WHEREABOUTS UNKNOWN

During the Great War numerous sportsmen enlightened those back home by writing revealing, expressive letters to various newspapers. Many thankfully avoided the censor's pencil, providing a revealing look at how dangerous and horrible life was on the frontline, and how the sporting contingent often banded together to revive spirits.

The Referee ran letter after letter from illustrious serving sportsmen. In June 1916 a letter was received titled 'Somewhere in France' from a Victorian Sheffield Shield player, Frank Lugton, who was missing his summer pastime.

'I am doing as well as can be expected by one at this game. It is different to cricket, and one wishes that the other side would bowl a few more wides and no-balls. I have had a couple of close shaves. Just heard the bails rattle once or twice, but not enough to knock them off. So long as they don't get closer I am quite satisfied. We still seem to be bowling against the wind, but I think our turn is coming this Summer. We have to get rid of a number of the other side, even if we don't finish the game.'

Lugton was the master of understatement. Close shaves! One of Melbourne's most revered sportsmen was lucky to be alive.

At Gallipoli he had been buried alive for more than six hours due to a shell explosion. He suffered from shell shock when firing at a Turkish sniper. An enemy shot knocked the bolt out of his rifle and ricocheted through the cap of a colleague standing nearby, just missing his skull. This led to a lengthy hospital spell in Malta with a 'defective right eye'.

But where Lugton excelled was grenade throwing. He was as good as any on the Turkish Peninsula, hurling them with pinpoint accuracy at enemy targets. Among those in the 24th Battalion, he was often called upon to lead the grenade charge.

Here he was a natural. As *The Leader* newspaper explained: 'Frank always had a splendid arm and could throw a cricket ball a hundred yards. He naturally took to "bombing" work at Gallipoli, and had charge of a grenade party. His CO told him jokingly on one occasion that on his return to Melbourne he could see him in his mind's eye putting a match to a cricket ball before he delivered it.'

His throwing skills came from years playing with the Northcote Cricket Club. He then became a regular member of the Victorian team in 1914, where as an allrounder he combined middle-order batting with fast-medium pace bowling. Lugton's career highlights included dismissing Victor Trumper and Charlie Kelleway and finishing just six runs short of a maiden century in his fifth first-class match. He was also an adept footballer, playing two seasons with the Melbourne VFL club as a tenacious centre half-back.

By May 1916, he was in France and struggling to make sense of his surroundings. He wrote: 'I have been in France a few weeks, and it has rained nearly all the time. Yesterday and today, however, are fine Spring days, the first we have had. We are in the trenches here and things seem fairly quiet, but the night we came out was rather funny. It was pitch dark and raining like anything. We had to go through a sap[13] about two miles in length. The bottom of the sap was full of mud and water and duck board was laid along the sap or built up as required. In some places the boards were a foot or so off the ground, and only a foot wide. The mud and water made the boards pretty greasy, and our chaps,

---

13 A deep narrow trench.

trying to walk along in the dark, would often walk clean off the boards into the mud and water, up to the waist in places. You can imagine the language flowed quicker than the water, and you picture what we were like when we got through.'

Two months later Lugton was gone, killed near Villers-Bretonneux on 29 July 1916 when part of a group that attacked a German parapet. Like hundreds of other Australians in that area, his body was never recovered. Some believe he may have been buried near Pozières. Where — no one knows.

He was wearing a silver wristwatch which the Northcote club had presented to him in May 1915 for 'his manly decision to fight for his country'. The watch, inscribed on the underside, was never found. In 1917, those from the Northcote club who had farewelled their representative star reassembled in the pavilion at the unveiling of his portrait. *The Preston Leader*, reporting the gathering, was told that Lugton 'would have undoubtedly become one of Victoria's mainstays as an all-round player had he been spared, perhaps such another player as Warwick Armstrong, who thought highly of Frank, both personally and as a player. Warwick on hearing of his death, said Frank was one of the nicest boys he had ever played with. So he was. His life had barely opened, the outlook bright and alluring, but who will say it was not complete?'

A month after Lugton's death, Tasmanian representative Lionel Butler, who was known as Leo, was killed in the same region. His rise to first-class cricketing status came relatively late. When 31, he was called in to bolster the Tasmanian batting line-up for two matches in 1914–15, scoring a meagre 24 runs in his four innings. His late promotion may have had something to do with his profession — a Hobart barrister, like his father, grandfather and great-grandfather. His battle life was relatively brief. Butler was on the Western Front for just over five months when at Mouquet Farm, Pozières, on 22 August 1916 he was called to relieve his captain. A shell exploded near him, blowing off one of his legs. Butler was carried out by stretcher-bearers to the closest aid post, where he died the following day.

By the end of the year, another Tasmanian notable had perished in France. The death of William Keith Eltham hit Hobart especially hard, as he was one of the island's most capable and versatile individuals, a master of many diverse crafts. Apart from playing 11 matches for the state, primarily as a middle-order batsman, he was a notable singer, actor, cartoonist, artist, writer, poet, essayist, draughtsman and rower.

His idol was his father, who taught him the importance of not wasting a moment. William Cooper Eltham was, apart from being *The Mercury*'s cricket writer, the chief scorer for the Southern Tasmania Cricket Association and one of the first ground umpires in the Southern Football Association. He was also a time judge and umpire of numerous athletic contests.

Eltham senior was the founder of the Hobart Orpheus Club, where he was honorary conductor, pianist, organist and vocalist for 30 years. A key member of the Hobart Choral Society, he organised and managed Tasmania's first 'jumble fair', where electric power was used for the first time in Hobart.

Keith followed his father in various fields, singing in the Orpheus Choir and appearing in vaudeville acts at various Hobart theatres. He received special praise in *The Mercury* in June 1912 for his encore at the Concert Comedy Company performance of 'If there hadn't been an apple in the tree would you still love me?'

His cartoons began appearing in Tasmanian newspapers during a period where he was a regular member of the state cricket team (between 1910 and 1914), batting at numerous spots in the order, including opening. His patriotism was intense, leaving Tasmania with the first contingent from Hobart in the 9th Australian Field Artillery in October 1914.

He was heavily involved in the Gallipoli campaign but had to return to Alexandria for treatment when in July 1915 he suffered extensive facial injuries from a piece of shrapnel smashing into his mouth. Even that did not deter him, as he was still able to contribute several line drawings of Gaba Tepe and McCoy's Reach which were included in Bean's *The Anzac Book*. The book was published in 1916 from stories, illustrations and poems submitted by the Gallipoli soldiers. Wherever Eltham went he had with him his sketchbook, colour box, pencils and fountain pen, as well as a book of poems.

Recuperating in Egypt, he sent several reports back to *The Mercury* on football and cricket matches involving the troops. This included Tasmania's epic football win over Western Australia in early 1916: 4.16 (40) to 4.13 (37).

Eltham reported: 'Eighty miles from Cairo, and few amusements for us, the good old Australian game has been booming here. The weather is rather warm, and the only available ground sandy and stony, but some excellent games have been played. Mr Jack Sharp, the popular League timekeeper, kindly forwarded a couple of balls to our Battery (9th). Poles from the wagons make adequate goal posts, and the boundaries are indicated by banks of sand.

'The Tassies owed their victory to their tenacity in sticking to their opponents, wearing them down for that last burst. The West Australians were a very even lot, in fact, there was hardly a passenger on either side, though Graham (an ex-League man) stood out most, and grey-haired old Chester did wonders.'

A month later, Eltham wrote to *The Mercury*'s sports editor to provide the latest Egyptian footy news. 'Since writing you last football has continued busily, matches being played every Wednesday and Sunday, and the 9th Battery is still unbeaten.'

There was one draw.

'A feature of this game was the commandeering of a soccer ball to complete the second half as a nail on a horse picketing post punctured our league ball. It was very windy that day and class of play poor.'

The reports dried up when he was transferred to France, to the 1st Australian Field Artillery, where he was elevated to first lieutenant in September 1916. Only weeks later he had to be moved to Wandsworth Hospital in England as he had been shot, with a bullet having to be extracted from his buttock. Just before Christmas 1916 he was back in France, and on New Year's Eve was having a rest in his dugout when he had a quick look, only to be struck by a German bullet. The dugout was then directly hit by a German shell. Eltham was buried alive. For some time his colleagues hadn't realised what had happened. They then tried to frantically dig him out. But it was far too late. Eltham was long dead. In his pockets were two notebooks which he used for drawings and for working out artillery aiming points. One which fitted snugly in his jacket pocket had the imprint of a bullet that had ripped apart the cover and numerous pages. Another pad had been shot straight through by a bullet on its way to hitting Eltham directly in the heart.

Adding to the pain of his friends was that, the day before the news of his death was announced in Hobart, several of them had received elaborate Christmas cards from him which included numerous drawings and illustrations wishing them season's greetings. That had buoyed their spirits, until 24 hours later ...[14]

In Eltham's last appearance for Tasmania, in 1914, his middle-order batting partner was Lawrence Gatenby. Later that year, Gatenby, a 26-year-old jackeroo, was a member of the 40th Infantry AIF Battalion, suffering from tonsillitis, typhoid, appendicitis, mumps and even, according to his medical records, 'suffering slightly from flatulence', before heading to the Western Front, where he was shot in early January 1917. He died of his wounds at the 2nd Australian Casualty Clearing Station on 14 January. When it came to organising a plaque, there was some confusion within the AIF over whether his first name was Laurence or Lawrence. The family confirmed it was Lawrence, ensuring the right spelling on his memorial.

The bereaved family of Hubert George Selwyn-Smith, who played three matches as an allrounder for Queensland in 1912–13, received what they thought was encouraging news following their son's death in Belgium when the *Brisbane Courier* ran a report of discovered war graves. For some time the paper had been told that Captain Selwyn-Smith, who had enlisted just before his final university law examinations, had not been recovered following

---

14 One hundred years on, the Hobart City Council honoured Eltham by naming the sporting pavilion at the Queens Domain after him.

several intense days of battle at Messines. How this tall, striking man, whose most telling feature was that he was missing nine teeth, had been killed in June 1917 is unknown, but the family knew he had been a mighty soldier. Nine months earlier he had been hospitalised after being hit in the neck by fragments of high explosives at Mouquet Farm. However, determined to get back to the front as soon as possible, he was among his colleagues in just over five weeks. The family had heard word in late 1917 that their son had died, but little else was known.

In 1919 the family wrote to the Base Records Office in Melbourne: 'Seeing in the Brisbane Courier of yesterday that photographs were being taken of the graves of those brave lads who had fallen in France and having lost a son, then it would be deeply grateful if we could have a photograph of our son's grave. He was killed at Messines on 7th June 1917 and we believe is buried at Despagues Farm, Messines Ridge.'

No reply was received. Instead Selwyn-Smith is commemorated on the Ypres (Menin Gate) Memorial. Nearby is the name of another notable cricketer, whose family also suffered dreadful years of uncertainty.

The relations of Fred Collins, who would be killed in action in Belgium four months later, suffered the anguish of discovering that where they originally thought he was buried was wrong, due to a mix-up with an identification tag that led to endless months of confusion — a distressing finale for someone who a few years earlier was on the verge of Australian Test selection.

A Scotch College student, Collins joined the strong East Melbourne Cricket Club straight from school. Even though only 17, he immediately became a key strike bowler, with a style described by club and state teammate Peter McAlister[15]

---

15   McAlister was one of Australian cricket's most controversial figures. A moderately successful Test batsman, he upset many players when appointed vice-captain and treasurer of the 1909 Australian touring team to England. McAlister, with strong allegiances to cricket's governing hierarchy, was at the centre of the 1912 player/administration dispute. McAlister was offside with many players for being too closely connected to officialdom, and as a selector using the position to ensure he was named in important line-ups.

as 'medium pace with a big off-break but also a fast ball which surprised many batsmen'. He was renowned for his express-pace yorker and deceptive slow ball. In his first senior match against Richmond, he took 8/78. The start to his next grade club was as profitable, with a five-wicket haul against Melbourne at the MCG convincing the Victorian selectors he was first-class quality. They promptly picked him for the away game against South Australia in in November 1899.

Even though aged only 18 years and one month, he was undaunted by opening the Victorian bowling with captain Hugh Trumble at Adelaide Oval. Collins enjoyed the most stunning of debuts, taking six first innings wickets for 81, with his victims including numerous notable Australian batsmen, such as Clem Hill, Joe Darling, George Giffin and Jack Lyons.

Thus began a highly productive decade-long career in which, in 37 appearances for Victoria, he tallied 146 wickets at an impressive average of 26.10, including 11 five-wicket-plus hauls. At grade level he was among Melbourne's most devastating, taking 422 wickets at 13.9. His batting, though, was hardly startling — a classic late-order batsman, coarse rather than class.

When the 1902 and 1905 Ashes tour teams were selected, Collins was among the final contenders, but each time missed out as the Australian selectors preferred Ernie Jones, Trumble, Jack Saunders, Monty Noble, Warwick Armstrong, Tibby Cotter and Charles McLeod to be the main strike bowlers. There was one last belated chance when he was selected to play in Monty Noble's testimonial match for 'The Rest' against an Australian XI at the SCG in March 1908. However, on a flat wicket, Collins was unable to provide any resistance as Australia's best made The Rest attack look second rate, scoring 569 in 362 minutes — with Syd Gregory and Armstrong scoring centuries even though batting No 8 and 9. Collins's only wicket was Clem Hill, bowling him after he had scored a half-century.

Constantly being overlooked by the Test selectors convinced Collins to focus more on his professional career as a commission agent with the AMP Insurance Company. However, his work-time diligence led to conflict with cricket officials, a problem also faced by some of his teammates — notably Warwick Armstrong and Jack Saunders.

During the 1906–07 season, Victorian officials were struggling to keep their belligerent captain, Armstrong, in check. They wanted him to play but Armstrong was selective as he had just taken up his first job in several years as a clerk with the Department of Home Affairs. He was nonetheless picked for the Christmas match against South Australia, but when he stressed to Victorian officials he could not play they tried to contact Department officials to allow him to play. That further riled Armstrong. McAlister took over the captaincy in Armstrong's absence, and Victoria was soon in disarray. On the final day, with Victoria batting to save the match, both Collins and Saunders failed to turn up. After Victoria batted only nine, South Australia won by 319 runs.

The Victorian Cricket Association (VCA) instituted an inquiry, where Collins explained that AMP had told him he had to work that day. Saunders said he didn't believe he would be required to bat until lunch, so spent the morning in his usual employ — caretaking at the Carlton club. Collins escaped a fine, while Saunders was docked 40 per cent of his £5 match fee.

Eventually leg injuries forced Collins to retire at the end of the 1911–12 season. A few years later, at age 34, it was the death of his cousin, Gunner William Collins of the 4th Field Artillery Brigade, from wounds received while in Gallipoli, which convinced Fred Collins to enlist.

Before leaving for France, Collins spent several months at the Broadmeadows Training Camp, where he became friends with one of Australia's most notorious business figures — John Wren. Describing himself as an entrepreneur, Wren ran illegal gambling joints in Melbourne, in particular a famous totalisator in Collingwood; was involved in numerous questionable sporting activities, including boxing promotion and fixing professional cycling races; and had strong political and business links to the top end of town. He was an intense nationalist and pro-conscriptionist, awarding Australia's first Great War Victoria Cross winner, Albert Jacka, with £500 and a gold watch, and later helping him in business. Wren, at the time 43, enlisted a week before Collins, describing his occupation as 'investor'. During their three months at Broadmeadows, he and Collins were close, not surprising considering Wren's intense sporting interests, which included being one of the Collingwood Football Club's most committed supporters. However, Wren was discharged after only a few months for being 'medically unfit'. His war papers state this very clearly, adding that it was 'not result of misconduct'. Clearly the AIF was aware of Wren's shady reputation and wanted to set the record straight — Wren was found to be deaf in his right ear.

While Wren was back in civilian clothing, Collins was in France by September 1916, where he was attached to the 21st Battalion, promoted to 2nd lieutenant and involved in fighting near the Belgium border. A fractured hand from a trench mishap saw him transferred to England, and a welcome return to the cricket field representing the 3rd Division AIF team against British Southern Command. The AIF cobbled together a reasonable line-up led by Private Charlie Macartney, who scored an easy century before Collins saw British Southern Command finish well short of a 270-run target by taking four wickets, the final dismissal involving a 'sensational' caught and bowled. A fair effort, considering he had a bung hand.

The frolic did not last long, as the following year Collins was on the frontline, north-east of Ypres, involved in an Australian assault. After arriving at Broodseinde Ridge, the superior officers found countless Australian soldiers had been killed or had gone missing. Among those was Collins, who had been in charge of a group of soldiers. No one had any clue what had happened to him. Another missing from the same action, later known as the 'carnage of Passchendaele', was John Cotter, the brother of Tibby Cotter, one of Collins's opponents for a Test pace spot. John Cotter's body was never found.

Within a fortnight the Collins family was told of their son's death, only for confusion to follow. They first heard he had been buried at Warlencourt British Cemetery, near Bapaume in France, about 90 kilometres from where he was supposed to have been fighting. They then received notification his body had to be elsewhere, because authorities were certain he had been killed near Ypres.

A letter from the Base Records Office to one of Fred's brothers states: 'It is manifestly impossible for his remains to have been removed for interment to within 2½ miles of Bapaume (France), some 55 miles distant from the scene of his death.

'A careful comparison of the Battalion records clearly indicates that Lieutenant Collins rejoined his unit on 22/9/17 following a period of hospital treatment, and undoubtedly participated in its operations up to the time of his death on 4/10/17, his name appearing with those of other regimental officers who became casualties on this date and who were buried in the neighbourhood.'

What led to the uncertainty was an identity disc, supposedly of F.B. Collins, which had been found with an unidentified body at Bapaume.

The Base Records Office letter continues: 'It transpires that the former report of burial originated with the recovery of a disc bearing the name of your brother from the remains of an Australian soldier interred in the above named cemetery, and it was erroneously assumed at the time that the grave was that of the late officer. It is not clear under what circumstances the disc came into the possession of another soldier, but it has been clearly demonstrated that the burial officers were at fault in registering the grave under the name of your brother.'

The letter ended: 'Assuring you of the Department's sympathy and profound regret at the distressing circumstances arising.'

The official records were changed to indicate the grave was of an 'unknown Australian soldier'. So where Collins is actually buried remains a puzzle.

Whether it was Collins's disc was also never verified, even though it was among the personal possessions the AIF sent back to the family in Melbourne. Unfortunately the ship bringing the belongings back to Australia was torpedoed and sunk by a German U-boat off the English coast.

Craig Reece's 2018 limited edition book *Patriotic Cricketers*, which provides extensive details of Collins's life, reveals that Wren later assisted the grieving family.[16]

---

16 In 2000, the Hawthorn-East Melbourne club was asked with all other clubs by the Victorian Cricket Association to nominate their Team of the Century. Collins was named in the team, along with Ben Barnett, Australia's wicketkeeper in the 1938 Ashes series, whose story is recalled later in this book. Collins's name is commemorated on the Ypres Menin Gate Memorial.

CHAPTER 6

THE BIG 'WHAT IF'

In April 1917, Private Norman Frank Callaway penned a letter from the Western Front to a cricketing mate in Sydney. It was succinct.

After a hooray, hello and indication of the delight that in France he was with several colleagues in a machine-gun company known as the Suicide Club, Callaway wrote: 'I've just had my 21st birthday and am now a man.' He would celebrate his elevation to manhood in a French inn.

No such letter was sent to his parents' house at 22 Ebley Street, Waverley, as they had still not quite got over the fact he'd falsified his age to enlist without their approval. The authorities thought he was 21 when he enlisted at Victoria Barracks on 7 May 1916. He'd written down his age as 21 years and one month, but he was exactly one year younger. Less drama on the home front if he didn't mention his birthday in a letter to his parents.

He had wanted to enlist for so long. He wanted to 'get in with the guns'. But he was told the artillery had too many recruits.

'Oh well, I'll go in the foot-sloggers. I can't hang around for a few weeks doing nothing,' he told his mate.

Callaway's time as a fully fledged adult was brief. Within a month of this letter, he was killed with thousands of other Australians during the second battle of Bullecourt.

Gone was a most special sportsman, the Australian cricketer with the best first-class batting average of all — over the 200-plus mark. Gone was someone who could have been a standout postwar international batsman.

Instead he left hardly a trace. His body was never found on the French killing fields. His death wasn't confirmed for six months. His name is alphabetically listed on the commemorative wall at the Australian memorial in nearby Villers-Bretonneux in line after line of Anzac deaths from that region. His name occasionally bobs up as a cricketing trivia question. But there are no monuments to this talent. A cricketer with the most stunning statistic of all became an overlooked war statistic.

But Callaway's life remains a crucial story in reminding all that war never discriminates. It takes the mediocre, the genius and everyone in between.

Australia has produced countless sporting prodigies. Many come from the bush — not surprising as competitive sport is a crucial release from the endless hard grind of country life. Sport is encouraged, often acting as a town's central social event.

The isolated NSW town of Hay on the slow-flowing Murrumbidgee River, 700 kilometres west of Sydney, soon knew that the only son of the town's soap factory owner was unique. This was a young town proud of its sporting prowess. After all, it had somehow produced an Olympic swimming champion in Theo Tartakover, who appeared at the 1908 games in London and four years later in Stockholm in the 100-metre freestyle, 400-metre freestyle and relay events. Tartakover had learnt to swim in the muddy Murrumbidgee. And one of the young tykes scrambling along the edge at the segregated Alma Beach learning how to dog paddle, while Tartakover was cultivating his freestyle stroke, was Norman Callaway.

In country towns, there's no option to ease your way into a sporting team. Numbers are often short, with towns relying on transient workers chasing whatever farming or service jobs are available across the country, moving on when the seasons change and the wool clip or wheat money runs out. A country sporting tradition is 'The Saturday morning roundup', with officials grabbing whoever they can from the local pubs to make up the numbers.

If you show any promise as a cricketer or footballer in the bush, you're immediately in. Norman, who showed himself to be mighty at all ball sports as soon as he could walk, was just 12 when he was playing club cricket for his father Tom's team — Waradgery Cricket Club — against the local townsfolk and farmers. For years the Callaways, including Tom and publican brother James, had been involved in any sporting activity the town tried to organise. Waradgery was one of the area's more powerful cricketing teams, but like all others in the bush often couldn't find players on game day. So one afternoon Norman had to fill in as two Waradgery players had gone missing. He made an immediate impression. The local paper, *The Riverine Grazier*, noted in March 1909 that in the game against Gymnasium, 'The fielding of the Waradgery players was good, young Norman Callaway being especially noticeable, he bringing off a magnificent catch at square leg.'

The following year, as a 14-year-old, he was described in the *Grazier* as 'the Trumper of the school' after scoring 117 and 64 against the Convent. Soon he was the most prolific scorer in the club competition, including the local derby against Hay in November 1910 when 'the boy champion ... again proceeded to show his grandfathers — not how to suck eggs — but how to play the Hay bowling' when scoring 32 of Waradgery's first innings of 117. In another game he belted three sixes into the Hay Park grandstand. The teenager became such a town identity that mishaps such as when he broke his left arm after falling over a clothes prop made the pages of the local paper. As did a dispute when in 1912 Callaway indicated he no longer wanted to play Saturday cricket for Waradgery, which, according to the Hay Cricket Association, 'considerably weakened' the club. He eventually changed his mind, and played. This was big news in the *Grazier*.

That same year a family tragedy forced the Callaways to leave Hay. A younger brother, Ernest, died with acute bronchitis at just three days old. Devastated by the loss, the Callaways moved to Sydney. The *Grazier* commented in November 1912 that they had 'succumbed to the attractions of the "big smoke"'.

Callaway joined Paddington and, after being promoted to first grade, scored a century against Middle Harbour. Then came a century in his first interstate fixture, for the NSW Colts against Victoria Colts at the SCG — an innings which saw a Sydney newspaper describe him as 'one of the most promising colts seen for some time'. He moved to Waverley, cultivating his batting even further by playing in the middle order with Alan Kippax. They became a devastating combination, especially with Callaway starting with four successive half-centuries and unbeaten centuries against Paddington and North Sydney.

Even though only 18 years and ten months old, he was promoted by the NSW selectors to first-class status for the final match of the season against Queensland at the SCG in February 1915. The team was short several players, and a middle-order batting spot needed to be filled. It was still a reasonable line-up, captained by experienced Test representative Charlie Macartney and with Arthur Mailey as the main leg-spinning strike-power. Queensland had numerous notable bowlers, including their first Test player — Jack McLaren.

Queensland won the toss, batted, came and went, dismissed mid-afternoon for 137. The pitch was described as 'perfect', but it clearly possessed some gremlins, as Callaway, batting No 5, was at the crease after just a few overs with NSW struggling at 3/17.

It was supposed to be time for restraint. But Callaway showed all the impetuosity of youth by immediately taking on the Queensland bowling. He had no interest in playing himself in. He was straight onto the front foot with lusty hits. After just ten minutes, he was on 20. His partnership with Frank Farrar reaped 41 in 13 minutes, before the opening batsman edged one behind. Out came Macartney, and the aggression continued.

The newspapers loved what they saw. The reports reveal that Callaway, a relatively small figure at just under 170 centimetres tall, was determined to convince all that he was older than he actually was. In its match report, the *SMH* said he was 20. As far as the *SMH* was concerned his 'display was one of the finest ever seen from a colt'.

'From the first ball he swung the bat with great power and precision at anything within striking distance, and the ball hummed to all parts of the field at an extraordinary pace,' the *Herald* reported.

He was in front of a relatively small crowd, with cricket interest dwindling, according to *The Referee*, because most people were 'centred on the battles of the Empire and her Allies on the trenched fields of Europe and among the mine-fields of the North Sea'.

'Nevertheless', *The Referee* observed, 'one was surprised to see in the pavilion so many of the regular patrons of the game, men who have been watching cricket for half-a-century, more or less, with unabated and unabating interest; men, too, who have given their sons to the Empire in the greatest war in the history of the world. Their interest in the "game of games" as it is to them, will remain keen-edged to the end of the human chapter.'

Charlie Macartney, dropped first ball at first slip, had no qualms about Callaway taking the senior role. The *SMH* said, 'Macartney was not feeling well, and seeing his partner in such great form told him: "You go right ahead: I'll keep my end up".'

The teenager responded with a flourish. Callaway's half-century came in just over an hour. The century was reached in 94 minutes.

At stumps on the first day, Callaway was unbeaten. The *SMH* headlined its report: 'Brilliant Batting. Callaway 125 not out'.

Underneath were paragraphs of praise: 'The three strokes in which Callaway excelled were the on and off drives and the cut past point. And he varied them.

'For instance, one stroke would send the ball along the carpet to the pickets, but the next would be lifted high. His lifting off-drives which cleared cover-point's head were a revelation, and reminiscent of H.H. Massie's famous strokes, and the more modest but equally effective efforts of the famous A.C. McLaren [sic].[17] Callaway's square cuts and those behind point were almost as powerful as an ordinary drive. From every point of view his effort was magnificent, and quite on a par with that of M.A. Noble, who as a colt made 152 not out against an English team in the early 'Nineties. Callaway is an orthodox batsman — plays very straight and uses his feet deftly. He certainly should rise to great heights, all going well with him.'

The headline in the *SMH*'s next edition was even more compelling: 'World's Record. Fine Performance by Callaway'.

Just before lunch, Callaway passed the double century mark, after his fifth-wicket partnership of 256 runs with Macartney ended when the skipper was caught at mid-on. After the break, Callaway was finally dismissed on 207 with an edge to first slip. The *SMH* discovered Callaway was now a cricketing record-holder, as it was the highest score by a first-class player on debut.

Luck was also with Callaway, as the Queenslanders missed chances on 41, 149, 163, 175 and 180, either through dropped catches or missed stumpings.[18]

Some hours later, NSW was celebrating an innings and 231-run win triumph after Queensland was dismissed a second time for 100. *The Referee* said Callaway's impressive strokes were a 'straight bat in defence to the lusty off-drive, which made the ball whizz past mid-off, or over the head of cover-point, or the shot inside point, and in front of third man'.

'Making good use of his feet, and swinging his shoulders into it, his drives were very fine, and though the turf was hardly any faster than it had been in the recent matches, the ball travelled from the bat with pace that carried it to the pickets.'

It was Callaway's lofted off-drives that most reminded *The Referee* of former Test batsman Hugh Massie. The NSW Cricket

---

17 Archie MacLaren.
18 Among those Queenslanders who dropped Callaway was George Poeppel, playing his one and only state match as a late-order batsman. Enlisting in the 15th Battalion AIF, Poeppel was seriously wounded when hit by a shell when trying to invade a German advance post at Guidecourt in the Somme in February 1917. He collapsed in a trench, where he was taken prisoner by the Germans. He died in captivity the following day.

Association executive noted in its minutes that Callaway's innings 'was a delight to old players'.

He was again compared to Victor Trumper. *The Mirror of Australia* said that, like Trumper, Callaway 'invariably attacks the bowling' and has 'a beautiful swing, the bat generally describing three parts of a circle, and finishing well over the left shoulder'. 'Callaway is a glorious batsman to watch, and is a coming world's player. He is the personification of confidence.'

This comparison was stinging because, four months after his epic innings, Callaway was attending Trumper's funeral, after Australia's most graceful player died, near penniless, from Bright's disease, aged 37.

Callaway was among a large entourage of first-class cricketers — including Dave Gregory, Charles Bannerman, Tom Garrett, Hanson Carter, Arthur Mailey, Monty Noble, Warren Bardsley, Tibby Cotter, Charlie Macartney, Charlie Kelleway, Frank Iredale, Charlie Turner and Syd Gregory — who followed the procession from Chatswood to Waverley Cemetery. That sad day reinforced in Callaway the uneasy feeling that not even the most notable cricketers, while adored by the public, as evidenced by more than 250,000 mourners lining the Sydney streets to pay their respects, are privileged or immortal, and can also be struck down by ill fate.

Callaway's cricketing opportunities had also shrunk, as the Sheffield Shield competition was suspended before the 1915–16 domestic season. So his one and only first-class match had come and gone, providing him with the most stunning of first-class averages: 207.

He was restricted to scoring grade centuries for Waverley. He also went back to Hay in December 1915 to play for an invitational 'Somerset' side against the local cricket association. This time he showed off his leg-spinning prowess, taking 7–61, then finished one short of his century while guiding Somerset to victory. In the winter, Callaway had also improved his athletic skills by being a capable baseballer with Paddington. *The Sydney Sportsman*'s baseball writer, 'Strike One', said Callaway had 'a good batting eye, which is only natural to such a brilliant cricketer'.

But he was restless. He hated being idle. With no first-class cricket planned, he wanted to enlist, but knew his family would stop him. One morning he walked to Victoria Barracks in Moore Park and convinced the AIF medical authorities he was older than he looked. Several days later he joined the Dubbo Depot Battalion.

In October 1916 Callaway left for Plymouth on the SS *Ceramic*, and just after Christmas was in France. His war records are brief, indicating that in February 1917 he was on the Western Front with the 19th Battalion. Three months on, he was reported as missing. By October 1917, that was changed to killed in action.

His Red Cross file provides some detail. It includes accounts from numerous fellow soldiers and eyewitnesses. Private Alec Matthews confirmed he 'was in a shell hole with Callaway during an attack Bullecourt on May 3rd'. Matthews had just asked Callaway how he was going. Callaway replied, 'All right,' then Matthews heard him say, 'Oh.' 'He was struck by a shell and the whole top of his head was blown off. He fell across me. I was so shocked at the time that I never thought of taking his disc or pay book or any proof of identity.'

Another 19th Battalion soldier, J.C. Hopher, confirmed that several members of his platoon had seen Callaway's 'head blown off by a shell while in a shell hole'.

Although no one could confirm what happened to the body, the assumption was that Callaway was buried where he had been killed.

Eerily, just a week before his death, *The Sydney Sportsman* had reminded all of his prowess: 'N Calloway [sic], the best bat in the Waverley team, left for the front early in October. He was looked upon as a likely man to become a champion batsman after his great score of 207 ... His batting was sadly missed by his club. May he return safe and sound at no distant date is the wish of his numerous friends and of Recorder.'[19]

---

19 Recorder was *The Sportsman's* cricket writer.

Like countless other families, the Callaways were treated callously by those in charge. They did not officially hear until late December 1917 that their son was dead. He remained missing for what would have seemed like an eternity.

In 1920 they were told some form of memorial would be made for their son and they were called on to provide an inscription. They obliged, only to receive an official letter stating: 'I have to point out that the inscription chosen by you greatly exceeds the limit imposed by the War Graves Commission, viz, sixty-six letters, each space between words counting as one letter. It will therefore be necessary for you to select a much shorter inscription conforming with his inscription.'

Callaway's mother responded in June 1920: 'Enclosing shorter verse re the inscription to my son, the late No 5794 Private N Callaway, 19th Battalion.

(A soldier and a man he died.

Honored by all, His country's pride).

Trusting it will be to your approval.'

The family did not receive a memorial scroll until 1921. The Victory Medal came in 1923. His memorial notice inserted by his 'ever loving parents and sister' did not appear in the *SMH* until 3 May 1924 — the seventh anniversary of his death.

For a time, a photograph of Callaway was hung in the Waverley Oval cricket pavilion. It was inscribed with the words of poet Robert W. Service:

'And though there's never a grave to tell,

Nor a cross to mark his fall,

Thank God! We knew he batted well,

In the last great game of all.'

After the war, other prodigies would be compared to Callaway, but before long the memory faded. Pleasingly, after his being a mere cricketing asterisk, numerous writers in recent times have been inspired by his short and tragic career. Former England captain Mike Atherton, when alerted about the Callaway saga in an article in *The Guardian*, was moved enough to track down details while in Australia in early 2018 for a *Sunday Times* feature.

The area where he grew up also now recognises him. Since the 2007–08 season, the Norman Callaway Medal has been presented to the most outstanding under-21 cricketer in the Murrumbidgee Cricket Council region.

He remains Australian cricket's greatest and most tragic 'what if'.

CHAPTER 7

CRICKET'S VC

All he could hear during the considerable walk from the dressing room to the Melbourne Cricket Ground wicket was rousing applause echoing around the stands. On the field numerous members of Australian cricketing royalty stood in a row applauding his advance.

Among those bowing to a suburban hero were three former Australian captains — Clem Hill, Monty Noble and Warwick Armstrong — and six fellow Test players — Hanson Carter, Ernie Jones, Roy Minnett, Peter McAlister, Jimmy Matthews and H.V. 'Ranji' Hordern. They led the three cheers, joined by the two guest umpires — Fred 'The Demon' Spofforth and Jack Blackham, cricket celebrities from the previous century. Their Test careers were long over but they had immediately agreed to be part of a specially staged match to raise money for the Returned Soldiers' Distress Fund and, as importantly, to celebrate the feats of Australian cricket's first Victoria Cross recipient.

It was seven years since the Great War had ended, but the extraordinary feats of Bob Grieve on the Western Front had transformed him into an idolised Melbourne figure. But he refused to be placed on a pedestal, remaining forever the common man, especially at his home cricket club of Brighton, where he remained their prime wicket-taking strike bowler.

Spofforth and Blackham were now in their 70s, and Armstrong, Hill and Noble in their late 40s or 50s, but each wanted to either adjudicate or see whether they could still bat or bowl with any ease. They all knew the aches and pains they would suffer from a rare appearance in their creams was nothing compared to what Grieve had endured during the Battle of Messines. If he was still able to play, so must they.

Robert Cuthbert Grieve, known to all as Bob, was from a committed cricket-loving family. His father, John, was a prominent early figure in one of Australia's oldest cricket clubs, Brighton, situated within sniffing distance of Port Phillip Bay just a few miles south of Melbourne. Bob followed his father. As soon as the Wesley College student showed promise, Brighton recruited him. Two years on, shortly after turning 22, Grieve was heading the first-grade attack with infuriatingly accurate left-arm medium-pace seam bowling. When war broke out four seasons later, Grieve was rated among the top two or three bowlers in the Melbourne sub-district competition[20] — hardly a surprise considering he had tallied 134 wickets at 13.6.

Shortly after the completion of the 1914–15 season, Grieve, a commercial traveller, was posted to the 37th Battalion. His selflessness and obvious leadership qualities saw him promoted to captain and he was soon given command of 'A' Company, which in early 1917 was directed towards the Flanders region of southern Belgium, where the Allies were attempting to capture the Wytschaete-Messines ridge near Ypres. A fearless assault at the Germans was required.

While waiting for the battle to begin, Captain Grieve, situated with his men in Ploegsteert Wood, experienced an odd sensation. 'We heard both the nightingale and the cuckoo for the first time,' he wrote in an official account of the Battle of Messines, which is now in the Australian War Memorial archives.

Venomous noises and odours took over. 'A hearty handshake all round, we started on our great adventure,' only to discover the Germans were bombarding them with gas shells. Putting on their gas masks didn't help, so intensive was the attack.

---

20 A subsidiary competition of Melbourne's district grade game.

Grieve wrote that his men displayed 'great grit and tenacity and an indomitable spirit' until they got to higher ground and away from the gas. It was distressing seeing 'horses and mules affected by it — gasping for breath as we passed them'. Adding to the pain was that Lieutenant W.F. Robertson, 'one of the finest officers we had', was 'killed instantly by a gas shell which struck him on the head before exploding'.

Grieve's men somehow negotiated their way through Ploegsteert Wood. 'Words fail to describe the condition in the Wood,' he wrote. 'Shells rained into it without ceasing — trees were falling in all directions and the whole place was full of gas. The duck boards in many places were smashed to atoms by direct hits and yet through all this we came safe and sound.

'[At 3.10am] suddenly bedlam was let loose. The earth seemed to vomit fire and was shaken as though by an earthquake — the air screamed shells and snapped bullets and above all the roar of the guns, the crackle of the machine guns and the hum of aeroplane propellers.'

Passing German bodies and countless bombed buildings, Grieve's men reached Bethleem Farm, near the Messines village, to discover Australian soldiers 'who had gone forward in the attack first were digging in'. 'Digging away for all they were worth they yet found time for a smoke and a joke and when we arrived it was more like a picnic than a battle.'

The festivities didn't last long, as Grieve's 4th Division were directed towards advancing the Oosttaverne Line. In his written report, Grieve downplayed what he did next, instead praising colleagues.

'We surged under a very heavy fire from machine guns which became more intense after we got through. Here we suffered many casualties — the whole of our Stokes and Vickers gun crews were knocked out and at this stage Lieut. Fraser did wonderful work. He brought the gun into action himself — located the hostile guns and brought continuous and accurate fire to bear on them. In this way he saved the lives of many men in my company and his actions were invaluable. His gun was twice knocked out.

'Meanwhile the company was held up by the fire from machine guns in a concrete building. These were put out of action by the aid of Mills Grenades and the company were able to get forward onto the objective allotted to us. We captured two batches of prisoners and No 2 Platoon did excellent work outflanking a large number of the enemy compelling them to surrender. At this stage I was struck through the right shoulder by a sniper's bullet but managed to keep going for a few hours after this.'

Grieve's involvement was somewhat more substantial than what he expressed here.

The German machine-gun fire had killed at least half his men and all of his officers. As C.E.W. Bean wrote in *The Official History of Australia in the War of 1914–18*, Volume IV *The AIF in France 1917*: 'To save the company from extermination, Grieve, who could see the machine-gun firing from a loop-holed blockhouse in the trench, signalled to his men to wait in shell-holes while he sought for a Vickers machine-gun and a Stokes mortar which were to have advanced with his company. He found that the trench-mortar crew had been shattered by a heavy German shell which had fallen among them early in the advance, and that the machine-gun and its crew had been hit by the German fire when in the entanglement.'

Grieve, carrying a bag of bombs, by himself attacked the German pillbox where the machine-gunners had been causing such devastation. He would throw a bomb, moving forward under the cover of the dust that followed the explosions. He did this several times, before lobbing a bomb close to the loop-hole which saw the machine-gunners stop firing. He rushed up to the loop-hole and rolled two more through the opening. Another explosion and Grieve barged through the back door, to find the Germans either dead or badly wounded. Grieve signalled to what was left of his company to capture the German prisoners and take the nearby trench. While standing on the parapet, he was shot by a sniper. He tried to keep guiding his men towards the Oosttaverne Line, but his shoulder was in a bad way.

Grieve wrote that he had to retire after 'losing a lot of blood'. He took refuge in shell holes. 'German dead were everywhere … many of our boys were walking cases and they were doing their best to help one another along.'

Grieve found a casualty clearing station, but they were too busy. Instead he had a meal with two stretcher-bearer friends.

After the meal, he went to battalion headquarters, 'and gave them all the history of the day and suggestions for further action'. He walked another 1000 yards and 'at last reached the dressing station and got bandaged up'.

'I was covered in dirt and mud — my tunic saturated with blood so I must have presented a pretty picture. I was that tired I could have laid down alongside the road and gone to sleep.'

When it was realised how serious his shoulder wound was, Grieve was sent to England for medical treatment. While recuperating, he was invited to Buckingham Palace to receive the VC from King George V.

His citation read: 'On June 7, 1917, at Messines, for most conspicuous gallantry in action during an attack on the enemy's position. He led his Company to the attack on the enemy's third line system in the face of heavy artillery and machine gun fire. After all his officers had been wounded and his Company had suffered very heavy casualties, he located in a house two hostile machine guns, which were holding up the advance and causing most of the casualties. He ran forward alone a distance of 50 yards in the open and under the constant fire from the two machine guns, he, singled handed, bombed and killed the machine gun crews. He then with great coolness, and ability, re-organised the remnants of his Company and succeeded in capturing his objectives. It was his action alone that enabled the advance to be continued, and objective reached. By his utter disregard for danger, his coolness under fire, and his magnificent conduct he set a splendid example to his NCOs and men, and when he finally fell wounded the position was finally in our hands and the few remaining enemy were in flight.'

The custom with VCs was for officers to put forward recommendations. However, Grieve's recommendation was different because every other officer had been killed in the lead-up to his heroic act. Instead two sergeants from his unit wrote the recommendation.

His award received extensive coverage in the Melbourne newspapers, with *The Winner* going overboard with its cricketing analogies. It wrote that Grieve 'has utilised his bowling arm with such deadly accuracy in France that he has performed the greatest "hat trick" ever accomplished by an Australian cricketer.

'His first two victims were Germans, who were using their machine guns with great effect. He actually clean "bowled" these with excellent length bombs. He then rallied his men, and with a third successive onslaught "bowled" the remainder of the Huns out of their positions.'

A few months later he returned to France, where Bean met up with him. The official war correspondent was impressed with the calibre of the man. Bean wrote in his diary on 8 November 1917: 'I met Captain Grieve who has just returned with his wound at Messines with the VC ribbon on his chest. He is a squarely built, square faced, fair haired man with a slightly quizzical humorous face. He doesn't seem to be spoilt tho' you can see that the others look up to him and do a bit of worshipping.'

Grieve was invalided to Australia in May 1918 with acute trench nephritis and double pneumonia. Before he left, he was looked after by an Australian army nurse, Sister Mary Bowman, whom he later married.

Within days of arriving in Melbourne, he was the guest of honour at a function at the Brighton Town Hall. One councillor representing the Brighton Cricket Club said the prime reason their man had won the VC was due to what he learnt from cricket 'and that was to aim straight'. 'He isn't known in the district for being a "deadly left" for nothing.'

The ever-modest Grieve tried to bring it all back to perspective by saying 'hundreds of V.C.s were won when there was a "stunt" on, but they were not awarded'.

Grieve was determined to return to the Brighton cricket ranks as soon as possible. He played only four games in the 1918–19 season but was back to full health and form the following season, when he was the competition's most effective opening bowler, taking 66 wickets at 9.43. This was followed by 55 and 54 wicket hauls the next two seasons by a player described by *The Herald* as 'modest, unassuming' and among 'the most popular Sub-District players'.

In 1922–23, Grieve captained Brighton to its first peacetime premiership, helped immensely by having as his opening bowling partner a future Test representative, Lisle Nagel. Between them they took 85 season wickets at 13.2, including seven in the final against Coburg. The decorated captain, getting to his feet at the premiership dinner — attended by numerous VCA officials, including stalwart Ernie Bean — used the moment to argue that Brighton should be admitted to the top Melbourne grade competition. Ernie Bean, knowing he could not mock a VC, bobbed and weaved, promising Brighton would be among the first to be considered if the district competition were ever remodelled. That went nowhere, even though Brighton won premierships in 1924–25 and 1925–26, continuing to rely on Grieve's bowling. After taking 503 wickets for the club at 12.03, including taking a 'ten-for' in a match on nine occasions, he gave it away before the 1928–29 season. This was understandable as he was approaching 40 and was now running a soft-goods warehouse in Flinders Lane.

In the winter Bob Grieve remained an avid follower of the Collegians Football Club, which had been formed by former Wesley College students. Again he was the ever-loyal, unselfish member. One time he wore a suit to the game, as that night he had to go to a military dinner. He discovered Collegians were four players short. So he placed his suit on a fence post, tucked his trousers into his socks, found a pair of football boots and a jersey, and ran on to help his mates. He was best on ground.

As for the 1925 Internationals–AIF match that lured so many luminaries, there were numerous game highlights. Grieve opened the bowling for the AIF, dismissing Carter, Armstrong and Jones, but could not stop them achieving a 161-run winning total. It was also the moment one of the most enduring of Australian cricketing rifts finally ended, when Clem Hill and Peter McAlister took the field as batting partners, then shook hands and at last 'let bygones be bygones'.

Back in 1912, at the height of the Australian players/administration rift, Hill and McAlister, who were in opposing camps, were in the same Sydney boardroom to pick a team for the Melbourne Test match. Hill had arrived late from Manly, and immediately began arguing with a journalist — Joe Davis from the *SMH* — yelling at him: 'A nice fucking judge of cricket you are.' A chastened Davis left the room.

Then Hill turned his attention to McAlister. Hill mocked McAlister for poor Victorian team selections. McAlister complained about Hill's dreadful bowling choices in recent Tests. The barbs became nastier and nastier.

When the selection meeting began, Hill told McAlister he knew nothing about captaincy. McAlister retorted that Hill was an appalling skipper, easily the worst he had ever seen.

Hill, glaring at McAlister, uttered: 'You've been looking for a fucking punch in the jaw all night, and I'll give you one.' He struck McAlister across the nose and side of the face. Hill reportedly tried to shove McAlister out of the third-floor window, before being restrained by Board of Control secretary Syd Smith and the other selector, Frank Iredale. Hill and McAlister wrestled for about 20 minutes. Smith eventually led Hill out of the room, prompting a bloodied McAlister to scream: 'You coward! You coward!' Hill countered that McAlister was drunk and that if he stayed on as a selector he would resign. Smith picked up Hill's letter of resignation later that night. In the interim, McAlister and Iredale picked the Test team, as well as the first ten names for the upcoming trip to England. Two days later, when McAlister arrived at Spencer Street Station in Melbourne, journalists noted his nose was cut, his left eye was bruised and there were numerous scratches across his face.

For some years, Hill and McAlister kept their distance. But being selected as teammates for this noble match in 1925 did the trick. *The Age* commented: 'One of the happiest outcomes of the match was the reconciliation between two veteran players, Hill and McAlister, between whom there had been for many years an estrangement.'

It was that type of day: healing wounds, celebrating courage, the rich camaraderie of cricket and the joys of peacetime. Bob Grieve made sure that was at the core of his postwar life.

He played several more seasons for Brighton, and then when retiring as a player, became a committed supporter of the club. In October 1957 Grieve died of heart failure, and was buried with full military honours in Springvale Cemetery. His Victoria Cross was donated to Wesley College.

CHAPTER 8

TIBBY

It is one of Australian cricket's saddest photographs — a dozen corpses in the desert all in a row. The bodies are covered by blankets. Nearby are several soldiers, including one who appears to be checking the identities of those lined up in front of him. The heads are hidden, except one.

A blanket has been partially pulled away, exposing his left-side profile. Unlike the rest, he has no pants, and his left knee is partially lifted. On the photograph someone has scrawled an X — just above his head, as if to indicate this was an important body. It was. The corpse is of Albert 'Tibby' (or 'Tibbie') Cotter.

As a dark army blanket hides part of Cotter's body, the photograph provides no clues to how he died. A century on, no one is exactly certain how he was killed in the epic Australian cavalry charge that captured Beersheba as part of the 1917 Palestine campaign. He died as he lived — with a touch of uncertainty, a dash of derring-do, and the whiff of controversy.

Australian cricket has relied upon reckless, ratbag pacemen. There is a long line of speedsters with little interest in conforming. One of the first was Tibby — a mysterious nickname given to him when he was a youngster growing up in the Sydney suburb of Glebe. The common assumption was that Tibby was a reference to his short stature. It is more likely to be a variation of Albert or Bertie.

Even though at 172 centimetres he was more stout than tall, Tibby knew how to intimidate, boasting a venomous bouncer that particularly irritated the English. His expressive slinging action was considered by some as suspect, earning him the nickname in England as 'Terror' Cotter. During the 1905 Australian tour of England, he incensed the local crowds and the press contingent by what they termed unnecessarily dangerous bowling, which included the ungentlemanly act of hurling head-high bouncers at tailenders. The Brits weren't impressed, especially the Trent Bridge crowd when Johnny Tyldesley was seriously troubled by Cotter's rising deliveries. Spectators screamed: 'Take him off.' He hit W.G. Grace in the chest with a high full toss. England captain Stanley Jackson even privately asked his Australian counterpart, Joe Darling, to instruct Cotter not to bowl at their players' bodies.

The Fleet Streeters targeted Cotter. *The Evening News* argued that he 'ought to be no-balled out of existence'. *The London Referee* described it as a 'monstrous style of bowling'. *Athletic News* labelled it 'dangerous'.

With bat in hand, he was similarly aggressive. He loved nothing better than to slog. In a Sydney club cricket game, he hit 16 sixes and six boundaries when scoring 152 in 85 minutes. A representative umpire observed: 'It was either four or out when Tibby was at the crease.'

He was not sophisticated, basically a simple soul, suspicious of officialdom, gladly played up to the 'larrikin' tag, and a central figure when just before the Great War leading Australian players refused to be reined in by administrators who demanded autocratic control of the game. He was among the Big Six who stood up to the Australian Board of Control in 1912.

A difficult man to manage, Tibby had altercations with police in his youth and his military superiors, because he forever stood his ground. There was always overwhelming public respect towards him, though, because at first-class and Test level he was an exceptional cricketer.

He developed his sporting prowess in Sydney's inner west, joining Glebe in March 1899 shortly after turning 15. As important were his final years of schooling at Sydney Grammar School, where he was coached by the domineering George Barbour, father of future NSW Sheffield Shield representative Eric Barbour, who succeeded in refining Tibby's bowling rawness, erratic direction and impetuous behaviour.

He was a handy rugby player, making Grammar's first XV and later spending several seasons with Glebe as part of an expressive backline that included future Wallabies Fred Wood and Chris McKivat.

But cricket dominated. He made the NSW team when 18. Two years on and boasting just three state appearances he was in the Test team playing the 1903–04 England tourists at the SCG. The highlight was knocking off a stunned Johnny Tyldesley's hat during the second innings. A short time later Cotter smashed Tyldesley's off stump as one of his three dismissals. Peter McAlister, also playing his first Test, was standing in the slips. 'I will never forget the dismayed look on Johnny Tyldesley's face as a fast-rising ball knocked off his hat. I doubt whether Johnny ever experienced a more narrow escape from serious injury,' McAlister wrote in the Melbourne newspaper *Winner*.

In the next Test where he took eight wickets including a first innings tally of 6–40, McAlister said Cotter 'bowled at an extraordinary pace and was almost unplayable'. McAlister was one of many seemingly in awe of Tibby's physique: 'A magnificent specimen of athletic manhood, with wonderful strength in his muscular and perfectly proportioned body.'

Cotter was fastidious about his appearance. Warren Bardsley declared him the best-dressed cricketer. Cotter's boots were perfectly polished; his shirt, creams and jumper spotlessly clean and ironed. A Glebe teammate once asked him for cricket advice. Cotter replied: 'Buy yourself a decent pair of strides for a start.'

For the next few seasons Cotter was an Australian regular, transforming the science of pace bowling as he was instrumental in the introduction of a slips cordon and the use of the rising delivery to strike fear into opposing batsmen. To be fast now meant being fearsome. As Bardsley explained, Tibby was the master of 'breaking stumps, breaking fingers and breaking ribs'.

Victor Trumper once had his middle stump split by a Cotter yorker — one of his most effective weapons. Impressed by Cotter's delivery, Trumper walked off the field, holding the two pieces of the stump aloft, so that everyone could see he was the victim of an extraordinary fire-and-brimstone performer. Other batsmen souvenired the stumps whenever they were smashed by Tibby. The shattered stumps became collector's pieces.

Cotter also broke convention off the field. With his supposed 'perfectly proportioned body' he was a female magnet. A persistent rumour was that a British barmaid had his child after the 1909 England tour. He enjoyed the pub life, falling victim to the effects of one grog too many.

In December 1907 Cotter played for an Australian XI against England at the Gabba and failed to take a wicket. Rain washed out the final day-and-a-half, so he headed for the closest hotel. Before his trip to Queensland was over he was in the Brisbane Police Court for assaulting police.

The Brisbane *Truth* picked the right day to walk into this courtroom. Under the headline 'Cotter Caught', the *Truth* wrote: 'Albert Cotter, Australia's fast bowler, has long posed in the limelight as one of the "flannelled fools" sung of by Bloodyard Kipling. But in the early hours of Sunday morning, the bowler must have broken out in a new place, for on Monday morning, he stood in the police court limelight, charged with assaulting two policemen and generally putting a head on 'em.

'Albert, in quite a gentlemanly manner, pleaded guilty. P.M. Ranking wanted to know the reason why. Sub-Inspector Broderick said he was one of the visitors from New South Wales, and they had been having a banquet or something, and Cotter had taken a few glasses too much, and was inclined to be rowdy, and when spoken to by the police had assaulted them.

'P.M. Ranking: That's right enough, but are the police injured?

'Sub-Inspector Broderick: No, your Worship, as a matter of fact, they are not injured.

'P.M. Ranking: Very well. You are fined £2 or one month. Stop the £2 out of his bail money.

'And this is how Australia's champions are going to recover the Ashes. In the middle of an important match their chief bowler gets full up to the neck, and goes roaring round the street looking for lash,[21] and bumps into two policemen. And on a Sunday morning of all mornings in the week. If there are many more of the same sort in the Australian Eleven the Ashes are pretty safe to go back over the sea.'

There were no reprisals from above. On the day the *Truth* report appeared, Tibby was playing in the first Test in Sydney.

Several years later, a paragraph in a country newspaper, *The Narandera Argus and Riverina Advertiser*,[22] revealed that Cotter had appeared in the Sydney Police Court for using indecent language. Pleading guilty, he was fined 20 shillings or seven days' hard labour.

Those in charge were wary of Tibby, and concerned his drinking was getting out of hand. He was dropped for the final Test of the 1911–12 England series after looking lost during the Melbourne international, getting belted for 125 runs off 37 overs. A letter from Frank Iredale to fellow selector Clem Hill provided the clues for Tibby's muddled performance.

Iredale wrote: 'Tibby unfortunately did not bowl at his best in Melbourne. I am afraid that late nights with Fred McEvoy (poor fellow that he is) is [*sic*] not much good to anyone playing cricket especially Test match cricket.'[23]

Drink and dissent had convinced the selectors to look elsewhere.

He continued playing club and state cricket, but the spark was gone. After taking 89 Test wickets — 67 of which were Englishmen — and 442 first-class dismissals, with a Test strike rate of 52.05 (similar to that of both Dennis Lillee and Glenn McGrath),

---

21 A fight.
22 Narandera is now officially spelled Narrandera.
23 David Frith in his co-authored book with Gideon Haigh, *Inside Story. Unlocking Australian Cricket Archives*, which revealed Iredale's letter, believed McEvoy was a cricketer who played once for Victoria in 1877.

the now book-keeper at the Riverstone Meat Company in Sydney needed something else to keep him occupied. The death of Trumper on 28 June 1915 affected him, and he was seen struggling appreciably at the funeral, where he was a pallbearer. By this time many of his state teammates had left for Egypt and beyond. Even though 31 years old, he followed, enlisting on 4 April 1915 at Liverpool with the 12th Australian Light Horse Regiment. He was originally classified 'unfit for service' because he was short-sighted. However, that assessment was changed, and Cotter joined as a stretcher-bearer. The AIF realised they could make mileage from Cotter enlisting, and they were soon using his image to convince others to join up. He left Sydney on the transport ship *Runic* on 9 August 1915.

By November that year, Cotter was at Anzac Cove. Old habits again let him down. Tibby hit the service issue rum hard. The following day army authorities found him a gibbering mess. He was charged with 'drunkenness' and punished with 'five days' Field Punishment No 2'. That involved latrine duty. For a week, he was picking up his superiors' turds.

After the Gallipoli evacuation, Cotter returned to Egypt, where he again suffered from another big night. This time he was sucked in by the depraved Cairo nightlife, including the notorious Wazzir brothel region, and for close to two days disappeared from camp. He was charged with being 'absent without leave', sentenced to 14 days' field punishment and fined £1.

When eventually able to stay out of trouble, Cotter played several cricket matches in Egypt, with claims that his last game was against England Test allrounder Johnny Douglas at a rest camp near the Mediterranean coast. England Test batsman and selector H.G.D. Leveson-Gower wrote in *The Strand* magazine that in an 'unofficial' Test match Douglas led the England team, which dismissed the Australians for 57.

'Douglas took first knock for his team, facing a young man clad in khaki breeches and grey shirt, who let loose a cannon ball delivery which spreadeagled Douglas's wicket. His 10 brother officers followed in quick succession, and the innings closed for four runs. And it was not until then that the jubilant Aussies revealed their "demon" was none other than the Albert Cotter of Test-match fame,' Leveson-Gower wrote.

Cotter also had time to write home to his father, explaining that Christmas was special as there were 'even Turkeys'.

When the battalion was again committed to battle, Tibby soon made a mark as a courageous frontline stretcher-bearer. During the Allied attack on Gaza, an important Turkish coastal strongpoint in Palestine, in April 1917, Cotter impressed many with his diligence. Even H.S. Gullett singled him out in the official war history *The Australian Imperial Force in Sinai and Palestine*.

'During this day's bitter fighting there were numberless fine instances of individual gallantry. Hour after hour the fearless stretcher-bearers worked in the open with no hope that the enemy could, under such conditions of fighting, respect their humane mission. Cotter, the international fast bowler, was prominent all day among the stretcher-bearers.'

For more than five hours, Tibby retrieved and tended to the wounded, until the failed attack petered out. His work at Gaza led to a promotion — lance corporal. But it was a short rise to the top, as he didn't like the extra responsibilities and wanted nothing to do with ordering fellow soldiers around. He asked if he could return to being a trooper, even if it meant a pay cut. He far preferred being a nuts and bolts man, mucking around with his mates.

After two failed attempts to capture Gaza, the Allied forces decided in October 1917 a wiser option was to turn around the left flank of the Turkish defensive line by capturing Beersheba, 40 kilometres to the east. The elaborate plan involved a cavalry charge featuring the Light Horse and its mounted stretcher-bearers, including Tibby.

During this famous and successful charge, Tibby was killed. How is not exactly certain.

The official Australian war history stated he died while the Australians raced towards the Turkish trenches outside Beersheba.

'The mounted stretcher-bearers rode forwards, as they always did, with the advanced light horse lines, and worked coolly in the midst of the dismounted fight round the earthworks. While so engaged Private A. Cotter, the famous Sydney fast bowler, was shot dead by a Turk at close range. As has been recorded already, he had at the second Gaza engagement been singled out for fine work under heavy fire; he behaved in action as a man without fear,' Gullett wrote.

Several months later, Private William 'Woz' Glazebrook provided *The Sydney Sportsman* with more detail of the death of Tibby Cotter:

'We [the Light Horse] were charging across ground that had been the Turkish trenches and were travelling so fast that the Turks, who were trying to stop us with artillery and machine-gun fire, could not get our range. Coming to a trench, Cotter's horse refused to jump it — the brute would never jump anything — and Al [Cotter] had to dismount to lead it across. Even then it would not budge, and he was standing in full view of the machine-gunners, a stationary target that they found immediately, and poor Cotter fell, mercifully dead before he touched the ground. He was the next man to me, so I had a clear view of the whole occurrence. His death was deeply deplored by us all, for Albert Cotter was as good a man as he was a cricketer and was the life and soul of the whole company,' Glazebrook wrote.[24]

Clive Single, a Glebe teammate, wrote in *The Morvada* magazine, the Light Horse journal, in 1919 that Tibby was 'shot from the saddle during a mounted charge on a Turkish position' and 'died a glorious death'. Single would have had some idea. This state cricket and baseball representative was in charge of the 4th Australian Light Horse Field Ambulance. Promoted to lieutenant colonel, Single was awarded the DSO 'for distinguished and gallant services and devotion to duty' while in Egypt.

Then came conflicting reports about Tibby's death.

---

24 Glazebrook had an eventful war. He was hospitalised for dysentery, placed in detention for being absent without leave when in London, and invalided back to Australia with serious jaw and ankle ailments.

Several cricketing ex-servicemen, including Bert Oldfield, had been told Tibby had been shot through the forehead after he raised his head from a trench to check where the enemy were. Bringing doubt to the story was that the players had also been alerted that Cotter was looking through a periscope before bobbing his head up. A periscope wasn't usually part of the stretcher-bearer's equipment.

An article which was reprinted word for word by *Smith's Weekly* several times in the 1930s provided a different finale. It was written by a Light Horse colleague of Tibby's who called himself 'Blue'. Blue wrote that before the attack on Beersheba he and Cotter were at Khallassa in Southern Palestine: 'Tibby was one of the best foragers in the AIF. He would come to light with a bottle of champagne in the middle of the desert, and the lads in the section all looked to him to turn up with something unusual.'

He had been told to go to Echelon headquarters for guard duty but ignored the instructions. Around 1.30am on the morning of the attack, he 'turned up at the unit'. 'He said to me: "Bluey, I've skittled a Turk in one hit; and what do you think he had on him. Here it is — a yard of ling."'

He said he would 'treat the boys' to a 'fish supper in Beersheba and be damned to the consequences.' 'We moved off at 4.30am from Khallassa and attacked Beersheba that afternoon. Tibby was next to me on one side of the charge, and Trooper Jack Beasley on the other. Rex Cowley was there also. The other three were skittled by a machine gun, and after we had cleared the Turks out the troops went back half-an-hour later to bury the dead.

'Tibby was still alive when I got to him and he recognised me. "Blue," he said, "you can have the fish supper on your own". He died shortly afterwards. He should never have been in that charge. Had he obeyed orders he would probably have been alive today.'

Blue ended his letter with an anecdote. 'Just before we left Khallassa, Tibby, who in a bowling competition at Tel-el-Fara, bowled over 18 single stumps at full pace out of 24 — took up a ball of mud, and throwing it into the air, said: "That's my last bowl, Blue, something is going to happen".'

Another theory was that Tibby may have been shot by a Turk who had already surrendered. Several light horsemen, including an Australian stretcher-bearer, were that day killed by surrendering Turkish gun crewmen. That stretcher-bearer could have been Tibby.

Cotter was buried the following week at the Beersheba War Cemetery. Near his grave are several Australian eucalypts.

Cotter's family wrote to the officer in charge at Melbourne's Victoria Barracks seeking 'any details' about his death. The army provided scant detail, explaining he had been 'killed in action'. His official war records provide nothing more than a stamp which says: KILLED IN ACTION. Many newspapers, including *The Sydney Morning Herald* and *The Australasian*,[25] in their reports of Tibby's death gave no details about what happened at Beersheba. Again it was just 'killed in action in Egypt'.

This was an especially trying time for the Cotter clan, as they had also been informed that Tibby's brother John had been killed during the Battle of Passchendaele. John's body was never recovered.

In January 1919, the NSW Cricket Association, which in its records noted 'those who knew him realise that as a man he asked for no better death than one in defence of his country', unveiled a brass tablet at the SCG to commemorate the life of Tibby. The Association called on each Sydney district club to donate ten shillings and sixpence to cover the cost. Some decades later the tablet disappeared, prompting the Sydney Cricket Ground Trust to organise a replica, which now sits in the back dining room of the Members Stand.

One hundred years on, cricket followers walk across the Tibby Cotter Walkway, a pedestrian bridge which allows those heading to the SCG to walk above the busy Anzac Parade. Like the person it's named after, the walkway has been the source of endless drama. The NSW Government was criticised for a massive cost blowout, along with complaints that it was built in the wrong

---

25   *The Australasian* was a long-running Melbourne weekly newspaper.

position and hardly used by sporting spectators. Many avoid it because an odd circular design adds several hundred metres to the journey. So even now people are cursing when they hear the name Tibby Cotter.

*

In the same month of Cotter's death, a teammate from his first Shield appearance with a backstory just as compelling, was also buried. Dr Gother Robert Carlisle Clarke was an expressive leg spin bowler who appeared seven times for NSW, a state lawn bowls title-holder, and from one of Sydney North Shore's most important and wealthy families. The Clarke family line included clergymen, headmasters, even successful gold diggers, while Gother was among the first to attend the Shore school at North Sydney. He lived in one of the best houses on the northern side of the harbour, and his medical practice was opposite Abbotsleigh School.

It was at the Clarke household that the opening scene of one of Australia's most notorious murder cases occurred.

In 1912, Clarke employed a 'Harry Crawford' as a sulky driver and Annie Birkett as his housekeeper. Harry and Annie fell in love and the next year were married.

However, Harry was a transgender woman called Eugenia Falleni, but appears to have hidden this from Annie. Later, Falleni was apparently deeply concerned Annie would tell the police, which would see Falleni arrested. In October 1917, while having a picnic on the Lane Cove River, they apparently quarrelled after Annie said she had had enough of their strange relationship and was going to leave. During the argument, Annie slipped, fell down a cliff-face, and according to Falleni could not be revived. Then Falleni burnt her body beyond recognition. Falleni was arrested on suspicion of murder in 1920 and, following a lengthy trial, was taken to Long Bay Gaol.[26]

---

26 In a bizarre twist, Falleni, while in Long Bay, was reputed to have had an affair with Dorothy Mort, who had murdered Claude Tozer (see Chapter 2).

By that time, Gother Clarke was involved in his own traumas. Appointed as the Medical Officer for the 34th Battalion, he was over-worked and under-resourced on the Western Front, with his first action at the Battle of Messines. The conditions were atrocious, and Clarke constantly attended to wounded men under virtually no cover. Emergency operations were conducted out in the open, and within sight of the Germans. Patients and their doctors were under constant threat of being killed. He kept a war diary, explaining one close call: 'At 3.10am, Mines were blown which sounded like the end of the world. What a barrage.'

It was while treating a soldier near an ambulance tent, about 300 metres behind the frontline at Polygon Wood on 12 October 1917, that Clarke was hit by a shell. In his war diary, Captain V.H. Collins detailed the moment. The aid post was 'situated about 100 yards behind our front line, on a ridge facing the famous Bellevue Spur', he wrote.

'We fixed our position and awaited the attack, a storm of German shells fell around our post, which was a concrete "pill-box". Casualties came in rapidly and we divided the work which was necessary in the open area around this concrete point. Major Clarke was at one side in a narrow trench and I was on the other. About 8am, a shell burst very close, about 3–4 yards from me. I sent around to enquire as to Major Clarke's safety and then went myself. He was lying in a trench instantaneously in the act of dressing a wounded man, and still had the dressing in his hand. He was not shattered or disfigured. His body was laid aside and covered and his regiment immediately notified. His death is greatly mourned by all of us who knew him.'

*

Australian cricket's final Great War victim is now long forgotten, but at the time was among the country's most respected versatile sportsmen.[27] Ernest Frederick 'Ernie' Parker was rated by many

---

27 The other Australian first-class cricketer to be killed in 1918 was Lance Corporal Osborne Douglas, who played seven games for Tasmania. The son of Sir Ade Douglas,

as Western Australia's greatest pre-First World War athlete. This is understandable, considering he is the only notable Australian cricketer to boast an Australasian men's single tennis title, several doubles conquests, and numerous intense duels with New Zealand's four-time Wimbledon champion and world number one, Tony Wilding. If he wasn't immersed in those two pursuits, Parker could have easily been a top-grade footballer, runner, golfer or hockey player.

As far as many in Perth were concerned, Parker should have been a far better known cricketer, but he was hampered by the tyranny of distance. A supposed Test batting candidate, he was often overlooked because he was too far away from the Australian selectors on the eastern seaboard. Parker was among the first of many whom Western Australians perceived to be unfairly treated by those with all the cricketing power thousands of miles away.

Educated at Perth High School, with a short stint at St Peter's College in Adelaide, Ernie joined his father at his Western Australian solicitor's firm. He was soon mixing cricket and tennis at a high level, astounding many with the power of his strokes in both sports, given his diminutive, almost spindly, figure.

As *The West Australian* newspaper observed: 'Frail in figure it was amazing where the power behind the strokes came from.

'He was truly a wizard with the bat and without a doubt was one of the greatest players Australia has had. Lack of opportunity alone barred his way into an Australian Eleven, for all who have seen him play freely admit that a season or so in regular first-class company would have put him amongst the most celebrated batsmen of all time.'

---

the Tasmanian Attorney-General, Osborne moved to Victoria, where as a barrister was a major figure in the country town of Nhill. After being seriously wounded during the Battle of Bullecourt, almost a year later in April 1918 he was killed in action near Albert. Charles Adamson, born in County Durham, England, who appeared in one match for Queensland in 1899 after remaining in Australia following the inaugural British Isles rugby tour of the country, where he appeared in all four Tests for the visitors, was killed in action on 17 September 1918 in Bulgaria whjle serving in the Royal Scots Fusiliers.

The Western Australian press tagged Ernie Parker 'The Trumper of the West'. When scoring 69 in 35 minutes against NSW at the WACA, one spectator yelled out: 'You're watching Trumper now!!'

His strengths and faults were close cousins. Ernie was aggressive and knew how to dominate bowlers. However, he sometimes wasted his wicket through his haste. His best shots were the pull and the hook, but he played them too often, regularly leading to his downfall. When on song he was the most attractive of batsmen. Former Test batsman Jack Lyons was a strong Parker advocate, arguing that he was among the best batsmen in the country, with 'a beautiful hook' and 'lovely square-cut past point, which travels to the boundary like a shot'.

Victorian opponent Bert Kortlang described Parker's 117 in the first ever interstate match between the two states in February–March 1910 as 'the finest century I have ever seen in my long career of cricket'.

'His placements left the fieldsmen standing and I remember well a remark made by Tim Scannell, who was fielding in the covers with me: "Korty, this bloke is not playing cricket, he is playing billiards."'

Kortlang believed Parker 'was fit for any team in the world'.

Unfortunately, the bigwigs who ran cricket didn't see it. Western Australia's first-class appearances weren't that often and were confined to Perth fixtures. As far as Australian cricket was concerned, it was a backwater. Ernie played all of his 10 state matches against South Australia, NSW and Victoria, in either Perth or Fremantle, scoring two centuries and four half-centuries.

The only time he was sighted in Sydney or Melbourne was when officials took note of what the visiting players to WA had said about Ernie, and he was picked in 'The Rest' side that played Australia in two matches in February 1909 as a selection trial for the forthcoming England tour. The Australian XI, led by Monty Noble, included eight who had already been named in an early tour party, and the other 14 were vying for the few vacant spots. Ernie's long boat trip to the SCG was fruitless, as he was bowled by Charlie Macartney for three in the first innings and dismissed first ball in the second.

The Melbourne trial three days later was more fruitful. Promoted from No 5 to opener, Ernie shared an opening partnership of 119 with Edgar Mayne, scoring 65 in 88 minutes. Asked about Ernie's innings, long-time cricket scribe Tom Horan, who wrote under the pen-name 'Felix', uttered: 'Yes, yes — the very champagne of batting.'

It wasn't enough for Ernie to make his way from left field into the touring team. As *The Age* commented, Parker was 'undoubtedly a first-class batsman [who] would certainly have been an Australian eleven man had he not been located so far away from the great centre of Australian cricket'.

Ernie devoted more time to tennis, and had a large fan club who delighted in his 'charming' approach to the game, as he was, in the words of *The West Australian*, 'quick, wristy and always looking for a "winner"'. His net play was exceptional, with his only weakness being his serve, which 'in his hands was merely a means of putting the ball into play'.

People were also intrigued by the unusual tattoo of a square on his right forearm. Ernie argued it wasn't a square but the dimensions of a tennis court.

At the 1909 Australasian titles, held at a court within the precincts of the Perth Zoo, Ernie lost the singles final to Wilding in three sets. He was successful in the doubles final with Vivian Keane.

Four years later at Subiaco, Ernie defeated NSW namesake Harry Parker to win the Australasian singles title with excellent play at the net, and the doubles with Alf Hedeman over Harry Parker and Ray Taylor. Ernie won eight Western Australian singles titles and eight men's doubles titles. Wilding later said that if Ernie had concentrated on tennis rather than cricket he would have finished with far more than one Australasian singles title and been a regular Davis Cup player. Charles Dixon, captain of the British Davis Cup team, said Ernie required 'only a little first-class practice to be right next to Norman Brookes in Australasian tennis'. Self-doubt was Ernie's biggest problem. Again, Western Australians believed it had more to do with eastern bias.

He eventually gave up both cricket and tennis because of failing eyesight. It was assumed he would fail his reading test when enlisting, but he avoided that problem. He delightedly told mates: 'I dodged the authorities while there was a rush of people wanting to be enlisted, and got in.'

He embarked from Melbourne on 11 May 1917, as a gunner in the 102 Howitzer Battery, 2nd Brigade, and was killed by an enemy shell on 2 May 1918. *The Referee* printed a report from an eyewitness:

'Parker was with his company, camped at a place called Caestre, and Ernest and a man named McCleery, and another were sitting outside their hut having tea (that is tea in the meal sense, the exact liquid being cocoa). They did not like the cocoa, and nearby they saw somebody lighting a fire to boil a billy, so McCleery went over to see if they could get some tea. He found that he could get tea, and returned for his own, and Ernest's mugs. He had not gone many yards when a shell dropped in front of the hut, killing Ernest and some other poor chap whose name is not known. McCleery said that Parker had five wounds, any one of which was sufficiently severe to be fatal.'

Ernie was buried in the Le Peuplier Military Cemetery, Caestre — just a haunting 25 kilometres from where his long-time tennis rival, Tony Wilding, had been killed in 1915 during the Battle of Aubers Ridge when a shell exploded on the roof of the hut he was sheltering in.

Ernie's final will and testament, signed in 1916, had a special sporting touch. It included the stipulation that his WA Tennis Championship Cup be bequeathed to the state lawn tennis association, and that it should be continued to be played for on the understanding that if someone won it three times it would become their property.

CHAPTER 9

THE AIF TEAM

The 1919–20 AIF touring team has been widely credited with revitalising Australian and English cricket after the Great War. Not so well chronicled was that it required a rescue mission by an Olympian to ensure this illustrious band of players, who delighted spectators across three nations, became one of Australian cricket's most admired teams.

Considering the talent available, forming a formidable cricket line-up from Australian soldiers in Europe celebrating peace in late 1918 seemed a reasonably simple assignment. There were however endless hurdles, including leading players, seriously affected by their frontline experiences and wanting to go home, showing scant interest in the concept. There were squabbles over seniority and rank within the team, as well as financial concerns. It finally required one of Australia's most revered rugby union and rowing representatives to mould it back into shape.

This AIF team is now rated among Australian cricket's most important touring outfits, with their successes in England, South Africa and back at home giving many the enthusiasm to pursue the game in peacetime.

It also provided the core of Australia's successful postwar Test line-ups, enabling the country in the 1920s to re-establish itself as the world's best cricketing nation. Arthur Mailey argued that the success and camaraderie of the 1920–21 team, which won eight Tests in a row against England, was that it included many of cricketers who had seen active service.

The players, and their enthusiasm for the game, were definitely there, even on the battlefield. Throughout the war, English, Australian, South African and New Zealander soldiers would often, away from the trenches, overcome the stress with impromptu games of cricket. As Bert Oldfield, who had played a few first-grade games for Glebe before enlisting, wrote: 'Our games, although they were played well within the constant roar of guns, were a great relaxation and were consequently in popular demand.

'While our division was moving towards Ypres for the great offensive of 1917, we still played cricket, at almost every resting place. In those circumstances we were not attired in cricket flannels. During such matches in France we generally played in riding breeches, puttees, khaki shorts, loose shirts, topees and sand-shoes. Despite the sordidness and grimness of those dreadful days, nothing could kill our love for cricket.'

Hessian from the officers' mess was often used to make a wicket on fields that were pockmarked with shell holes and bricks from nearby bombed buildings. Some grounds were better than others. Oldfield thought the Ghezireh Sporting Club ground in Cairo, with coir matting laid over buffalo grass and maintained 'by a regular army of Egyptians', reminded him of Newlands in Cape Town. Such a ground attracted numerous notable cricketers, such as Tibby Cotter, Eric Barbour and Johnnie Moyes, who whenever possible made themselves available for any AIF team.

'I still remember the friendly touch on the shoulder from that delightful teammate, Tibby Cotter, as we left the field one match, when I had substituted in the first AIF XI,' Oldfield said years later.

Oldfield believed cricket helped him overcome the trauma of dreadful war moments, which included an incident in June 1917 in which, as a stretcher-bearer with the 15th Field Ambulance at Polygon Wood, he was buried alive and suffered shrapnel wounds to his face and back when a German shell exploded underneath his stretcher. His three colleagues, and their patient, were killed. Oldfield was the only one to survive the explosion.

'You know I had no right to be here at all,' Oldfield said a half-century later during an interview with *The Sydney Sun*'s David Jack. 'But my mates dug me out. With God's help, naturally.'

'The fact that I was buried is, no doubt, responsible for me being the sole survivor. I think of those pals frequently and reverently. The Flanders offensive was indescribable, and the horror of conditions at Passchaendale, Polygon Wood, Merin Road and Ypres were terrifying and deadly,' Oldfield would say in his final years during his regular Anzac Day speeches.

Oldfield, who refused to put up with too much nonsense — as evidenced by his spending eight days in the Abbassia Detention Barracks for being 'insolent' to a non-commissioned officer — later developed shell shock and, invalided in England, spent five months in hospital. Working at a kit store in Hammersmith, Oldfield was playing club cricket when, as he wrote in *Behind The Wicket*: 'the news of the Armistice reawakened the love for serious cricket and other sports'.

The feeling was contagious.

There had been numerous major games in England during 1917–18 involving Australian Services players, prompting interest from the MCC in financing an AIF cricket team to travel the country as a way of improving morale in the months after the Armistice. One of England cricket's most notable figures — Plum Warner — was among the most committed to an AIF tour coming together. A fixture list was organised for 1919.

Australian Services selectors, including Barbour, were organised, as well as a manager, Gordon Campbell, a South Australian wicketkeeper. But it soon started to fray.

Campbell, who had won a Military Cross, withdrew as he wanted to return to Australia. So too Claude Tozer (a close friend of Barbour's), Jack Massie, Moyes and the man who was expected to be their key player, Charlie Macartney. While the official reason for the prized Test batsman being unavailable was that he wanted to get back to Sydney as his father had just died, many believed Macartney had been traumatised by his war experience. An admired soldier, winning the Meritorious Service Medal, he witnessed events in France that deeply affected him. Teammates noted in the final months of war and early peacetime that he would often be sullen, lost in his thoughts.

The clue came in 1924 when numerous Australian newspapers revealed that Macartney had to take a break from cricket because of a nervous breakdown. It was written as fact. *The Sporting Globe* headlined its report: 'Macartney. Unfortunate Breakdown'. In later life, Macartney was described as 'reclusive'.

The fourth Australian Test player to enlist alongside Cotter, Macartney and Charlie Kelleway — Jimmy Matthews — was also unavailable, as he had been sent home from France with a gastric ulcer.

Matthews was a teammate of Kelleway and Macartney on Australia's underwhelming 1912 tour of England. While Matthews was, with several others, reprimanded for his involvement in some unsavoury tour incidents, he at least had the distinction of taking with his wrist spin two Test hat-tricks on the same day, against South Africa in Manchester during the triangular series. Enlisting in the 12th Reinforcements, 14th Battalion, Matthews served in Egypt and France, even sending a blade of desert grass to the curator at his Essendon cricket club ground to remind him that his mind was still on the game. In France in July 1917, while awaiting a boat to take him home to Melbourne, he became ill with dyspepsia and was instead transferred to England. He at least had time to be reunited with Kelleway and Macartney in an Australian Army–English Army match played at Lord's. He was back home in December 1917, where he was docked two days' pay for disappearing from a Caulfield hospital for 48 hours so that he could visit his wife and children, whom he hadn't seen in almost two years.

The next withdrawal from the AIF team was Eric Barbour, because he wanted to return to his medical practice.

In February 1919 *The Referee* reported that the AIF tour had been abandoned: 'That something has gone wrong with the organising of the AIF team in England has been apparent for some time. The Board of Control has received no news of the selection of the team, and players of splendid parts have been returning to Australia with little or no likelihood of returning for the purpose of playing in the suggested campaign. It has been hinted that financial considerations have proven a stumbling block, and also that questions of military rank have arisen.'

The MCC withdrew its offer of financial support.

There was also dissent among those who had been approached to play. Back in Sydney, Barbour was contacted by *The Evening News* over rumours the AIF tour 'had fallen through owing to the fact that some of the officers desired to retain their rank in the field and draw a larger share of the profits'.

Barbour denied it.

'As a matter of fact', Major Barbour said, 'we would have retained our ranks if the tour had come off because we would have been on leave from the Military Forces. When a number of prominent players found that for business and private reasons they would not be available, it was decided to abandon the proposal, because it was recognised that we would not be sufficiently strong to play Test matches.'

To the rescue came the AIF Sports Control Board, which took over the tour organisation. The Board had been organised to avoid a serious problem — how to keep the thousands of Australian troops still in Europe occupied until they could get them home. There were genuine concerns about bored, restless, virile Australian soldiers causing civil unrest in Britain and France. To keep the soldiers entertained, a vast range of sporting competitions was organised, including boxing, tennis, golf, rugby, swimming, rowing, athletics and cricket. The organising secretary was the remarkable Australian rugby representative Syd Middleton, now Major Syd Middleton of the 17th Battalion.

A prominent member of the first Wallabies touring team in 1908–09, which won a gold medal at the London Games, Middleton was also in the 1912 Australian Olympic rowing eight that made the quarter finals. A fearless soldier and leader,

Middleton received the Distinguished Service Order in 1919 for his battalion command near Amiens the previous year.

Middleton diligently went about getting the AIF cricket tour back on track, successfully negotiating with the MCC and confirming that the Sports Control Board would financially back the tour. The counties and clubs which the Australians were to play responded, many allotting half of the net proceeds to the AIF.

The selectors — Roy Park, Clarence 'Nip' Pellew and Ted Long — organised selection trials at The Oval, deciding on a squad of 14, including just one Test representative, Charlie Kelleway, who was named captain. An extensive 34-match tour of England and Scotland from 14 May to 10 September, with numerous matches at Lord's and The Oval, was scheduled. The players — deemed amateurs — received their normal army pay and an entertainment allowance of eight shillings per day.[28] They received all their clothing, and an official team blazer with the AIF 'rising sun' emblem on its pocket.

In the end, 18 played for the AIF. They were: Gunner Eric Bull, Lance-Corporal Herbie Collins, Captain Cyril Docker, Lieutenant Jack Gregory, Chaplain Henry Heath, Captain Charlie Kelleway, Sergeant Albert Lampard, Captain Ted Long, Sergeant Hammie Love, Gunner John Murray, Gunner Clifford O'Connor, Corporal Bert Oldfield, Captain Nip Pellew, Staff Sergeant William Stirling, Captain Bill Trenerry, Gunner Johnny Taylor, Lieutenant Carl Willis and Staff Sergeant Charlie Winning.

There was a smattering of state representatives, such as Collins, and little-knowns, such as Gregory, who had played a few first-grade games for North Sydney before the war, and, as a late call-up, Oldfield. In Gregory's case, there was a strong cricket heritage, as the Gregory clan had produced six first-class cricketers, three of whom had played Tests. He had made an impact in numerous Services matches during the war, including one involving

---

28 At the same time as the AIF cricket tour, Middleton was a successful member of the AIF rowing team that won the King's Cup at the Royal Henley Peace Regatta. After the race, the London *Times* paid tribute to the 'gallant old major in the middle of the boat, who must be nearer fifty than forty'. Middleton was 35.

Macartney, where on a matting wicket on Salisbury Plain a Gregory delivery jumped and smashed a batsman's eye.

As for Oldfield, on the recommendation of Essendon VFL footballer Ernie Cameron he was invited to be the keeper after Long was cleaned up by a Gregory bouncer that went through his gloves and crashed into his face.

Then an unexpected captaincy change. After six matches, including victories over Essex and Cambridge University in May–June 1919, Kelleway was suddenly replaced as skipper by Collins, who during the war had been driving supply trucks. Collins had ensured his batting skills remained intact, playing several matches on the Western Front. In a letter to *The Referee* editor, J.C. Davis, Collins described how he had played in a village 'under fire of German guns'.

'Great was my surprise to find a turf wicket rolled and chalked out and bearing evidence of having had a lot of work put in on it. The Royal Engineers were responsible,' Collins wrote.

The reason behind Collins's promotion has always been a bit muddied. There are at least four theories. The official line was that Kelleway, who had risen to the rank of major, had always stipulated that he was going to return to Australia in June. He had suffered during the war, with several stints in hospital for a gunshot wound to his right buttock, being 'dangerously ill' with a bullet to his forearm, and incapacitated with gastritis. Some Sydney newspapers made out that it had something to do with a war wound to his leg.

But there was more to it, especially as Kelleway was in such fine form, scoring centuries against Essex and Cambridge and taking wickets with his medium-fast bowling. The reliable Ray Robinson wrote in *On Top Down Under* that Kelleway's control of the team ended 'after a dispute about the list of games in 1919'.

There were accusations Kelleway had made disparaging remarks to a groundsman. In his book *Masters of Cricket*, Jack Fingleton provided more details:

'It was during the third game of the tour, against Surrey at The Oval, that Field-Marshal William Birdwood, of the Australian troops, sent for Collins.

'Collins,' said Birdwood, 'I want you to take over the captaincy of this side from Captain Kelleway.'

Collins was staggered.

'Captain Kelleway is a good cricketer', said Birdwood, 'but unfortunately he quarrels. I understand that he has already had three arguments — including one with the caretaker here before the game began. I'm sending him back on the next ship.'

But Kelleway didn't agree with the Field-Marshal. He refused to be 'sacked' and went to Brighton for the next match. Collins approached him as he was unpacking his bag.

'Charlie,' he said, 'this puts me in a pretty awkward position. Won't you think it over?'

'I'm playing,' said the dogged Kelleway.

A delegation of players confronted Kelleway and told him they wouldn't take the field if he did. Kelleway had no option but to leave.

In letters to J.C. Davis, Kelleway admitted he abhorred army officialdom. In one letter, he explained newspapers reports he had received a Military Cross were wrong and that 'the only honor I have is a machine gun bullet wound in my right buttock'. Kelleway admitted he originally wanted to remain in the army after the war, before realising it was only for those with 'an empty head'.

While admitting to Davis he had suffered difficult war moments, including having 'a bad fit of the blues', he also had reservations about his fellow troops. 'There are no better fighters. But they should be taught deportment … It makes your blood boil to see the manner in which they slouch about in the untidy clothes they wear,' Kelleway wrote to Davis.

The impish, streetwise Collins took over as captain, following a player vote. They ignored that his military rank was lance corporal and that there were at least seven others of a higher rank. He convinced them all he was a master leader. Oldfield rated Collins as 'unquestionably the best captain I have played with … a compliment because I played under Armstrong, Ryder, Woodfull and Bradman — all good captains'.

'Collins developed a knowledge that made it possible for him to nominate his move to dismiss a batsman. In a crisis he remained unruffled, and his sane temperament was a grand influence and example,' Oldfield said. 'He was a psychologist, and had the marvellous ability to lead and develop talent.'

Similarly, Collins thought Oldfield the best wicketkeeper he ever saw.

Oldfield, who described his period with the AIF team as 'one of the most enjoyable times I have ever had … we emerged from the horrors of war to the happy days of peace — from the hardships of the trenches and bully-beef to the luxuries of hotel life', blossomed under Collins's tutelage.

So did Gregory, an artillery gunner and bombardier who, with an extravagant kangaroo-hop at the end of his bowling run-up and a whirl of arms and legs at delivery, transformed himself from a brittle, uncoordinated player into a world-class performer. Collins was soon explaining to the British press: 'Gregory is the best fast bowler in the world.'

His bowling aggression was matched by reckless but highly effective lusty left-handed batting, often without gloves. He also refused to wear a hat. No one was sure whether he even wore a protective box.

He became an exceptional slips fielder after spiking his hand while chasing a ball in the outfield. Collins decided for his own safety to bring Gregory into the slips.

Collins knew how to use one of his AIF discoveries to rile another. A tiring Gregory had slowed down appreciably during one of his bowling spells. Collins told Oldfield to stand up to the stumps for the next delivery. Oldfield was aghast.

'He'll knock my head off.'

'You'll only have to be there for one delivery.'

Gregory turned, saw Oldfield, glared at Collins, and bounded in, producing the fastest delivery of the whole tour. Wickets soon followed. He finished with 6/40.

Gregory was like Oldfield in believing that Collins — a master of being able to mix with the elite and the downtrodden — was instrumental in ensuring this AIF team was a memorable outfit.

'Almost every rank in the army was represented in the team, from private to major, but our motto was "Abandon rank all ye who enter here",' Gregory said.

As fascinating were some of the lesser-known players, such as the team's most successful batsman, Carl Willis.

Willis hailed from a prominent Victorian family. His father, Rupert, was a founder of Melbourne University's student medical society, a Wesley College old boy and one-time Mayor of Malvern.

Carl, who boasted a boisterous, carefree manner which earnt him the nickname of 'Smiler', was given every chance — educated at Wesley, where the development of his football and cricket skills lured him to the prestigious Melbourne Cricket Club, and, in the winter, the University Football Club, which in 1908 had, with Richmond, been introduced to the VFL competition.

In his first VFL season Willis was the talk of the competition when suspended for a month for belting an opponent. He learnt his lesson and for the next three seasons kept away from trouble, including when he was once punched in the neck. (Others were more sensitive about the incident, prompting a 15-minute crowd invasion.) A committed, rather than talented, footballer, he was one of University's most consistent goalkickers, with 41 from 46 games. His most notable University teammate was Roy Park, who after the war played one Test for Australia, suffering the indignity of a first-ball duck in his only innings. His wife was reputed to have looked down to pick up her knitting and missed his Test batting career.

Willis made the Victorian cricket team in 1914, scoring 40 as a No 4 in his debut against New Zealand at the MCG that year. He played four more first-class games and another season of VFL after moving from University to South Melbourne before global matters overwhelmed him.

Willis was a free spirit with an inquiring eye. When signing up in November 1915 with the 3rd Pioneer Battalion, the 22-year-old qualified dentist was brazen enough to write on his enlistment papers that his religious denomination was 'agnostic'. He was also eager to provide the public with an insight into what was going on on the other side of the world by writing for a weekly sporting broadsheet newspaper called *The Winner*. The paper had an interesting collection of correspondents, including Olympian Frank Beaurepaire as its swimming writer, while Willis had been its provocative cricket editor since its inception in July 1914.

Willis knew how to upset officials and opposing players and clubs. One week he was complaining about 'obnoxious spectators' attending club cricket games who attacked even their own players with 'witticisms and sarcasm', the worst being at Collingwood home games. The next he was describing the pennant competition as a 'farce' because the Victorian Cricket Association had opted for a fortnight's break between the first and second day of a final.

He thought it ridiculous authorities wanted to call off cricket because of war, arguing that not everyone was going to the front and should be allowed to continue playing sport as it was their 'only chance to take their mind off their work and worry for a few hours a week'. If cricket was banned, it would give the idle every excuse to waste their Saturday afternoon drinking themselves to oblivion in a local pub.

He even castigated cricketers who did not purchase Australian-made gear.

Heading off to army camp didn't stop the barrage. He caused uproar when in April 1916 he accused Test batsman and Essendon captain Edgar Mayne of being selfish by doing everything he could to win the club's batting average award.

Under a headline of 'Unpleasant Rumours', Willis wrote that some Essendon supporters believed Mayne was not giving a fellow batsman, Paddy Shea, a fair chance, as they were 'running close for the batting average'. That included Mayne ensuring he was always ahead of Shea in the batting order. Eleven Essendon players, including Shea, wrote to *The Winner* saying Willis's 'slanderous' article was blatantly wrong. They argued that Mayne gave Shea every chance to be the team's prominent batsman.

Another letter-writer entitled 'Fair Sport' said Willis's writing 'is most unpardonable, for he is one who attempts to uphold the manly sport of cricket, and yet he rushes in without first obtaining the true facts'.

Willis defended himself the following week. 'What I stated then I now state again. There were unpleasant rumours being circulated about Mayne's action; in fact, it was more than rumour, as several people made no secret of it at all, and told me definitely that it was a fact. Now I personally have nothing at all against him ... Mayne should be extremely grateful that he and the playing members of his club have had the chance of explaining openly an action which otherwise would have been discussed to his disadvantage in the dark.'

By that time Willis, with a gift of a silver cigarette case and matchbox from *The Winner* staff in his kitbag, was learning with numerous other notable sportsmen how to be a sharpshooter at the 3rd Pioneer Battalion training barracks near Broadmeadows. They soon discovered the rifle range was a dangerous area.

'When the shooting commences there are many humorous remarks and scenes. It is a remarkable fact that men who are champions at one form of sport cannot imagine how they are not champions at shooting at practically their first attempt, and get quite annoyed when the target is not hit. I had never realised the truth of the old saying, "Bad workmen always blame their tools" until this trip ... In common with many others not accustomed to rifle shooting I had the idea that all you did was to lie down, point the rifle straight, and pull the trigger; but it is not so, as I found out.'

The battalion left Melbourne for Europe in June 1916. Willis decided to send articles to *The Winner* whenever he could, explaining a soldier's life.

Meningitis struck down many of the troops on the leg to South Africa, with one of the few moments of relief occurring when they berthed in Durban: 'a launch, with about half a dozen girls in it, circled around the ship, and they all threw oranges and cigarettes.'

'It was awfully good of them and much appreciated, as we had had no fruit since leaving Fremantle. Those girls must have got sick and tired of throwing, and goodness only knows how many black boys were throwing. I would not like to say how many oranges came on board, but there must have been thousands.'

It was only when the troops saw a lighthouse near Plymouth that they comprehended that their final stop-off was England.

'There was not a single person on board not overjoyed at the idea of going on shore again. Towards the end it got deadly monotonous, and one felt inclined to argue about anything, no matter how trivial. There was also far too much time to think.'

Willis believed after a few weeks in England they would all soon be heading home.

'The idea here is that the war cannot last six months longer, and we may never see the real thing,' Willis wrote.

The first few months were tranquil, allowing him to keep his sporting skills in tune by being called to play for the AIF against the British Southern Command at Tidworth, described by Willis as 'the prettiest ground I have ever seen'. Surrounded by seven grass tennis courts and a polo green, the ground had as its centrepiece 'a pretty little red-tiled roofed pavilion with a verandah outside'.

Jack Massie was supposed to be playing for the AIF, but withdrew after falling off a horse. Macartney took over and outscored the opposition with an innings of 134. It was here that Willis sighted Jack Gregory for the first time.

Then he was involved in a special Australian sporting moment. General John Monash, like all Melburnians having an intimate knowledge of how that city revolves around its winter sporting code, was eager for those in England waiting for the call-up to the Western Front not to be idle. When asked by an AIF provost officer about the possibility of staging an Aussie Rules exhibition match in England, especially as there were so many VFL footballers in the Old Dart at the time, Monash responded, making the necessary calls to ensure it was played at one of London's most famous tennis venues — the Queen's Club in West

Kensington. Monash got the approval, then Beaurepaire, who was involved in organising sporting events for the troops, ensured it happened.

The match was between a 3rd Division team headed by South Melbourne's renowned Bruce Sloss, and including Willis, and a Combined Training Group that included players from Victoria, NSW, Western Australia and South Australia. On a dull London day in October 1916, the teams walked out onto the somewhat cramped ground, which was appreciably narrow as well as being ten metres short. Not surprisingly it was a congested game, but Willis was a standout, kicking two goals that helped the 3rd Division win 6.16 (52) to 4.12 (36) in front of about 5000 spectators, most of whom were Australian soldiers on weekend leave. The British media was confused by it all. *The Yorkshire Post* thought it 'a tear-away affair from start to finish, but too higgledy-piggledly to make a spectacle'.

This frolic was soon forgotten, because Willis and co had been transported to hell. In late November 1916, he landed in France and marched towards the trenches. First night he found a bed in a drenched tent. 'We went to bed, but not to sleep, as it was too cold. It blew and hailed all night. Every hour or so we had smoke-ohs and a general hymn of hate on the camp and soldiering generally.'

It didn't get any better, as the next leg involved a 37-hour trip in the back of an 'evil smelling' cattle truck. He eventually found himself in a French town, the name of which had been cut out of *The Winner* article by the war censors. They were billeted in a badly bombed building.

'There are holes in the walls and scarcely a pane of glass left whole. When the Germans occupied the place they stripped it of all the fittings. Every bit of copper or brass is gone, even to door nobs [sic] and taps. We had our first hot meal at dinner time for five days, and most acceptable it was too, bully beef and potatoes stewed together.'

As for what was going on around them, 'we know nothing at all, in fact, less of the war by far than you do in Australia'.

'The only things which worried me at all here were, firstly, the want of a smoke, and, secondly, the cold. The latter is awful. It penetrates right into the joints and absolutely hurts. For the sake of warmth nearly all of us make our beds together. I slept for a couple of nights with another fellow, and was still cold, but now four of us make the one bed and sleep in it with a fair amount of comfort. I have not had a bath for eight days now, and there seems little immediate prospect of getting one: in fact I have not had my singlet, shirt and underpants off for that time.'

His experiences on the front were confronting. He experienced shell shock victims who were 'never quite the same afterwards', and was gassed on his first day of involvement in the Battle of Messines.

'I got gassed after seeing about 5 or 6 hours of the show,' Willis wrote in a letter to *The Winner*. 'I can honestly say that I got the one thing I was really frightened of … I was not bad from it when one considers what some of the other fellows got, but quite bad enough for my liking. I would sooner see men blown to pieces than see them die from gas. It is the most ghastly death.

'We duly marched off at the appointed time, and everything went smoothly until we walked into that greatest horror of the soldier, gas. Gas shells were raining over. There is no chance of mistaking the gas shell when you have once seen or heard one. The first time one lands you will probably think it is a "dead" shell [one which has not exploded] owing to there being no report; but soon you distinguish them easily, as they have quite a different sound in the air to the ordinary shell.

'Instead of a scream or whirr, the gas shell seems to make a buzzing sound, and when it hits the ground there is simply a dull plop. The gas is fairly heavy and easily visible in small white clouds hanging to the ground like an early morning mist, which is being gradually dispersed by the sun.'

Wearing a gas mask worked to a certain degree, 'but when you are going along with fighting equipment on and carrying a pick and shovel, breathing becomes difficult'.

'It is, I think, just about the most awful invention of a diabolical brain ... Somehow in war you expect to see terrifying sights, such as men with extensive wounds and men cut into pieces by shellfire, but to see them gassed is unnatural. A man comes toward you rolling and staggering about for all the world like a drunken man.'

Willis was hospitalised after the gas attack, before being transferred back to Salisbury Plain to take charge of a dental unit. This also had its pitfalls. Dealing day in day out with serious mouth disease, suffered by countless soldiers due to poor frontline hygiene, was demanding work.

'I have been back on the "Dental Job" now for three months, and am deadly sick of it already; it is so monotonous, especially after the other side of the Channel, but this is the trouble about this game, it is either terribly dull or too damned variegated.' He now wished he was 'back with the boys'.

Thankfully there was the occasional game of cricket, including an appearance at Lord's with a combined Australian and South African Services team in 1917. The following year he was among the first lured to the AIF team. Willis was their highest run-scorer in first-class games during the England leg, with 1652 runs, including four centuries, at 41.30. He became a team selector.

Several others overcame hardships or disabilities to be among the AIF cricketing entourage. Bill Trenerry was a colleague of Gregory's at Shore school, and on the verge of making the NSW team as a middle-order batsman when war intervened. He was 'accidentally wounded' at Gallipoli and nine months later suffered a head wound in France. He was soon back at the front, with his courageous actions in November 1916 earning him the Military Cross for 'conspicuous gallantry'.

His citation read: 'In the attack on the Gird Trenches near Flers on the 14 November 1916, this Officer was in command of the Lewis Machine Guns and displayed great gallantry and coolness under fire. After the position had been captured and the troops on the right of the 19 Battalion had retired, he was given command of the right flank. During the night of 14–15 November he was attacked by enemy's bombing parties, and each time repelled them. He showed an excellent example to his men and was responsible for the right flank being held securely, until relieved the following day.'

Cyril Docker, one of the AIF tour speedsters, had an agonising war, suffering from a hernia that involved an operation near his scrotum, epiphora (an overflowing of tears) in both eyes, pharyngitis and a dislocated shoulder. He also required treatment for shell shock. He suffered nervous fits and insomnia, after being bombed at Pozières in 1916. His bout of epiphora forced him out of active service in 1918. Amid all these traumas, he was widely praised at Pozières for leading a group that charged into the German trenches, killing 60 of the enemy and capturing four others.

Somehow he got himself right in time to be picked as one of the AIF's key bowlers, with the selectors well aware of his one and only first-class game before the war, when, opening the bowling for NSW against Queensland at the Gabba in December 1909, he finished with nine wickets — eight clean bowled. However, his many war ailments worked against him, and his appearances during the British leg were intermittent. Instead, one of the unknowns — Gregory — took over, with Collins and Oldfield becoming the key attraction of the AIF team, prompting sizeable crowds wherever they played. Gregory was at times in his own league, finishing with 131 wickets at 18.19, including three seven-wicket hauls, from his 25 matches, while also scoring 942 runs at 29.43, including a century against Northamptonshire.

The AIF enjoyed numerous notable victories. One of the most special was against a quality Yorkshire side — which included Wilfred Rhodes, George Hirst, Herbert Sutcliffe, Percy Holmes and Roy Kilner. The highlight was a last-wicket 54-run stand by Gregory and Ted Long which enabled the AIF to secure a one-wicket victory, and the admiration of the British cricketing community.

The military heavies also occasionally attended matches to cheer on their men. At the Surrey match, General Birdwood, who was in command of the Anzac troops at Gallipoli, strode into the AIF dressing room, boomed Oldfield's name and shook the keeper's hand.

Oldfield was staggered the general knew his name, until Collins later told him Birdwood had asked him, 'Who's that little chap in the corner?'

After winning 15 and drawing 15 of their 34 matches, the AIF team found other countries haggling for their services. South African cricketing officials tried to sway Australia to travel their way on the team's journey home. Near the end of the England leg, the AIF Sports Control Board received a cable from the South African Government requesting a six-week tour. The players weren't keen. They wanted to get home. But the Australian Minister for Defence, Senator George Pearce, comprehending the diplomatic advantages of travelling to the land of a now close war ally which they had fought against during the Boer War only a few decades previously, overruled them. With that another ten matches were added to their schedule.

Before they left for Cape Town, the AIF team was feted by England's most notable cricketing, military and political figures at the famed Café Monico in Piccadilly Circus. The hundred guests included Lord Harris, who had captained England to victory over Australia in the first Test match on English soil in 1880. Countless dignitaries sang their praises, with *The Referee* reporting that Plum Warner felt it imperative Australia was told 'what this team has done for English cricket'. Warner said Collins's men were so popular because they were 'a team of thorough sportsmen'.

Then to Plymouth to board the transport *Ascanius*, where Collins reiterated to the British media that Gregory was the world's best pace bowler, and that the South African matting wickets will make him virtually unplayable.

He was proven right. They were unbeaten in their eight first-class games in South Africa — including two unofficial Tests — victorious in six and drawing the other two. The biggest difficulty was, according to Oldfield, getting accustomed to the coir matting, 'which caused the ball to fly'.

Then they heard that the Australian states were bickering over who should play them when they at last returned home in January 1920. South Australia, Western Australia and Tasmania were all miffed when told that the only three games would be on the eastern seaboard, against Victoria, Queensland and NSW.

The team arrived in Melbourne on 9 January and was transported to Scott's Hotel for early morning champagne, canapes and cheerful speeches. The team was given a week off before the first game against Victoria. To get their eye in, the players were invited to the Fitzroy ground for a practice match and a 'longest hit' competition. The winner was John Murray, who hit the ball over the top of the football stand and onto a lawn bowling green 154 yards away. If that wasn't enough froth, the AIF scored 500 runs in a few hours in the practice game, Collins and Docker making 100 in 22 minutes, and Nip Pellew hitting ten sixes — four in the one over.

At the MCG, after being visited by the Governor-General, Sir Ronald Munro Ferguson, in the dressing rooms, they were greeted with a rousing three cheers from the crowd. They then lined up while two buglers sounded the Last Post.[29]

Edgar Mayne and Warwick Armstrong were first to confront Gregory on a wet wicket which had delayed the start of play till 3pm. This did not deter the AIF, as they still had Victoria dismissed before the end of the first day for 116. Collins was beaming as Gregory showed exactly what he had been telling everyone. Even though no one had seen him in Australia, he was still the best paceman in the land. Taking 7/22 off 12 overs, including the wickets of Armstrong and Jack Ryder, was the perfect arrival card. As Gregory was sight unseen, the local newspapers set about explaining his style and attributes.

'Gregory runs only half the distance of Cotter,' *The Age* reported; 'he shows irregular movement in arms, legs and body, executes a jerk a pace or two before reaching the wickets, and then brings limbs into harmony before delivering the ball. He is the embodiment of physical energy, and is a decidedly spectacular

---

[29] The war had taken its toll on the Melbourne grade competition. Due to a shortage of cricket balls, only one was used per game, rather than a new one for each innings.

bowler, as well as being a successful one.'

The Referee correspondent 'Onlooker' wrote: 'Tall and spare, but big-framed, active and agile, Gregory has a run that bespeaks vigour, determination and endurance. Lacking the graceful ease of Tom Richardson, the Surrey star, or Albert Cotter, the New South Wales express, who died the death of a soldier, Gregory has more the style of Barnes, the Englishman, a trifle stilted, with a quick halt and high delivery.'

The following day, in front of more than 18,000 spectators, Willis was the local hero, scoring 111 in 162 minutes to bring about a six-wicket win by the AIF. Onlooker thought it could even put Willis into Test calculations, with England touring Australia the following summer.

'Watching Willis, one was reminded somewhat of the wonderful mastery A.C. MacLaren, the gifted English captain, had over the ball. There was much of the same watchfulness, the cool deliberation, the sweet stroke so exquisitely timed, and the quick, twinkling feet. Truly, these soldier boys seem destined to upset all previous calculations as to the personnel of the next Australian Eleven,' Onlooker wrote.

The AIF team was again invited to Scott's for a banquet. Special presentations were made to Gregory and Willis, while Sir John Monash told the gathering that sport was crucial in maintaining morale during wartime.

'Every unit had its teams and the keeping of the spirit of sport alive was an important factor in maintaining the morale,' Monash said. 'An appeal to the men that never failed was the appeal to their sportsmanship. This was the inspiration which took them to many victories. The appeal "It's up to you to play for your side" always told,' *The Weekly Times* reported.

This remark prompted resounding cheers from the audience.

Following a tepid draw against Queensland, in which Collins scored the team's 30th century of the tour, and the skipper's eighth, the AIF came to Sydney for their final, and ultimately their most important, fixture against Australia's strongest cricketing state — NSW.

If they could excel against them, then the AIF could confirm its status as a special cricketing breed. They did.

Every person of note in Sydney cricket was at Central Station to greet the Brisbane express. However, the two notables — Gregory and Willis — weren't among the entourage. Gregory had left the train at Hornsby to meet up with his family, whom he had not seen for several years, while Willis stayed in Brisbane for leg surgery.

The endless speeches continued, with the *SMH* reporting that Hugh Massie, a member of the 1882 Australian team and father of Jack Massie, believing that despite not having at their disposal every cricketer, they had 'proved themselves the best all-round team that ever represented Australia'.

'When originally selected some critics asserted the men were on the young side, and lacked balance and experience but the results showed that it was wise policy for the older men to stand aside and give the young men a chance,' Massie said.

On the first day, more than 13,000 were at the SCG, primarily to see Gregory bowl. They had heard so much about this phenomenal talent. They had also heard the rumour that he was going to disappear at the end of the tour — so better witness it while you could. Even *The Sydney Morning Herald* threw out the line that Gregory was expected to 'retire from big cricket after this match'.

In the Members Stand were countless past notable cricketers such as Monty Noble and Syd Gregory; the latter, a 58-Test veteran batsman, was a cousin of Jack Gregory's but had never seen him play. Syd had every right to feel at home here, as he was born in a cottage near the main pavilion.

When the crowd heard Collins had won the toss, a groan echoed around the ground. 'There was a feeling of disappointment,' the *SMH* reported, 'as everybody wanted to see Gregory bowl.'

Realising the crowd wanted Gregory, Collins promoted him to open the batting. It was a masterstroke. Collins was gone first ball, and Pellew soon followed. Gregory, confronting an attack that included Hunter 'Stork' Hendry and Arthur Mailey, decided the only way to get the AIF back on track was to take the initiative. Anything slightly off line by Hendry, Mailey and co was swatted away with contempt. Just over two hours later Gregory had completed a century. When he was dismissed on 122, the crowd stood as one and 'wildly cheered' him all the way back to the dressing room. 'No batsman has returned to the pavilion of the Sydney ground amidst cheers more heartfelt than Gregory received on Saturday,' the *SMH* said.

Gregory was not done for the day, though, as he then opened the bowling.

The *SMH* observed: 'After the interval, it was possible to feel the pulse of the 13,000 people waiting for Gregory! Carter[30] took strike, and it seemed an unfair attack by a giant bowler against a somewhat diminutive batsman. A run of 20 yards brought Gregory to the crease, where, with a herculean twist of the arm and shoulder muscles, whizz went the ball, and Carter knew very little about the first six.'

Shortly after, Carter was on his way, bowled by Gregory for 17 — the first of five wickets that also included Hendry, Tommy Andrews and Alan Kippax.

The team members were guests at another official luncheon, one in which they were paraded in front of the NSW Governor and Premier. The *SMH* reported Collins reiterating what everyone thought: 'There seems to be a wonderful revival of interest in cricket all over the world, and I am glad to see that this is so in Australia. I hope our team has done something to assist in this revival.'

That was definitely the case when Collins and his favourite player provided endless entertainment in the AIF's second innings, combining in an exhilarating 188-run third-wicket partnership in a mere 101 minutes that saw each perfectly finish their time with the AIF with centuries. With it came endless plaudits, especially as Gregory finished the game by bowling both NSW openers,

---

30 NSW wicketkeeper Hanson Carter.

Warren Bardsley and Carter, resulting in a convincing 203-run triumph.

After leaving the field, the team was feted by the NSW Cricket Association, with its leading official, Syd Smith, saying this was a special team because it had done so much to 'revive the interest in cricket'. Then the players were off to The Tivoli for a performance of 'As You Were' as guests of notorious wheeler and dealer H.D. 'Huge Deal' McIntosh.

The *SMH* headlined its report 'Brilliant Victory', describing the AIF success as: 'A wonderful victory! In a three-day match for a side to win so decisively on an Australian wicket, perfect in every respect, is a memorable achievement.

'The match will go down in sporting records as a splendid triumph for J.M. Gregory.'

The Referee's highly respected editor J.C. Davis — using the nom de plume 'Not Out' — was effusive in his praise: 'We take off our hats to the AIF team, to their captain, H.L. Collins, for his brainy, shrewd and expert leadership, his batsmanship and his bowling. And to J.M. Gregory for his unique, scintillating cricket in all departments. And to all the others for being such excellent cogs in the wheel.'

Davis, a mate of Collins, said the AIF skipper 'showed us far the best in captaincy seen this season'.

'We take off our hats to J.M. Gregory for rising to greater heights than we could have anticipated from the reports of his powers by critics in England, South Africa and elsewhere. Having seen the young Cornstalk in action, one can know that the truest assessment of his peculiar all-round powers that I read was that of H.L. Collins in letters to me, and which were published in *The Referee*. He said that as a slip fieldsman Gregory was a freak — and that is what he is. As batsman he said he was fit for any eleven — and that is what he is, though likely to improve, especially when dealing with the length ball on the off stump or outside it when it is going away. As fast bowler he is one of the best we have seen, possibly the best in the world today, and certainly the best in Australia. That was all told to us by Skipper HLC, without any boasting, and the Sydney crowds have had the extreme good fortune to see the young man demonstrate its correctness by his strikingly versatile qualities, his great genius for the game. In every department he is a champion.'

Frank Iredale, the NSWCA secretary and former Test batsman, tried to soften Gregory with praise. He had a regular column in the *Sydney Sun* in which he constantly pushed Gregory's barrel. After the AIF win in Sydney, Iredale wrote: 'As a bowler, he runs 15 yards, has the Oxford jump, swings them a bit and makes them fly — the higher they go the better he likes them. If he is in the field and not bowling he is gathering them up in the slips, with either hand, in a manner painfully reminiscent of cricketers other than Australians. He is a man of action now, and his name is J.M. Gregory.'

Clearly Davis, Iredale and Collins, concerned about the rumours, were doing all they could to convince Gregory not to retire. It worked. Collins took over as NSW captain for the next match against Queensland, while Oldfield was the new state keeper. Gregory took a little longer, as he was considering a non-cricket life in Queensland.

Iredale revealed in the *Sydney Sun* in August he had 'received a letter from J.M. Gregory, from Queensland, containing the welcome news that he is coming to Sydney during the approaching season. He will accordingly be available for the big matches against the Englishmen.'

J.C. Davis was miffed *The Referee* did not get the scoop. The following week he wrote that he had known 'for some little time' that Gregory was available for NSW and Australia, but 'I was asked not to make it public yet awhile'. He was unimpressed that Iredale, 'who writes notes for a Sydney paper', had broken the news. 'This is hardly playing the game.'

Iredale had told Davis to keep quiet on Gregory, but then out-scooped him. Gregory made his debut for NSW a few months later, and became a mighty Australian performer, taking 85 Test wickets at 31.15 and scoring 1146 Test runs at 36.96 over an eight-year period. After the war, he repeatedly intimidated

English batsmen, forming a formidable opening combination with Ted McDonald under the astute control of Test captain Warwick Armstrong. Armstrong always made certain Gregory, who by bowling wide on the return crease angled the ball dangerously into the batsman's body, had the wind whipping in behind him. As he was such an expressive character, Gregory became the cricketing hero of Bill O'Reilly and many other Australian schoolboys. It also appeared O'Reilly may have patterned part of his expressive, elongated, bouncy run-up on Gregory's style.[31]

In the first Australian Test after the war, the AIF team provided six players — Collins, Kelleway, Gregory, Pellew, Oldfield and Johnny Taylor — against England at the SCG in December 1920.

Oldfield, who credited the AIF team with turning him into a Test player, remained Australia's number one keeper until just before the next World War, while Collins, an obsessive gambler who became a bookmaker, stipendary steward and commission agent (and ultimately penniless), was one of Australia's most successful and controversial captains. The high side was that he only lost two of the 11 Tests as skipper. The low side was that there were strong claims that in two of those Test matches he may have been involved in match-fixing. Teammate Stork Hendry was adamant Collins 'threw' a 1926 Test in England. Monty Noble was 'suspicious'.

Several AIF players returned to the grade ranks, and some — Hammy Love, Harry Heath, John Murray, Bill Stirling and Bill Trenerry — played Sheffield Shield cricket. Cyril Docker had a flourishing business career before being the head of the Australian Comforts Fund during the Second World War. As a bank inspector, Docker constantly dealt with cantankerous newspaper magnate Sir Frank Packer, father of Kerry — the mogul who transformed Australian cricket in the 1970s and 1980s.

Asked by R.S. 'Dick' Whitington when he was writing Packer's biography in 1971 why Sir Frank upset so many people,

---

31 After his Test career and marrying a Miss Australia, Gregory was reclusive, refusing interviews after he had 'been burnt by the press' late in his career, retiring to the NSW South Coast to fish and play lawn bowls.

Docker replied: 'He is often too outspoken, he never suffers fools, or bludgers, gladly and he harbours a complex about his father [R.C. Packer].'

Carl Willis continued a varied life after the war. For a time he was considered a Test possibility, but missing the NSW match through injury proved costly. Davis wrote in *The Referee* that it was 'a pity' Willis did not play, because 'all reports agree that he is a very fine player'.

He was back in the Victorian team the following month, but his form fell away in the lead-up to the 1920–21 Ashes series. Demoted to No 8, he would get starts, but failed to transform them into sizeable innings. For the next eight seasons, Willis played for his state but wasn't always a first-choice selection. He even played several games with the 19-year-old Don Bradman in Arthur Mailey's Bohemians outfit that played in the NSW bush. Willis's VFL career continued, including a stint as captain of South Melbourne in the 1921 season. He eventually gave sport away so he could concentrate on his dentistry. This single man flitted between Victorian and NSW country towns, playing in the local cricket competitions in Jerilderie (where he became the town hero by taking all ten Leeton wickets in a challenge match), Numurkah and Tocumwal, but he was hampered by the gas attacks he had suffered on the Western Front. The 37-year-old finally settled in Berrigan, where on 12 May 1930, after attending a Bachelor and Spinsters Ball, he died of pneumonia at a female friend's house.

The feats of the AIF team were gradually forgotten, as a country devastated by four years of war wanted to move on. But the impact of these valiant soldiers in ensuring that Australian cricket began on a solid footing from 1919 onwards ensured that this country's summer game was soon back to full health and its Test XI a potent international force. It was an immense help that several of the key AIF players, such as Gregory, Collins, Oldfield and its early tour captain Kelleway, were at the core of the highly successful Australian Test line-up for several years after the Great War. They gave Australian cricket backbone. Oldfield remained a critical part of the local cricket landscape until 1937, playing a dramatic role during the 1932–33 Bodyline series when his skull was fractured by a Harold Larwood delivery during the volatile Adelaide Test. Hammy Love would be his replacement, playing his only Test.

As Oldfield wrote in the 1939 Original AIF team versus Contemporary International XI match day booklet: 'We had emerged from the horrors of war to the happy days of peace — from the hardship of the trenches and bully beef to the luxuries of hotel life.

'The tour was an unqualified success. The spirit of comradeship which developed during those months was one of the most pleasing features of the tour, because it brought together on a common level, officers and men of the ranks. A great spirit of camaraderie was apparent almost from the team's inception, and this invaluable asset of a match-winning quality has been of inestimable help to Australia's subsequent Test teams.'

PART THREE
SECOND WORLD WAR

CHAPTER 10

BARNEY, ROSS AND THE GREATEST EVER

Now is the era of the driven, myopic specialist. In the past, versatility was encouraged, applauded. It was a badge of honour if you excelled in numerous pursuits, especially sporting. Some took it to extremes. Reginald 'Snowy' Baker claimed he excelled in 26 different sports. But this notable boxer, swimmer and Test rugby representative was also a snake-oil salesman. He knew how to spin it. Nonetheless, in Baker's time it was usual for elite athletes to be proficient at countless sports. Talented athletes did not have to make a decision between playing cricket or football, because the seasons did not conflict. One was regarded as an ideal way to get fit for the other.

Some, like Harold Hardwick, combined a flourishing swimming career that included an Olympic gold medal triumph with boxing ring success that saw him win the Australian heavyweight title as well as knocking out Les Darcy's front teeth. For several seasons Hardwick was a regular Sydney first-grade rugby footballer.

Barney Wood is not so well known, but his accomplishments are on a special level. They are certainly diverse. But his achievements were cut short, as he was Australian cricket's initial first-class representative to die in a Second World War battle.

Percival Barnes Wood was born in Wellington, New Zealand, in 1901, moving to Victoria as a youngster. The Melbourne Grammar School prefect excelled in four sports — cricket, football, boxing and golf. He also had a passion for adventure, speed and endurance — holding numerous trans-continental records driving his Essex Super Six motor car across rough, often dangerous, outback tracks.

He was first noticed as a cricketer with the Melbourne Cricket Club. But, after winning the school boxing title, he considered a life in the ring, fighting for the 1923 Victorian amateur welterweight title. He lost, but the *Weekly Times* and *Australasian* newspapers believed Wood was robbed. 'A large section of the crowd considered Wood the winner, and expressed their feelings accordingly,' *The Australasian* reported.

He caught the bug to see Australia as quickly as possible. With friend Alan Mackay, he decided to beat as many overland car speed records as possible. In 1926 Wood and Mackay clipped two-and-a-half days off the fastest drive between Darwin to Adelaide. The following year, in the same Essex Super Six, they took a 'leisurely' trip from Melbourne to Darwin, via Sydney, negotiating numerous treacherous tracks and rough terrain via Lithgow, Bourke, Cunnamulla, Longreach, Urandangi, Newcastle Waters and Daly Waters. When arriving in Darwin, they immediately turned around and attempted to break the record. The 5576-kilometre trip was finished in six days, three hours and 58 minutes, breaking the previous record by a day and a half.

A few months later the pair motored from Fremantle to Sydney, via Melbourne, breaking the record with a trip of four days, 23 hours and 51 minutes.

This was in between Wood playing for the Victorian amateur football team against South Australia, which, shortly after the Fremantle–Sydney trip, saw him lured to the Melbourne club, where he played five matches in 1928. *Football Record* described the defender as having 'plenty of dash'.

He didn't hang around, though, heading to Perth the following year to run a sports goods business. He was also adept in selling baby-food. His sporting endeavours did not dim, with Wood playing first-grade cricket as a left-handed batsman for West Perth, football for Perth, and becoming captain of the Royal Perth Golf Club.

In March 1932, the South Africa team was on its way home after an exasperating 5–0 Test drubbing from Australia and was hoping for a late psychological boost against Western Australia at the WACA. After a consistent season with West Perth, the WA selectors included Wood as a No 6 batsman. He failed, scoring six and two, which included being dropped in either innings. As for the match, it was a non-event, with South Africa winning by an innings and 242 runs, with the lopsided three-day game described by *The West Australian* as a 'bad advertisement' for the local competition.

After his forgettable one and only state appearance, Barney focused on golf and business. When the threat of war emerged some years later, he enlisted, even though in his late 30s he could have avoided serving due to his responsibilities as a businessman and merchant. Many of his sporting mates were joining up, so why not he? He had experienced the Great War as a teenager, and the pressures applied to those who stayed at home, including white feathers being sent to those whom an unkind society thought were traitors. He was placed on the Reserves list, but, sick of waiting for a call-up, joined the 2/16th Australian Infantry Battalion as a private.

By October 1940, he was in the Middle East to bolster the AIF stocks at various critical early battles of the war. This time around, though, there wasn't as frantic an influx of sportsmen desperate to join up.

Some sports, particularly rugby union in Australia, had learnt a crucial lesson from the Great War. The game had shut down between 1915 and 1918 as its administrators had transformed themselves into active AIF recruiters, and had even disappeared in Queensland until 1929.

When cricketophile Robert Menzies announced on 3 September 1939 that Australia was at war with Germany, rugby authorities were less keen to be pro-military. They realised the dangers of closing down the head office. They also comprehended that sport, rather than keeping the idle, lazy and unpatriotic entertained, could provide a necessary distraction to war. District competitions were encouraged.

Cricket in Australia followed a similar line. Officials believed that playing the game could lift home spirits. The tone was provided by the often combative, often confusing Labor figure and NSW Cricket Association vice-president Dr H.V. 'Bert' Evatt, who wrote to another of the Association's officials that, although 'cricket must take a second place owing to the necessity of defending our country against aggression', the Association was also 'trustees of the game for the benefit of the youth of the nation'.

It was imperative to 'give every opportunity for playing not only grade, but first-class cricket, so long as we are sure that the war effort will not be interfered with'.

The NSWCA even complained to local newspapers and radio stations about giving increased publicity to 'horse-racing and dog-racing' at the expense of cricket, where 'youth' could improve their 'physical and moral well-being'.

District and Sheffield Shield cricket continued in the 1939–40 and '40–41 seasons, until Japan's imminent entry into the war convinced administrators that the first-class competition had to be stopped. Instead of the Sheffield Shield in 1941–42, an 'Interstate Patriotic Competition' — in which 75 per cent of net profits would go to the war effort — was to be staged. Only one of the eight planned matches was played, however, as the competition was immediately called off following the attack on Pearl Harbor that heightened fears of a Japanese invasion of Australia.

Officials were soon providing facilities and equipment to the defence forces, as well as agreeing to allow the military to use cricket grounds as training camps. There was the occasional drama, as in 1941 when the South Australian Cricket Association lent cricket nets to the RAAF, only to see the lorry sent to collect them demolish the northern gates of Adelaide Oval.

Cricket associations had to be frugal. Due to rationing, there was a shortage of cricket balls, while coir yarn for matting wickets, canvas for cricket boots and rubber for composition balls were near impossible to find. The NSWCA stopped providing free cigars and cigarettes in its SCG meeting room.

The MCG, renamed 'Camp Murphy', became the home of the United States Army's Fifth Air Force, then of the First Regiment of the First Division of the US Marine Corps.[32] Overseas, a West Indies touring team had to call off its final five games of its 1939 England tour, England's proposed tour to India was abandoned, and the Ashes urn was moved from Lord's to a secret location in case of a German bombing attack.

The Australian state associations were soon paying their respects to lost cricketing soldiers. One of Australia's first critical battles in the Second World War revolved around the capture and siege of the north African port town of Tobruk. Among those from the illustrious 2/48th Infantry Battalion — which became Australia's most highly decorated Second World War unit — involved in holding the Tobruk fortress for eight months in 1941 was Bob Christie from the South Australian country town of Angaston. He was the town's gun sportsman, a masterful footballer, baseballer and cricketer. Just days after winning the Mail Cup for the fastest century in Adelaide grade cricket when he hit a ton in 58 minutes in the last match of the 1938–39 season for Glenelg — beating Don Bradman, who came second with an 80-minute ton — he enlisted and was on his way to the Middle East. The only son of an AIF private killed in France during the Great War, Christie died of wounds in Libya on 7 May 1941.

Along the coast from Tobruk, Australian troops were involved in numerous battles, including at Litani River in southern Lebanon as part of a campaign to take control of the French colonies of Lebanon and Syria from the pro-German Vichy government. On the frontline was Barney Wood, who was part of a 40-kilometre advance in June 1941 in which he was struck by

---

32 The camp was named after William Murphy, an American Signal Corps colonel who was killed in Java.

a bullet. While being attended to, he was hit by a mortar bomb. Shortly after, his brother-in-law, W.M. Irvine, wrote a letter to Wood's old school, Melbourne Grammar, explaining: 'From what I heard, he went out in the way you would expect of him — in the very van where things were hottest, and in front of his men he got what he was apparently destined for. No one could ever question his courage. I only wish I had half as much myself.

'He was, I gather, wounded, and was being treated by the first-aid men, when a mortar came along and completely wiped out the whole party. He would know nothing about it. He met the finest fate a man can meet — a quick and painless death in the face of the enemy. We all know that this is the way he would have chosen it. I am writing this from one of the most famous of the holy cities [Damascus] of the world, and as I write on this peaceful Sunday morning, the church bells are telling their story to the world. To me, this morning they toll for Barnes, as two thousand years ago they tolled for another Man.'

Barney Wood was buried at Sidon War Cemetery, near Beirut.

Due to the twin threats of Germany in Europe and Japan in the Pacific, Australian troops, including numerous cricketers of note, were soon placed across the globe. Many went to England to help in the aerial campaign against the Nazi forces; some were embedded in the Middle East, Greece or Crete; some were lured back by Prime Minister John Curtin, who, standing up to Winston 'Germany First' Churchill, demanded their return to provide support as the Japanese infiltrated New Guinea and threatened Australia's north; while others were caught up in numerous Asian battles and debacles, including Malaya, Burma and the fall of Singapore. In spite of the many battles, cricket of a good standard continued to be played near the frontline. Competition was encouraged. Thomas Blamey, the Australian Commander-in-Chief in the Middle East, and Gordon Bennett, commander of the AIF in Malaya and Singapore, were both adamant sport was crucial for soldiers' morale and general fitness. Soon AIF and Services matches were being played within earshot of the front in numerous locations.

Blamey took it so seriously he gave permission for NSW allrounder Albert Cheetham to leave Tobruk in October 1941 to play for the AIF against the British Services team in Alexandria. After receiving the directive, Cheetham's astounded superior, General Leslie Morshead, replied to Blamey: 'Don't you know there's a war on?' Blamey shot back that in this instance cricket came first.

Blamey won this battle, as the AIF team, with Cheetham and Lindsay Hassett guiding them, passed the British Services' score of 171. In the crowd was acclaimed journalist and poet Kenneth Slessor, who wrote for *The Argus* that the game brought back 'memories of the famous AIF side which grew out of the last war'.

'Every Australian in Alexandria seemed to be present, and there was a large party of Australian hospital patients and a sprinkling of Australian nurses. There was a little good-humoured barracking at the expense of the Australians,' Slessor wrote.

Even during the darkest days of Tobruk, cricket was played. One semi-serious inter-service match in July 1941 between the 20th Australian Infantry Brigade and 107th Royal Horse Artillery at the Tobruch (Tobruk) Cricket Ground included the stipulations that 'play will NOT cease during shell fire', 'All players will supply own Beer. Rum issue, before and after match, is being arranged by Manager', 'Umpires will wear with coats (if available) and will carry loaded rifle with fixed bayonet', 'Tin hat to be used (on head only) by wicket-keeper, if desired', 'Remarks to umpires on receipt of adverse decisions to be confined to those words used during dive-bombing attacks', 'all players will be searched for concealed weapons before start of play', 'all weapons found, other than ST grenades, Mills bombs and revolvers will be confiscated (this does NOT apply to umpires)' and 'any other rules may be added or deleted as a majority of players, umpires or onlookers think fit'.

Back at home the game continued, heartily endorsed by Curtin, a committed cricket and Aussie Rules follower. The Prime Minister had played grade cricket with Brunswick in Melbourne, was the club's delegate to the Melbourne Junior Cricket Association, and, on moving to Perth, a lower grader at the Cottesloe club. He would where possible umpire club games and was a member of the Western Australian Cricket Association.[33]

In November 1941, as reported in the *Cairns Post*, Curtin emphasised the importance of Australians being able to play sport or attend cricket matches.

'I cannot agree that participation in games and sport in moderation, either as players or spectators, need be in any way detrimental to our war effort,' Curtin said. 'On the contrary, those who are working through the week have at least as much to gain by spending their afternoon off at a sporting event as they have by spending a night at the pictures. In the balance, they are probably better occupied at an open air sports meeting than at indoor entertainment.'

Sports participation improved 'physical wellbeing' and 'morale'.

'The fact is that our race does not live by bread alone. I think it would be an entirely commendable thing and a demonstration to the world at large of the spirit of the British race if immediately after the war ends England and Australia resumed Test cricket matches. I think these things just as important to the British race as the performance of Shakespeare. The two things go together in making us what we are.'

Following Pearl Harbor, however, Curtin decided midweek sport should be called off. Then the fall of Singapore to the Japanese, leading to thousands of Australian soldiers ending up in prisoner-of-war camps or enduring hardship, including constructing the Thai–Burma Railway or suffering the Sandakan Death March, convinced him the war had taken such a bad turn that those obsessed with sport had to rethink their priorities.

On 16 February 1942, in an address to the nation, Curtin described Singapore as 'Australia's Dunkirk'.

---

33 Arthur Mailey wrote in *The Sunday Telegraph*: 'Curtin had read nearly all the cricket classics, but in 1942 I found he had not read [R.C.] Robertson-Glasgow's *The Brighter Side of Cricket*. I lent him the book. He read it until 4am next day, and on the following night he made one of the most moving of all his speeches — his appeal for the Austerity Loan. He wrote to me later saying that staying up late reading cricket stories had freshened his mind for the speech.'

'Our honeymoon has finished. It is now work or fight as we have never worked or fought before. We can put play-time aside. The hours previously devoted to sport and leisure must now be given to the duties of war.'

Curtin didn't go as far as banning sport. Still, many got the message and either enlisted or focused on the war effort on the home front.

The week before Curtin's address, a player who had been a regular Victorian representative between 1937 and 1939 suddenly went missing. Frank Thorn, a penetrative off-spin bowler who took 24 wickets at the impressive average of 26.83 in seven games, was best known for dismissing Bradman for only five in a 1939 Shield match against South Australia in Adelaide, thwarting him from making a record seventh consecutive hundred. The biggest ever Adelaide Oval Shield crowd, 17,777, was there to witness Bradman break C.B. Fry's world record. Bradman misread a shorter delivery by Thorn, turning it straight into Les 'Chuck' Fleetwood-Smith's hands at backward short leg. The bulk of the crowd immediately left the ground. Thorn laughed at the mass exodus.

Thorn, whose club coach, Jack Baggott, was adamant he was of Test quality, joined the Royal Australian Air Force the following year, and shortly after was married. However, his time with his wife, Bertha, was sadly short, as he was transferred to New Guinea.

On 11 February 1942, Thorn was flying as part of a formation of three Hudson bombers with the assignment of destroying several Japanese cargo ships berthed in Gasmata Harbour on the southern coast of New Britain. However, near the target, the squadron was intercepted by four Japanese fighters. Thorn was part of a four-man crew who headed inland, where the bomber was seen crashing into a ridgeline and then disappearing. That was the last sighting of the four-man crew.

Thorn's wife's grief was near immediate, as three days later Victorian newspapers reported he was missing in New Guinea, but provided no details. In *The Australasian*'s report that Thorn was missing, cricket correspondent Percy Taylor wrote: 'But for the war he was a possibility for the Test side.'

The authorities had no idea where Thorn's body was. More than 60 years later, a missionary, Mark Reichman, accidentally found the wreckage while trekking through dense jungle. Several large pieces of wreckage were discovered, with the upside-down cockpit partially buried in mud. The tail section was battered with bullet holes. There was no trace of any bodies.

It also took an eternity for anyone to find out what had happened to South Australian batsman Gilbert Jose, who played against the 1920–21 MCC tourists. Jose hailed from a notable South Australian family. His father was the Dean of Adelaide, working as a missionary in China, where Gilbert was born in 1898. Gilbert became a surgeon, having three children before joining the Royal Australian Army Medical Corps in October 1940. He was among a multitude of Australian soldiers captured by the Japanese in Singapore. He was taken to Changi, where he died of dysentery in March 1942. The family was not alerted of his death for another 11 months.[34]

As with Thorn, Jose's death received minimal press coverage.

It was only when Australia's first Test fatality of the Second World War — Ross Gregory — was widely reported that the devastation of war really hit the local cricketing community. Heightening the pain was that the Australian pilot who suddenly disappeared over the Bengal floodplains was such a popular figure, a cricketer of boundless, untapped talent who had the fresh-faced features of someone sitting at the front of a family photograph. He looked like the younger brother you wanted to humiliate on a dodgy backyard pitch.

His was an Australian face — boasting a wide, impish grin, pronounced parting of the hair, childlike features and complexion that made him look considerably younger than he actually was. He was constantly referred to in the press as the 'baby' of whatever

---

34 Gilbert's son, Tony Jose, played first-class cricket as an opening bowler for South Australia, Oxford University and Kent. He was South Australia's Rhodes Scholar in 1949.

team he was picked in. Newspaper cartoons of Ross Gregory often mocked him. Sometimes he was perched in a pram with a dummy stuck in his mouth, or portrayed as a midget wielding a gargantuan cricket bat.

Gregory was a boy in a man's uniform. And that was what endeared him to so many. The Australian public felt an instant affinity. In one of the first newspaper references to him, he was described at 14 as 'a thorough little gentleman'.

Little changed over the next decade or so. He was short, pushing 170 centimetres, but that did not stop him from being a fearless batsman, or the most resilient of fighters in peace and wartime.

He hailed from a Melbourne school cricketing stronghold — Wesley College — which also educated the game's VC recipient, Robert Grieve, as well as Test cricketers Ian Johnson, Keith Rigg and Sam Loxton. A precocious talent, Gregory, in his final year, was rated by the college's magazine as close to the best allrounder the school had produced.[35] In his favour was that his mentor at Wesley, P.L. 'Percy' Williams, was ranked among the game's most respected and successful cricketing coaches. Johnson, another Williams protégé, said there was 'no greater cricket coach in Australia — and if there is one elsewhere in the world I've never seen nor heard of him'.

Williams, who coached a tribe of Test players, drove the students hard — even demanding fielding practice during their lunch breaks. But he had a knack of producing determined competitors.

Sighting Gregory for the first time, Williams remarked: 'It was so plain that he can bat.'

'But it was rather ridiculous to consider this 15-year-old boy for any first XI. He was far too young and anyway he was far too small,' Williams said. Williams ignored those instincts. He picked Gregory at 15 in the Wesley first XI for his early-order batting and leg-spinners.

---

35 Wesley College is also where a group of officials met in 1905 to form the Australian Board of Control for International Cricket.

'Though he took bags of wickets, made centuries and was in century, double-century and treble-century partnerships, I remember chiefly a slow and humble innings of 15 in his first year — with the whips cracking, runs worth gold, the wicket sodden. He wouldn't get out. He just wouldn't get out. He was hit everywhere but he kept on stepping in behind the bowling. It was typical — I don't think he ever drew away from trouble in his life,' Williams told the *Sporting Globe*.

While at school in February 1934, Gregory made the Victorian team two weeks before his 18th birthday — picked more for his bowling abilities — against Western Australia at the MCG. He immediately acquitted himself, taking five wickets — four caught and bowled — and also had to rue a dropped chance. By the end of the year, *The Age* was describing him as 'a young Grimmett'. Some matches later, he could proudly say he had taken Bradman's wicket in a Shield game.

Within two seasons Gregory was considered Test quality, but now as a batsman, after scoring a century for Victoria against the 1936–37 England tourists. The press were on his side. They liked his modesty and how spectators and fans gravitated towards him. Former Victorian batsman and Wesley College student Roy Park wrote in *The Sporting Globe* that Gregory reminded him of Bill Ponsford.

Williams explained: 'He could have been spoiled. Hero worship was thrust upon him. He was immensely popular but it was not a cheap popularity of his own seeking. He remained always the same lovable character. With men he was at home, for he was a man's man. With elderly people he was the soul of consideration, with children he became a kid again. He was a Christian in the truest sense, but he did not thrust his Christianity at you.'

Like Victoria, the national selectors did not hold back, selecting him for the fourth Test of the 1936–37 series — 30 days before his 21st birthday — making him the then 14th-youngest Australian player on debut. Replacing Len Darling in the Australian middle order, the newcomer could not have chosen a more eventful first-up Test. In the end the result revolved around one of the most extraordinary of deliveries, and an intriguing backstory.

Bradman, after winning the toss, infuriated the visitors when his long-time ally, umpire Jack Scott, gave him the benefit of the doubt after England heartily appealed for a caught behind. David Frith writes in *The Ross Gregory Story* that England keeper Les Ames took the ball in front of first slip, prompting a raucous shout, only for the bowler (and captain), Gubby Allen, to be told by Scott that he couldn't give Bradman out because he hadn't heard anything.

A furious Allen was reputed to have said: 'No, because the ball went off the face of the bat.'

Shortly after, Allen won that battle by bowling Bradman. Replacing Bradman at the crease to accompany Stan McCabe was a nervous Gregory.

Gregory was jittery for some time, as when he was later joined at the crease by Arthur Chipperfield. C.B. Fry remarked that the pair were 'having an impudent try to run one another out and are shocking innumerable ladies. Three spasms in five minutes is a lot for decorous Adelaide.'

He lasted an hour and a half before misreading a Wally Hammond medium-pace seamer and was trapped leg-before. His second innings was similarly edgy, but this time the pressure wasn't so stifling. At the other end, Bradman was on song, accelerating towards a double century. Still many observed how out of place the debutant looked. 'Boy Gregory makes his slim, pale, imperturbable entry,' Fry remarked.

The Age described his early overs as 'an ordeal' but added that 'fortified by frequent and almost paternal advice from Bradman, he displayed his usual grit, and remained with his captain for over two hours'.

England tried every tactic, with Hedley Verity causing him trouble with his masterful slow left-armers. Within arm's length was a tribe of England fielders. He refused to be distracted. Yet his innings finished strangely. After almost three hours at the crease, and only one boundary, Gregory straight-drove Allen. By running two, he advanced to his half-century, but was called through for a third by Bradman. A direct throw by Charlie Barnett saw Gregory out of his ground and on his way to the pavilion. The 38,000-plus crowd didn't know what to do. Applause for his half-century was interspersed with groans, and questions about what might have been. Cartoonists had a field day. The following morning, they portrayed 'little Ross Gregory' hugging his bat and seemingly sobbing. Another showed him smaller than the stumps and calling down the wicket to Bradman 'How'm I doin' Pop?'

But Gregory's 135-run partnership with Bradman had the desired effect of giving England a sizeable run chase to win the game. It also established Gregory as a player of Test standard. Bill Woodfull wrote that he had already shown enough to be in serious consideration for the 1938 Ashes tour. Gregory relished the international scene, explaining to his old cricket coach: 'This Test cricket is the best of good fun. I wish the game had lasted a month.'

Gregory also knew — due to his close affiliation with Victoria's Test players — he had joined a deeply divided national team. Three weeks earlier, Australia had easily defeated England in the third Test in Melbourne. However, the gloss was taken off the victory when the Australian Board of Control summoned four players — McCabe, O'Reilly and two of Gregory's Victorian teammates, Leo O'Brien and Fleetwood-Smith — to appear before a tribunal of Board members. The players thought Bradman had dobbed them in for reckless behaviour. Bradman denied it.

The players were told at the meeting that some players had 'been indulging in too much alcohol and making no effort to get into top physical condition'.

There were thinly veiled suggestions that one of the four was not 100 per cent loyal to Bradman. O'Reilly immediately assumed he was the man in question. He asked chairman Dr Allen Robertson whether the four were being held responsible for being the disloyal slackers and boozers. The answer was 'no'. O'Reilly asked what they were there for. He didn't receive an answer, and the meeting petered out. The players were incensed they had been targeted. They were forever wary of Bradman.

Fleetwood-Smith was particularly annoyed his fitness had been questioned at that meeting. Before the Adelaide Test, he had to convince the selectors he was match fit. In a net session Fleetwood-Smith bowled The Don three times in 15 minutes. He was passed fit. As an irritable Chuck left the net, he told Melbourne journalist Percy Taylor: 'I'll show them and I guarantee I'll get ten wickets.'

He proved true to his word. One delivery stood out. On the last day England needed 244 runs with plenty of wickets left and Hammond still at the crease. Fleetwood-Smith had already taken two second-innings wickets when Bradman walked over to him and said: 'Chuck, if ever we wanted you to bowl that unplayable ball, now is the time.'

He responded. In the air the heavily spun ball swerved away from Hammond's bat and pitched on a worn spot outside the off stump. Hammond was drawn defensively forward but was caught in no-man's-land when the ball viciously spun back between bat and pad, accelerating from the pace it made from the pitch, to conclusively bowl England's best batsman. Fleetwood-Smith slumped to his knees. He turned to Bradman and said with a hint of sarcasm: 'Was that what you wanted?'

Bradman proudly shook his hand, followed by Gregory, still trying to comprehend what he had actually witnessed. O'Reilly described it as one of the greatest deliveries, if not the greatest, he had seen. That was the end of the England campaign. Australia won by 148 runs, and Fleetwood-Smith finished with ten wickets.

Gregory's next Test appearance also had a distinct edge to it. He witnessed a furious opposition determined to stand up to Bradman.

The tourists were unimpressed the abrasive opening bowler Laurie Nash had been plucked from the wilderness to pepper them with dangerous bowling. Nash was only 173 centimetres tall but always attempted to tower over all, in particular batsmen, provoking them with deliveries aimed at the throat.

Nash was a renowned footballer, captaining South Melbourne in the VFL and adjudged by *The Sporting Globe* as the best defender since the Great War. Jack 'Captain Blood' Dyer was adamant Nash was Australian football's greatest player. So was Nash. He encouraged the media to tag him Laurie 'The Greatest Ever' Nash, because after all that's what he called himself.

Nash anecdotes abound, such as the time he was a spectator at a game and a player was attempting a difficult kick at goal. Asked 'would you be able to kick it?', Nash replied: 'In my dressing-gown, pyjamas and carpet slippers — either foot!'

Having such a high opinion of himself turned many off him. He often squabbled with sporting officials. He was abrasive, rarely diplomatic — a proud 'working man's son'. While admiring his athletic skills, Dyer still thought him bombastic and an ego maniac.

The ever-belligerent Nash, who had moved from Victoria to Launceston for work, opened the bowling for Tasmania in 1929–30, and was soon called for throwing. He later said these deliveries against Victoria in Launceston were deliberately thrown because he was furious with his fielders. Then a fierce spell against the 1931–32 South Africans in Hobart, where he broke Eric Dalton's jaw with a wild bouncer while taking 7/50, convinced the Australian selectors to play him as their only speedster in the fifth Test in Melbourne. Tasmanian captain Jim 'Snowy' Atkinson, realising he couldn't control Nash, was so concerned about the South African batsmen's safety he took his strike bowler off. Nash castigated his captain for being 'weak'.

In the Test, the ferocity of Nash, who had the rare distinction of playing Test cricket before appearing in a Sheffield Shield match, again shook up the South Africans. The game was over in five hours and 50 minutes — after the tourists struggled to get to 36 and 45. Nash, with five wickets, appeared destined for a long representative career.

Instead his often uncouth behaviour saw him overlooked for several seasons. When Douglas Jardine's touring Englishmen transformed the 1932–33 Ashes series into the vicious Bodyline encounter, many, including Australian vice-captain Vic Richardson and Jack Fingleton, believed Nash had to be selected to counter Harold Larwood and co.

But Australian officials did not want to inflame the issue any further. The often cocky Nash told friends he would have ended Bodyline in two overs, and without a leg-trap field. It was not to be. Now living in Melbourne, where his football career had blossomed, Nash was thought by the Victorian selectors to be too difficult to handle, and so wasn't sighted in first-class ranks for three-and-a-half seasons. He kept getting wickets in Melbourne district cricket, and was finally selected for Victoria against England in the lead-up match to the 1936–37 fifth Test in Melbourne. It had the desired effect. He bowled short, at the body, and had Barnett and Hammond bobbing and weaving. Bradman, now a selector and still seething over what had happened to him four seasons earlier, pushed for Nash to be brought into the Test side ahead of NSW's Ginty Lush. Bradman knew Nash's inclusion would infuriate Gubby's Englishmen. It did. Allen was beside himself when he saw Nash named in a 13-man Australian fifth Test squad. Allen organised a pre-match lunch with Bradman at which he asked: 'What! Are you going to have a go at us?'

Allen said that if Bodyline tactics were introduced he would publicly blame Bradman, and retaliate.

Bradman stood his ground, stating that Allen could not dictate who played for Australia, but assured the England captain the use of the bouncer would not be excessive. Allen told umpire Jack Scott that if Nash bowled 'straight at my men' he would immediately take his team off the field. 'Nash deliberately bowled Bodyline in our game against Victoria,' Allen fumed.

Bradman kept the peace by telling Nash to restrain himself and rely more on pace, line and length to make his impact. The tension also eased as Australia batted first. Gregory was noticeably nervous, as he had been reminded all week how this would be the most crucial five days of his life. Only two days earlier, he and teammate Keith Rigg had been guests of honour at the Wesley Old Boys luncheon, where the chairman, L. Cole, told the room: 'Australia is in the shadow of an event of great international importance. Within 48 hours Melbourne will be swept out of its orderly routine into a maelstrom of feverish excitement and conflicting interests and emotions. The cables will run hot. Hitler, Mussolini and the "Yes" campaign[36] will cease to be front page news. Business men will find it almost impossible to make engagements, and if they do the venue will have to be in the vicinity of Jolimont. In other words, the fifth Test match begins on Friday.'

Buoyed by making 86 for Victoria against the MCC in the lead-up match, Gregory had at least 24 hours to compose himself as he sat in the dressing room all the first day while Bradman and McCabe scored centuries. He was eventually required in the first ten minutes of the second day when, in front of 77,000 spectators, he came to the wicket to replace Bradman, who had been bowled by Ken Farnes. As Australia was 4/346, it was time for Gregory to really push home the advantage; and he did, combining in a 161-run partnership with Jack Badcock. Badcock finished with a century, but Gregory was a standout. In front of his home crowd, he played with poise. Up in the press box, the critics were preparing to eulogise Gregory as he approached three figures, but he dabbed a rising delivery from Farnes straight to Verity at forward short leg to be out 20 runs short of a century.

This was ultimately the most tragic dismissal in Test cricket history — as all three involved were soon to be war victims. In Sicily in 1942, Verity was shot in the chest. Captured by the Germans, he underwent several operations but died in an Italian hospital. Farnes, a pilot officer, crash-landed during a night flight in Oxfordshire in 1941 and was killed instantly.

Neville Cardus wrote in *The Advertiser* that Gregory's innings had revitalised the game: 'We have again witnessed strokes in a Test match, gay and handsome and cultured strokes.' *The Age*'s 'Mid Off' said succinctly: 'Another champion in the making!' J.C. Davis in *The Referee* commented: 'In sound batsmanship Gregory

---

36 Australia was about to vote on a national referendum on protection of primary producers and on legislation concerning air navigation and aircraft.

is exceptional for one so young. To the on-side he was high-class in front of the wicket and behind it, with the power of a champion.'

A perfect start, as it was two victories out of two for Gregory, as well as being part of an Ashes series triumph. But it stalled. Gregory was not sighted in a Test team again. Nor was Nash.[37]

The next major Australian assignment was the 1938 Ashes tour. Gregory was a serious contender for a batting or allrounder spot, but Chipperfield was chosen ahead of him. It wasn't the most staggering omission, as Clarrie Grimmett was inexplicably overlooked for one of Bradman's mates, leg-spinner Frank Ward. It proved an ineffective selection as Ward failed to take a wicket in his only Test appearance of the tour, at Trent Bridge. The players, in particular O'Reilly and Fingleton, blamed Bradman, believing he was too close to Ward. Bradman was also furious Grimmett had recently chastised him during a Shield match in Melbourne. Grimmett, angry Bradman had thrown his wicket away late in the day, said to his state captain: 'You clearly don't like the idea of facing [Ernie] McCormick again with the new ball, do you?'

O'Reilly said: 'To my mind these few words marked the end of Grimmett's career.'[38]

Comparing Ward with Grimmett was in O'Reilly's eyes 'like comparing Bradley's Head with Mount Kosciusko ... absolute poles apart'.

---

37 Keith Miller agreed with Leo O'Brien that Nash's controversial career, which involved only two Test matches, was 'the greatest waste of talent in Australian cricket history'.
38 Bradman argued that Grimmett was overlooked as he was 46, and Ward's strike rate was better. In a letter to biographer Jack McHarg in 1991, Bradman said Ward's strike rate on the tour, in the non-Test matches, was better than O'Reilly's, while Grimmett had been taking wickets against 'very weak opposition'. Statistics 'debunk O'Reilly's florid and unjustifiable claim that Grimmett was discarded like an old boot', Bradman wrote. 'O'Reilly's trouble is that he shelters behind emotional statements about what Grimmett MIGHT have done (pure conjecture) but he never attempts to analyse the facts of the case.' McHarg replied to Bradman that his defence of Ward against Grimmett was 'statistically sound' except when he compared Ward's tour strike rate against O'Reilly's. As O'Reilly had played in all the Tests and Ward only one, the former would be affected as 'bowling in Test matches would tend to worsen strike rates'. The ever-defensive Bradman again vehemently argued that Ward remained a better option than Grimmett.

Many came to the defence of Gregory. 'Poor little Ross Gregory' was the immediate reaction of Bert Oldfield when told of the squad. Oldfield was also privately peeved he missed out himself, and shortly after retired from international cricket.

Gregory continued playing Shield cricket for Victoria, but there were now distractions. He was among the first to enlist in the Royal Australian Air Force, while he was also infatuated by a woman, Barbara Thompson, who had been introduced to him by the new Test wicketkeeper, Ben Barnett, at a Melbourne cricket match in 1938. Just before Gregory, one examination away from becoming a qualified accountant, was to head to England as an air navigator in 1941, they got engaged. As with so many young Second World War couples, their time together was fleeting. Within a year, he was dead.

What occurred in his final 12 months, including his emotions and feelings, was chronicled in his personal diaries, which in 2001 were purchased at an auction by cricketing historian and author David Frith and used as a basis for his comprehensive biography *The Ross Gregory Story*.

Delighted that on the same day as he announced his engagement he won £7 on a 50/1 outsider at the races, Gregory was the same week on his way to Sydney, New Zealand and Canada before arriving in Bournemouth in late July 1941 to report to the Royal Air Force's Personnel Dispatch. On the same ship was NSW wicketkeeper Stan Sismey. The first few weeks in England were leisurely, including a day at Lord's with Plum Warner — 'a grand old man and keen as mustard on the game'.

The following day he met Gubby Allen over lunch, along with another former England captain, Percy Chapman, who wanted him to play in a charity match. But that had to wait as Gregory had been posted to 99 Squadron RAF at Lossiemouth, on the north coast of Scotland, for training, which included pilot land navigation lectures and flights in Vickers Wellington planes.

He soon tired of the surrounds and its inhabitants, questioning the English level of hygiene and unimpressed that in his opinion they were narrow minded. Gregory was suffering from trench mouth due to a lack of fruit, but played several social cricket games, including an RAF–Army match in which Bill Edrich was a teammate. Gregory's respect for the English waned, as he believed it a 'declining nation'. But he admired the Scots, as they were 'kinder, better fighters & certainly better & harder workers'. 'They realise there is a job to be done & immediately set about it in a businesslike manner, but the Eng[lish] people — in very many cases — I blame the so-called upper class for I detest them — like formality & side issues & lose sight of the actual job in hand,' he wrote in October.

He had been involved in bombing raids over Germany, explaining matter-of-factly: 'We flew in the morning & dropped bombs, in the afternoon & dropped more bombs.' His first major operation as a navigator was in December 1941 in an attack on Le Havre, where they had 'to bomb hell out of the docks'. It was a tense trip, especially when the pilot 'passed out' and the plane went into a spiral dive. Gregory described it in his diary as 'the most frightening and harrowing experience I or any of us had ever had'.

'To be in a plane out of control and not able to do anything because you are pinned to the ceiling by centrifugal force is most frightening to say the least.'

Finally the plane was steadied by the second pilot. Gregory had his concerns about the chief pilot, who had put their lives at risk, believing that he was too highly strung.

This was followed by several raids over Norway and Germany to bomb battleships. After some R&R in Dublin — 'a city with so few unattractive girls — they were mostly really beautiful and attractive' — Gregory was transferred to 215 Squadron as a pilot officer with the directive to head to India to take on the Japanese. In early 1942, the Japanese had swept across Manila, Singapore and Rabaul, and invaded Burma. With countless British troops driven out of Burma to India, British and US aircraft provided some resistance. On 10 June 1942 a six-man crew, including Gregory as its navigator, in a Wellington Mark IC bomber left Bengal for Burma. The plane was sighted flying across East Bengal, where it encountered an electrical storm. Some witnesses claimed seeing smoke billowing from the plane before it disintegrated. The bodies were found and buried in a grave near the crash site. What exactly happened is uncertain, especially with Defence officials initially believing that rather than bad weather it may have been due to enemy action.

Details were scanty, with newspapers reporting a fortnight later that Gregory was officially reported to 'have lost his life in operations overseas'. Where was not revealed. *The Cricketer* magazine in England took a punt and said he had been 'killed in air operations in Libya'.

In *The Sporting Globe*, E.H.M. Baillie echoed the thoughts of many by writing on 27 June: 'War has claimed as a victim a young man who had Adolf Hitler not gone mad might by now have created a record in Test and other cricket that would have ranked among the best among Australians. Ross Gregory was apparently on the threshold of a great career when the war dogs were let loose, and created chaos throughout the world.'

The Gregory family received several depressing letters from the Australian Department of Air. The family was told, 'your son and the members of his crew were buried with full military honours near their crashed aircraft. I deeply regret to say that the graves are situated in a remote locality, and have since been covered by flood waters.'

These graves have never been found. At least the family received most of his belongings, which indicated his vast interests. His personal effects included Masonic booklets, the New Testament and Psalms, a *Wisden Cricketers' Almanack*, a biography on Rudolf Hess, and Daphne Du Maurier's *Rebecca*.[39]

Of far simpler tastes was Gregory's one Test teammate Laurie Nash. He had a ratbag of a war. Strict military officialdom couldn't even contain him. He served briefly in New Guinea in a transport regiment, but most of the time was on home soil, where he often disappeared — even bobbing up in suburban football

---

39 The St Kilda Cricket Club's Ross Gregory Oval is named in his honour.

matches. In September 1943, Nash was fined £1 and 28 days' pay for being absent without leave for almost a month. The next year he was court-martialled and arrested on another charge of being an 'illegal absentee' and had to appear in Hawthorn District Court. He received a 60-day detention suspended sentence.[40]

Nash was shortly after released from the army for being medically unfit because of arthritis in both knees. Despite this serious ailment, which would normally stop a man from playing sport, the 35-year-old Nash almost immediately resurrected his VFL football career, playing in the infamous 1945 VFL 'bloodbath' grand final for South Melbourne against Carlton, where, amid numerous brawls, which included even spectators, he threw a left hook, breaking the jaw of opposing captain Bob Chitty, who 'went down as cold as mutton'.

Nothing less was expected from someone who, when asked the best he had ever seen, would reply: 'I just happen to see the greatest player of all time in the mirror every morning when I have a shave.'

---

40 Frank Ward was another Australian cricketer to go AWL, fined a day's pay when he disappeared for 24 hours in March 1941. However, Ward, who had problems with foot ulcers and scabies, was soon on side with military authorities, promoted to sergeant in the Australian Canteen Services. Don Tallon, Australia's premier keeper immediately after the war, was fined £1 after being AWL for three days in June 1941. Tallon, a private with the 47th Battalion, Citizen Military Forces, was discharged from the army in 1943 as 'medically unfit'. Returning from leave, he was at Bundaberg station waiting for a train when he collapsed with pain. He had a duodenal ulcer. Part of his stomach was later removed in an operation.

CHAPTER 11

OUR COUNTRY'S KEEPERS

After suffering horrific wartime experiences, Ben Barnett was not allowed to forget. He had to recall it all for the Australian War Crimes Board of Inquiry. He chronicled how he had been beaten, punched and kicked while in POW camps and working on the Burma–Thailand Railway by Japanese and Korean guards.

'They are sadists … It is in their nature. They are even cruel to animals. They take great delight in, say, tying two dogs together by the tail and seeing what happens. I think they are just fanatical school children.'

The memories were grim. But as he spoke to the inquiry, which was determining which Japanese be convicted for war crimes, Barnett's humanitarian side came through. He was not seeking revenge — when probed, he did not blame the Japanese officers for anything he had not witnessed, and always saw the big picture. He was compassionate, intelligent, thoughtful.

Benjamin Arthur Barnett is one of Australian cricket's most important figures. He deserves greater recognition. His was a broad, sympathetic life — a flourishing prewar international sporting career, in wartime always supporting his fellow man, and postwar having vast influence in various international sporting spheres as well as doing what he could to right past wrongs.

A classmate of future Victorian Governor Sir Henry Winneke at Scotch College, he captained the prestigious private school's football team, but was consumed by cricket. An effervescent figure, he began as a batsman and spin bowler but, when joining the Hawthorn-East Melbourne grade cricket club, decided on another pursuit when the regular wicketkeeper took ill on the morning of a game. At 21 he was his state's keeper, holding that role for the next decade. Selected as Bert Oldfield's understudy for the 1934 Ashes tour, Barnett was popular, especially when his teammates discovered his hobby was magic tricks. An impish humour helped. Just before the team visited Windsor Castle, Barnett bruised his right hand. King George V asked him about it. Taking a dig at the strict rules which forbade Australian players from providing any information to the media, Barnett replied: 'Well, Your Majesty, speaking quite privately and not for publication, it is very much better.'

His teammates were also convinced he could read the future. Victoria was playing NSW in a Sydney Shield match and was being slayed by Don Bradman and Stan McCabe, each scoring centuries. The Victorian fielders were exasperated. Len Darling asked Barnett if he could come up with one of his conjuring tricks. Barnett stated categorically that he would catch McCabe the next ball. He did.

Barnett waited until 1938 to be the Test keeper, surprisingly chosen ahead of Don Tallon for the Ashes tour. The first congratulatory telegram came from his other rival, South Australia's Charlie Walker, who had been selected as his understudy.

The Barnett and Walker pairing was unexpected, as many thought Tallon was now the country's premier keeper. However, some thought Tallon 'too rough around the edges' for an England tour. Tallon would have to wait until after the war to establish himself as probably Australia's greatest glovesman.

Barnett's second Ashes tour is unfairly remembered for one blunder. The fifth Test at The Oval revolved around Len Hutton's epic 13 hours and 20 minutes at the crease, breaking Bradman's record for the highest Test score with 364. Yet it almost never was. When Hutton was on 40, Les Fleetwood-Smith, with whom Barnett had developed a strong relationship as Victorian teammates, lured the batsman forward. Hutton, at least a metre out of his crease, misread the line. It was a mere formality for Barnett to stump him. However, Barnett, thinking the ball was going to hit the stumps, kept his hands down. The ball missed the stumps and fell to the ground, and Hutton scrambled back. Barnett later admitted the ball had turned so sharply it baffled him as much as Hutton. It was still a basic error, among the most crucial in Test history. Even the sympathetic Neville Cardus described it as an 'easy chance'.

Watching from the grandstand was Oldfield, following the tour as part of a working holiday which included radio and newspaper commentaries on the Tests. When he returned home, Oldfield targeted the man who had taken his spot.

In a broadcast, Oldfield said: 'I feel diffident about the wicketkeepers, because I might be misunderstood. But, as I am no longer available for selection for international matches, I will say that neither Walker nor Barnett came up to expectations on the English tour. Barnett failed at critical moments to cooperate with the bowlers, and he made mistakes costly to Australia.'

Oldfield was shot down for his comments. Arthur Mailey, writing in *The Daily Telegraph*, said 'members of the Australian Test team' considered Oldfield's criticism of Barnett 'unjust'.

Mailey wrote: 'I regard him as the most improved member of the team. This view is shared by Bradman, who, at a luncheon in Adelaide, referred to him as a great "keeper and a splendid influence on the team. Barnett doesn't profess to be either a Hitler or an Oldfield," Bradman said. "He is just an ordinary being, like the rest of us."'

Victorian Cricket Association president Canon Hughes, known as 'the Fighting Parson', told the Melbourne press: 'It is hard for a champion to step down and look on, but if he were wise he would realise that silence is golden. It is unfortunate that his predecessor has not given Barnett his due.'

Oldfield refused to back down, pointing out several other stumpings Barnett missed during the series. Barnett laughed it all off. Even though O'Reilly escaped the barbs himself, his relationship with Oldfield cooled from that moment.

The Victorians emphasised their support of Barnett by making him state captain, until war intervened. He then joined the AIF, sailing to Singapore in 1941 with the 8th Division Signals, leaving behind a wife and five-month-old son.

On arrival in Singapore, Barnett was treated as a celebrity, called to the microphone at the wharf to send a message home that the Australians had arrived safe and well.

He was soon involved in organising mock Australia–England Test matches that were covered by the local press, and an Australian Armed Services game against The Rest at the Singapore Cricket Club. The Rest surprisingly won, with one Services player later complaining their supposed quality keeper had dropped three catches off his bowling. Then came the fall of Singapore, and Barnett was imprisoned in Changi. This did not deter his acute organisational skills, as he was the instigator of the celebrated Changi 'Australia versus England Test' cricket series in 1942–43 that had the desired effect of revitalising a dispirited group of POWs.

After a prisoner smuggled in a cricket kit with stumps, bats and new ball, the matches were staged on the Changi playing field, which boasted a clay pitch. Matches were taken very seriously — being described as the Sydney, Brisbane and Melbourne Tests and played in front of more than 1000 captive spectators, with typed scoresheets, umpires and official scorers. In the early matches, the players appeared in their creams. The English team included Geoff Edrich (brother of Test batsman Bill Edrich), who went on to play 339 matches for Lancashire after the war, tallying 15,600 first-class runs.

One British soldier wrote with great delight in his diary of the day he bowled Barnett, which prompted 'a tremendous cheer' from the crowd, which included bemused Japanese guards. The 'Australian team' even went on 'tour', playing various barrack teams in the compound.

As another diversion Barnett held lectures on cricket for the British troops, engrossing them with stories of Bradman and the wicketkeeper's two Ashes trips to the motherland. Barnett was as instrumental in Australian Rules matches being played in Changi, mimicking the VFL by organising a league where POWs were assembled into various premiership club sides.

Sport fervour in the camp was curtailed in 1943, however, as the building of the Burma–Thailand Railway required Australian POWs as labour. Among those departing with 'F' Force from Changi was Barnett, transported in cattle trucks to Banpong, the Thai starting point of the railway, followed by a two-week march to the Thai–Burma border. Under the authority of Lieutenant Hajime Maruyama, a scowling former police officer and judo expert from the Imperial Japanese Army Engineers, they were given the exacting work of bridge and road construction. Taking its toll was a cholera outbreak among the Australians which led to 60 deaths.

On the railway, Barnett proved an admirable and unselfish leader. Captain Roy Mills, the only doctor for the more than 700 Australians at their isolated railway work camps, developed a close relationship with Barnett during these terrible days of 'slaving on the Thai–Burma railway'. In his memoirs Mills wrote: 'Ben Barnett was a gentle person. His steady unflinching gaze masked a steel resolve. He was not only trusted, but admired, by all ranks.' And that he 'possessed a brain capable of quick analyses' which was of great use when working on the railway.

'As medical officer I had each officer and man, each day, classified into one of seven groups: — H (hospital), NO (no duty), L3 (extremely light duty), L2 (very light duty), L1 (light duty), MD (medicine and duty) and D (duty),' Mills wrote.

'After the last sick parade late at night, I would inform Captain Barnett how many there were in each category. Next morning I would modify this report after the 0700 sick parade. The Japanese would then demand from Captain Barnett so many men to work. He would barter; sometimes he would succeed; most times he would not. If the demands were absolutely unreasonable Ben would stand up for the men and, as likely as not, sustain a beating. Accordingly, as medical officer, I was spared daily confrontation.'

Captain James Hardacre said the only man who could handle Murayama was Barnett, who was prepared to take a belting to protect his men.

Hardacre, who was also subjected to beatings, said Barnett was fearless when dealing with the Japanese. He became the only POW Murayama would talk to, referring to him as 'Captain Barnetto'.

Barnett shared with his men any extra food or provisions he received as an officer. His war diary revealed that a common meal was a rudimentary rice onion stew. He and Mills repeatedly protested to Murayama that their starving men needed more food. Mills, punished by the Japanese with repeated blows to the head with bamboo sticks, became so emotional during one argument that Murayama demanded a fight to the death, using Japanese weapons. Mills agreed, but it had to be a fist fight. Barnett would be the judge. Murayama suddenly showed no interest.

Mills often demanded Barnett brighten their spirits by telling him and the other POWs cricket stories before trying to sleep 'on the ground under the open sky'. They were usually forced to sleep on wet mud. Barnett often told of the unflappable Lindsay Hassett during the 1938 Ashes tour when, at a fashionable London hotel, a waiter spilt a bowl of soup over his trousers. Hassett called for the head waiter while asking the other players to move their chairs closer. He handed his trousers, which he had taken off, to the waiter, politely asked to have them cleaned immediately, and continued his meal.

Near the end of the railway construction, Barnett almost bumped into a man who would go on to be one of Australian cricket's most heroic postwar figures — Ern Toovey. Toovey, who had played Brisbane grade cricket from the age of 15, had been working on the railway and was taken to a large camp where there were countless other Australian POWs. In an interview for the Imperial War Museum, Toovey told David Frith: 'I saw this officer, this captain, and I said to one of my mates: "Do you know who he reminds me of?" He said: "Who?" I said: "Ben Barnett." He said: "What would he be doing here?" I replied: "Well what are we doing here?" It was years later and I was talking to a former officer and I told him how during the war I saw someone who was a dead-ringer for Ben Barnett. He said: "That was Ben Barnett." I was sorry I never got to meet him.'

In Toovey's memoirs, held in the Australian War Memorial archives, he wrote that Barnett 'even in his well-worn army clothes, still looked smart'.

Toovey had arrived at that POW camp in a bad way but amazingly he was still alive. His war experience had been one trauma after another.

Enlisting when 18, Toovey was on the HMAS *Perth* as an ordinary seaman when during the Battle of Sunda Strait the ship was sunk 'on a beautiful starry night' off the Java coast in February 1942. Among the 353 killed, more than half the crew, was its admired captain, Hector 'Hard Over Hec' Waller.

In darkness, Toovey, who was below deck, scrambled up ladders, stumbled his way over numerous dead bodies, took off his boots, and dived over the side of the sinking ship. He crashed into part of the stern, damaging his right knee. On top of that he had several shrapnel wounds in his thigh. In the oily sea Toovey, who in rushing to get off the boat had lost his 'Mae West' lifejacket, attempted to hold onto any object available. He found a 44 gallon drum with a plank attached, and he and several others grabbed onto it.

'Strange situations cause strange things, and it does seem silly to have an argument about cricket, while swimming around and going nowhere in particular,' Toovey wrote. A survivor, 'an argumentative bloke from the south', questioned him over who was Australia's best wicketkeeper. Toovey, forever the diehard Queenslander, while trying to stay afloat among all the debris, vehemently pushed Tallon's credentials. The other crewman soon realised it was smarter to just shut up. Over the next day, which included several excruciating hours in the sun where the oil smeared across their bodies burnt them, Toovey's dozen-strong group drifted towards the Java shore, where in the distance 'Krakatoa seemed to be standing guard'.

Australian soldiers playing a game of cricket in South Africa during the Boer War, around 1900.
(AWM P00295.700)

In his prime, J.J. Ferris was rated one of cricket's best left-handed medium-pace bowlers. In 1899 he volunteered to fight for the Empire in South Africa, but a year later he was discharged for unknown reasons. He died penniless in Durban.

Alan Marshal played for Surrey and his home state of Queensland. At Gallipoli, he was struck down with typhoid and did not recover. A talent described by *Wisden* as 'a cricketer of unfulfilled promise' was gone.
(Photograph by George Beldam)

Gother Clarke was an expressive leg-spin bowler who appeared seven times for NSW. In 1917, as Medical Officer for the 34th Battalion, he was treating a soldier about 300 metres behind the frontline at Polygon Wood when he was hit by a shell and killed instantly. (SLNSW)

This advertisement is representative of two common recruiting devices used in Australia during the First World War — a well-known local soldier and an appeal to a sporting fighting spirit. The campaign to enlist sportsmen was fuelled by a strong belief that by playing sport young men developed specific skills and qualities that could be used on the battlefield.

ABOVE: Tibby Cotter was an exceptional cricketer, transforming the science of pace bowling to strike fear into opposing batsmen. A courageous frontline stretcher-bearer, he was killed in the epic Australian cavalry charge that captured Beersheba in the 1917 Palestine campaign.

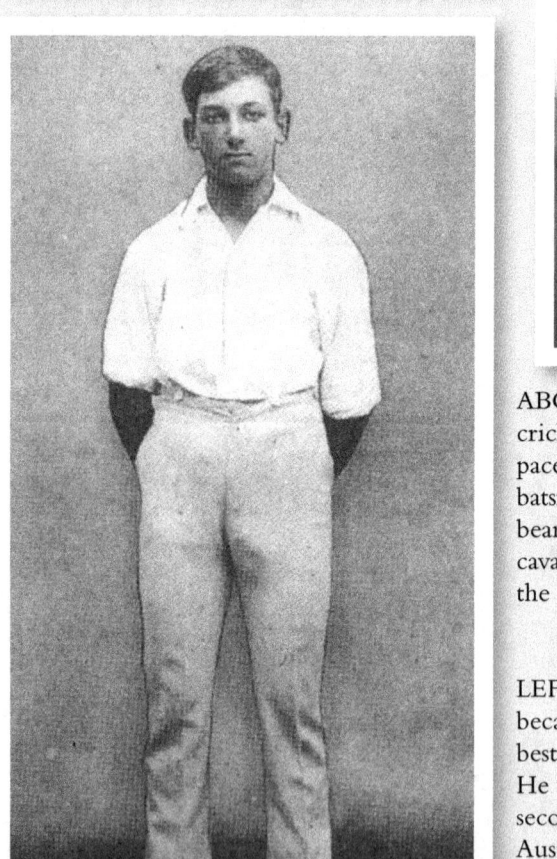

LEFT: While in his teens, Norman Callaway became the Australian cricketer with the best first-class batting average of all — 207. He was killed in 1917, aged 21, during the second battle of Bullecourt. He remains Australian cricket's greatest and most tragic 'what if'.

A group of Light Horse soldiers playing an impromptu game at Anzac Cove in December 1915 to distract the Turks into believing they were there for the long haul. It was a masterful display of deception and planning. The Anzac soldiers would soon be gone from Gallipoli without suffering any more casualties. (Photo by C.E.W. Bean / AWM 601289)

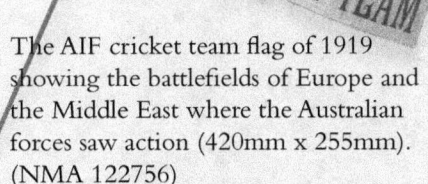

The AIF cricket team flag of 1919 showing the battlefields of Europe and the Middle East where the Australian forces saw action (420mm x 255mm). (NMA 122756)

Victorian bowler Bob Grieve was awarded the VC in 1917 'for most conspicuous gallantry in action during an attack on the enemy's position'. He ran 50 yards in the open, carrying a bag of bombs, alone and under fire from German machine gunners. He used his bowling arm with deadly accuracy.

Tradeable cigarette cards were a popular medium for celebrating sporting heroes in the early 20th century. These examples feature (left to right): 1919–20 AIF team players Herbie Collins and Carl Willis; along with Charlie Walker and Ross Gregory, both of whom died in action with the RAAF in the Second World War.

Batsman Ben Barnett, bowler Les Fleetwood-Smith and keeper Stan McCabe going to lunch after play was abandoned at Old Trafford, July 1938. A year later, war began and Fleetwood-Smith enlisted in the AIF. McCabe enlisted in 1943 but was soon discharged due to ill-health. Barnett enlisted in 1941 and was taken prisoner when Singapore fell to the Japanese; he was in Changi Gaol and then forced to work on the Burma–Thailand Railway.

Two RAAF intelligence officers, Flying Officer Harold Moschetti (left) and Stuart King, examine aerial photographs of the Japanese-held Kahili airstrip on Bougainville Island through a stereoscope. King was a fine sportsman, excelling at cricket and in the VFL. In February 1943 he was an observer in a Catalina flying boat that disappeared off the coast of Cairns while on anti-submarine patrol. (AWM NEA0164)

As a physical and recreational instructor for the AIF, Don Bradman was involved in the Australian Fighting Forces Athletic Track Championships at the MCG in November 1940, where all proceeds went to *The Sporting Globe*'s 'Fags for Fighters Fund'. Bradman led his army men in the march-past around the ground, where almost four years earlier he had scored a Test century against Gubby Allen's England tourists.

ABOVE LEFT: Member of Australia XI Ben Barnett, Victorian wicketkeeper, in 1934. His was a broad, sympathetic life: a flourishing prewar sporting career, in wartime always supporting his fellow man, and postwar having vast influence in various international sporting spheres as well as doing what he could to right past wrongs.

ABOVE: Ern Toovey, who had played Brisbane grade cricket from the age of 15, enlisted aged 18. During the Battle of Sunda Strait his ship was sunk 'on a beautiful starry night' off the Java coast in February 1942. He survived and was captured by the Japanese. To motivate himself he thought about cricket, convincing himself he would again play the game. McCabe was his idol. He'd even named his dog Stan.

London barrister Betty Archdale captained the first women's Test tour to Australia in 1934–35. England finished the tour unbeaten. After joining the Wrens she sailed to Singapore to be a wireless operator (listening for signals from Japanese submarines) and teach Japanese Morse code. In 1946 she became principal of the Women's College at Sydney University, and in 1958 progressive headmistress of Abbotsleigh school. Her mantra was: 'With education, women can do and be anything.'

Australian soldiers stage an impromptu cricket match in Malaya, 1941. Gordon Bennett, commander of the AIF in Malaya and Singapore, was adamant that sport was crucial for soldiers' morale and general fitness. (AWM 009963)

Keith Miller (left) and Jim Brown with a Bristol Beaufighter, February 1945. Years later, when Miller was asked about how he handled pressure as an elite cricket player, he said: 'Pressure? Pressure is having a Messerschmitt up your arse!' (AWM P10332.002)

The Australian Services cricket team, India 1945–46.
(SLNSW PXA 801.31)

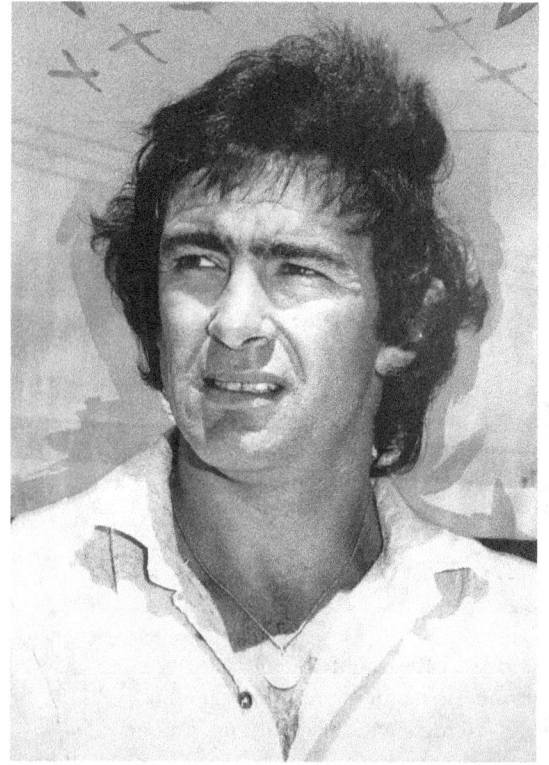

Tony Dell went to Vietnam as a gentle giant and returned damaged by what he had witnessed in battle. Aggression and stamina transformed Dell into a serious first-class cricketer. He played five seasons of Sheffield Shield cricket with Queensland and two Test matches for Australia. But his life began to fray. Eventually diagnosed with post-traumatic stress disorder, he founded the support group Stand Tall for PTS.

While the cross-current swept many survivors out of the bay and into the Indian Ocean, never to be seen again, Toovey willed himself on by telling the rest he was determined to survive for his family's sake, and he had to get home to play cricket for Queensland.

The next chore was to bury at sea their colleague Neville McWilliams, who had been badly wounded when a port torpedo hit. They had dragged him, unconscious, onto their raft of sorts, but eventually realised he had died. A quick service was held.

After several hours avoiding Japanese cruisers, Toovey and co eventually clambered onto a beach, prompting shocked looks from the locals. Toovey couldn't comprehend why they kept gesticulating at them, until realising they weren't used to being confronted by naked white males. The natives gave the ravenous men bananas and coconuts, and one of the group had to hand over his wedding ring and watch for an earthenware jug of water, only to spill the contents just seconds after providing his possessions.

After four days of hiding, they were taken prisoner by the Japanese.

The Japanese Army soldier asked them: 'What do you want me to do with you?'

The reply: 'Tell the bludger we want to go home', prompted a belting across the face with the soldier's sword.

Toovey was marched to Batavia Railway Station, and transported to Singapore on a dilapidated boat in which the Australian POWs were crowded below deck and fed minuscule amounts of rice and thin soup. Several days at Changi was luxury compared to what they had just endured. Toovey said following the dreadful trip from Java, Changi felt like a palace. The cement floor felt like an inner spring mattress.

To motivate himself he kept thinking about cricket, convincing himself he would again play the game. McCabe was his idol. He had even named his dog Stan.

Following another dreadful boat trip, in which 'we were practically sitting or lying on each other', they found themselves in Burma as part of 'A' Force, the first group of 3000 Australian soldiers put to work on the Burma–Thailand Railway. Toovey spent day after day swinging a square-nose pick.

Toovey's superior was the remarkable Colonel Charles Anderson, who during the Japanese invasion of Malaya commanded a small force which destroyed ten enemy tanks near Muar. The next day the South African-born Anderson destroyed two machine-gun posts and shot two enemy soldiers with his pistol, breaking through the Japanese line. Then cut off, Anderson led his forces through enemy lines and, while suffering heavy casualties, attacked an enemy-held bridge. Now surrounded, he ordered all heavy equipment to be destroyed, which enabled them to escape from the enemy. His exceptional leadership, which enabled around 500 Australian and 400 Indian troops to reach the British lines, saw him awarded the Victoria Cross, just two days before being taken prisoner in Singapore. He stoically defended the rights of the POWs on the railway, for that getting numerous severe beatings from Japanese guards. Toovey was one of many indebted to Anderson.

Days were torture, nights uncomfortable — stuck in bamboo huts in which each had only about 'two feet of space'. Familiar faces appeared, such as Wallaby five-eighth Cec Ramalli, whom in 1938 Toovey had seen play his first Test at Brisbane's Exhibition Ground against New Zealand. Both player and spectator at the time were teenagers.

There were constant frightening moments, including Christmas Eve 1942 'when a sergeant Ron O'Donnell was murdered by a guard who from then on we nicknamed "Dillinger"'.

At another camp, there was an overwhelming smell of 'death', from hundreds of natives who had died of cholera.

While working on the railway, Toovey would hear the Last Post played several times a day, having to wait until they returned to camp to find out which colleague had died.

Men were buried in graves, 'not in coffins, but wrapped in bags'.

Sometimes there were 'hardly enough fit men available to carry the bodies'. As humiliating was watching 'hungry men fighting over food scraps thrown out by the enemy' or seeing colleagues crawling on their stomachs 'to and from evil smelling latrines' because there weren't enough fit men to help them.

Adding to the pain was that Toovey suffered badly from jungle ulcers. He was admitted to camp hospital with malaria, dengue fever and dysentery, and at times thought he would just 'give up' as it appeared easier 'not wanting to live'. He was also suffering from facial injuries.

One day he had ignored a Japanese guard giving hand signals. His punishment was a 'nice karate chop to my jaw, breaking an upper tooth'.

A close mate, Charles 'Chilla' Goodchap, 'heard that I was crook'.

'One day he came into the so-called hospital and gave me a serve, casting reflections on my ancestry, besides calling me a "Catholic bludger etc …" It must have awakened the Irish in me, as others said I wanted to fight him. It must have helped as I was back on the line again in a week or two,' Toovey recalled.

Another day, there was a good reason why he didn't want to work. On 16 May 1943 Toovey deliberately went on sick parade. The reason? His 21st birthday. He told the doctor he didn't want to tell his parents when he returned home that he had worked for the enemy on his 21st. Following the railway construction, Toovey's group were moved to build an airport in another part of Thailand.

Barnett, after looking after those members of 'F' Force too ill to go back to Changi, returned to Singapore in April 1944, moving from Changi to Selarang Barracks, where he reintroduced Australia–England 'Test' cricket matches. Despite what he had endured, his enthusiasm never dimmed. He remained focused on improving the wellbeing of his fellow soldiers.

When the war ended, his priority was reacquainting himself with his family, in particular his son Ian, whom he had not seen for five years. But the sadness did not disappear, as it was only then that Barnett discovered that the person who was the first to telegram him on making the 1938 Ashes team, and on that tour had become a close friend, was among the war fatalities.

Charlie Walker (like Charles Goodchap, also nicknamed 'Chilla') was a long-time South Australian wicketkeeper, playing more than 100 first-class games. But his two Ashes tours — 1930 and 1938 — were marred by hand problems. In 1938 he played in only nine tour games because of a damaged left forefinger, broken before the first game. When he appeared against Somerset after almost a seven-week absence, teammates playfully told him he had to reintroduce himself to everyone.

He was part of South Australian sporting royalty, especially as his sister, May, was married to renowned Port Adelaide footballer Bob Quinn. In 1941 Walker joined the RAAF, and transferred to England, where he flew Lancaster bombers. On 18 December 1942 he was shot down over Soltau, Germany, and his body was never recovered. There was no other detail, except that the aircraft had left its England base at 5.05pm and 'no communication was subsequently received'. Six months after his disappearance, military authorities contacted Walker's wife in Adelaide to inform her that 'efforts to trace your husband have proven unavailing and it is feared that all hope of finding him alive must be abandoned'.

His name is remembered every year when the South Australian Cricket Association awards the Charlie Walker Trophy to the best wicketkeeper in Adelaide grade cricket.[41]

Someone who once replaced Walker behind the stumps for South Australia also did not return home. Ross Moyle was a Bradman clubmate at Kensington in Adelaide, and the pair often decimated opposing attacks, one time sharing a 199-run partnership in 89 minutes against Sturt. They also shared the gloves when Walker withdrew from a Shield game against NSW in Sydney due to a hand complaint. Bradman took the gloves in the first innings and Moyle the second, stumping Arthur Chipperfield off Merv Waite's bowling.

---

41 Walker's cousin, Ron Hamence, played three Tests for Australia in 1947–48 after serving in the RAAF for four years, including seven months in 1943 in Milne Bay at the Medical Receiving Station. Hamence was in Bradman's famous 1948 Invincibles squad but did not play a Test on that tour.

A sergeant in the 2/8 Field Ambulance Australian Army Medical Corps, during the second battle of El Alamein he died of wounds to his abdomen and right thigh. Moyle was Mentioned in Despatches for 'gallantry'.

For Ben Barnett, cricket remained an intense passion. Within months of returning from war and regaining the many kilograms lost through deprivation, he was again playing for the Hawthorn-East Melbourne club and the Victorian Sheffield Shield team. He believed the only way to heal the wounds of the previous years was to move on. Remain positive. Ignore the negativity. And be compassionate.

On 14 December 1945 Barnett was back behind the stumps for Victoria in their first first-class game of the season against Queensland at the Carlton Cricket Ground, scoring a half-century in the first innings. In the opposing team was his old 1938 Ashes teammate Bill Brown, an RAAF flight lieutenant who had returned from the Philippines only the previous day.[42]

But, as Roy Mills explained: 'The three-and-a-half years as prisoner of war had taken their toll.

'Prolonged starvation, prolonged untreated illnesses, prolonged physical and mental stress had robbed him of that vital physical spark.'

Nonetheless, Australian selector Don Bradman believed the now 38-year-old Barnett was in fine fettle and should be considered for the 1946–47 series against England. Bradman wrote to fellow selector E.A. 'Chappie' Dwyer that, after 'some uncertainty' over Don Tallon's keeping on the short Australian tour of New Zealand, 'without any hesitation at all I recommend Ben Barnett as the next man on the list'.

'Ben kept beautifully last year and is a much more valuable batsman than he is given credit for,' Bradman wrote. Furthermore, Barnett's understanding with Victorian spinner George Tribe, also in contention for a Test spot, was crucial.

---

42 Brown described his experience in New Guinea and Philippines as: 'I class mine as a gentleman's war. Never got dirty doing anything.'

Barnett was occupied, though, as he had to appear at the War Crimes Tribunal, which was sitting in Melbourne. The tribunal was determining whether numerous Japanese officers, including Maruyama, should be killed or imprisoned for inhumane treatment of Australian soldiers. Barnett provided a fair, objective view of what he and his troops had endured.

When asked 'what type of man was Maruyama?', Barnett replied: 'He was originally one of the Gestapo in Japan. He was a very hard man … He was originally a secret policeman in Japan. He was imbued with the Bushido spirit and his only consideration seemed to be the getting through of that railway line.'

The food — a small amount of rice and occasionally whitebait — was inadequate, and his men 'became very debilitated because of the absence of suitable food and the appalling conditions under which they were forced to work'. This often included having to sleep in wet clothes on a rain-sodden bed.

Barnett tried to convince Maruyama to give his men occasional holidays, but was refused. Maruyama told Barnett that sick men could no longer be protected and had to work on the railway. Recreation was forbidden, which didn't upset Barnett. 'It would not have been much good, as the men were either too tired from working or too sick to partake in any form of recreation,' he told the tribunal.

Barnett recalled that in August 1943 Maruyama had ordered a camp parade to choose a working party. Mills had stipulated that there were six officers and 98 men fit to work. Murayama wasn't impressed, even calling on those in hospital to be paraded in front of him. 'He personally examined them and sent out a further nine officers and 68 other ranks. He turned out the sick men. Most of these men were suffering from malaria, beri beri, bad feet and ulcers.'

All Maruyama and other Japanese officers were focused on was getting the railway completed as quickly as possible. Asked whether the POWs — if the Japanese had treated them better by providing better facilities, proper meals and medical supplies — would have been more thorough, faster workers, Barnett replied:

'That is what we were pointing out to them all the time. They were not concerned with that. They seemed to be more concerned with the number of bodies they could get out there, irrespective of whether they were fit or otherwise. If they wanted 200 bodies and they got 200 bodies, they would be quite happy despite the fact that 50 fit men might have done as much work.'

Maruyama was also 'ropable' that Barnett had decided to brighten the spirits of some hospital patients by organising a concert in which five of them sang. Maruyama demanded they be punished, telling Barnett: 'You never hear Japanese men singing. Have you ever heard Japanese men singing?'

Barnett said he should be the one to be punished. Instead Maruyama put the five men in a line and smacked them across the face.

Maruyama never attacked Barnett, because 'he seemed to respect me'.

Not so with other Japanese and Korean guards. One Korean guard with a 'raging temper' hit him with a closed fist, kicking him in the stomach and shins.

He later discovered it was because some Koreans hated being called Koreans. They preferred to be known as Japanese.

He had been struck several times by Sergeant Toshio Aoki, who was in charge of the Korean guards. Barnett had also seen Aoki 'beat up a medical officer on one occasion'.

The person most to blame for the Australians' plight, though, was Maruyama. Asked late in the hearing if the 'behaviour of the higher officers' was 'all-right', Barnett replied: 'The behaviour of the officers with whom I came into contact, with the exception of Maruyama, was.' Of other Japanese atrocities Barnett 'had no personal knowledge'. He even said several Japanese officers were 'good fellows and treated our lads well'.

But what person could have alleviated the conditions in the Australian camp?

'Maruyama,' Barnett said.

Barnett's testimony, along with that of several others, was instrumental in seeing Maruyama sentenced to 15 years — the first part of which was served in Changi Gaol. Barnett, after the Australian selectors opted for Tallon for the 1946–47 England series, had no qualms about returning to Singapore. He was keen to ensure Singapore re-established itself after the war, and, when employment with a pharmaceutical company enabled him to travel there straight after the war, he seized the opportunity.

One of the first places he visited was Changi. A British officer approached him, saying they had an 'old friend' of his there. It was Murayama.

Barnett asked Murayama if he remembered him. He did, standing to attention and calling him 'Captain Barnetto'.

Barnett asked if there was anything he could do for him.

Murayama produced a letter for his family, hoping that he could post it.

Captain Barnetto did.

In 1948 Barnett moved his family to Singapore, including his son Ross, who had been named in honour of Barnett's lost close mate Ross Gregory. With the move came a season of playing with one of his favourites — the Singapore Cricket Club. He attempted to revive the game in Malaya, even trying to tempt Bradman, whom he was close to, to lead a 'team of star Australian cricketers' to the country in 1949–50. Bradman was not interested, as he had just retired from Test cricket, and wanted to focus on his Adelaide business interests.

One of the most important moments was taking his family to see sections of the Burma–Thailand Railway he had been involved in, so they could pay their respects to all his POW mates who never left.

Barnett was then transferred to England, where he took on several crucial sporting roles. Apart from leading a number of Commonwealth XI teams and playing until his early 50s, Barnett was for many years Australia's representative at the International Cricket Council, where he was involved in several crucial issues, including the policing of illegal bowling actions and the barring of South Africa due to apartheid. Between 1969 and 1971 he was also president of the International Lawn Tennis Federation, at a time when the game was split due to a breakaway group of high-profile professional players.

Barnett died in 1979 when visiting his POW mate Roy Mills in Newcastle. On the drive from Melbourne, Barnett suffered a recurrence of acute pancreatitis. Taken to Royal Newcastle Hospital, he suffered a fatal heart attack. At a small family service, there were two cricketing figures — one of which was Arthur Chipperfield, at whose wedding Barnett had been best man — and eight of his POW mates.

As for Ern Toovey, his war had an unexpected ending. He and a group of men had spent weeks clearing the jungle to make an airstrip, before being told to dig a huge hole. Toovey assumed they were 'digging our own graves'. Suddenly the Japanese guards disappeared. When peace was declared, Toovey 'simply couldn't believe it'. The first plane to land on their airstrip was an Allied Dakota, which flew them to Rangoon.

Having dropped from 73 to 44 kilograms while a POW, he received urgent medical treatment.

'It was here in this camp that a South Australian friend, George Walker, invited me to meet a cricketing legend — Vic Richardson, who was over there in his capacity as an RAAF Welfare Officer. We invited him to our hut for a drink and we all enjoyed his company. Unfortunately he had to break the news to George that his brother Charlie, the former international wicketkeeper, had been killed while a member of the RAAF. He also told us that Ross Gregory had died,' Toovey wrote in his unpublished memoirs.

This chance meeting with one of his cricketing idols intensified Toovey's resolve to get home and resurrect his cricketing career. Relying on painkilling injections in his knees so that he could play, the middle-order left-handed batsman made his Queensland debut in January 1950 against South Australia at the Gabba. Over the next six seasons, he played 37 times for Queensland, tallying 1346 first-class runs. Yet that was not the limit of his sporting prowess.

When a POW, numerous American soldiers convinced him to play in an impromptu game of baseball. He immediately took to it. Back at home, he made the Queensland and Australian baseball teams. However, he knocked back the chance to play overseas with the Australian team. As he explained: 'It took me three and a half years to get back last time, I am not going to risk it again.'

Playing days over, he was a respected Queensland cricket selector for 28 years, and was awarded the MBE — for, in Toovey's words, 'Made Bloody Eighty'.

The best decision he made?

Easy. In a 'dirty disease ridden' POW hospital camp, a Dutch doctor had checked a small ulcer on his left shin. 'He reached for a scraper, then with a couple of quick cuts had opened my leg, as if it was a small trap door and it suddenly hurt like hell. Evidently it had healed externally, but was rotten on the inside.'

Strangely Toovey discovered the best way to ease the pain was placing his foot into warm ashes.

Shortly after, the distinguished Victorian surgeon Colonel Albert Coates, the chief medical officer at the POW hospital, told Toovey his leg had to be amputated. Coates told him he could get him home with one leg or leave him here with two.

Toovey fervently refused to let any doctor anywhere near his leg.

'You can't take it off,' he repeatedly told medical staff. 'I've got to play cricket for Queensland.'

His wish was fulfilled.

CHAPTER 12

WOMEN AT WAR

In the 1930s, Betty Archdale and Barbara Peden had been intense rivals in the first Australia–England women's Test cricket series.

Now a few years later they were side by side walking along a London street to attend a Women's Army meeting. Archdale, the England captain, was working for a legal firm, while Peden, the Australian allrounder and slips specialist, who had married a Scot, was pursuing a career in architecture after being one of Sydney University's first graduates in that subject.

Archdale was leading the first women's international touring team to Australia in 1934–35 when she first met Peden. They became close friends.

'We careered all over Australia and New Zealand and enjoyed every minute of it,' Archdale recalled for the book *Against the Odds*. 'I was now doing my year as a pupil in chambers when joy of joys another invitation came from Australia. I made the team again and we were due to sail in October 1939. Hitler put an end to that.'

After the Munich agreement, the pair decided to go 'to a recruiting evening with the Women's Army'.

'As an architect and a barrister we thought we were pretty hot stuff and the Army would be glad to get us. We were asked whether we could cook or type. We both lied and said "No" and they remarked "no qualifications" and wrote us off as useless.'

That was far from the end of their Second World War adventures. Instead Archdale was swept up in one of the most diabolical disasters of the war, while Peden suffered the agony of years of uncertainty over the whereabouts of loved ones, but alleviated that by actively helping fellow sufferers.

The snub from the British Army recruiters was nothing new for the pair. In pursuing an international sporting career, they were used to prejudices and being rated as useless. That happens when you're trailblazers.

While women's cricket is now a well-established, popular product, its history is dotted with failures. A crucial moment in this history was when Archdale's party of 15 players embarked on the first major tour by an international women's team, arriving in Fremantle in November 1934 for a 14-match three-month tour involving games in Perth, Melbourne, Deniliquin, Sydney, Wollongong, Newcastle, Brisbane, Canberra, Goulburn, Leeton and Junee, before another seven in New Zealand. The highlight was three Tests against Australia, and one against New Zealand.

This was a significant journey as, apart from exposing women's cricket to a new audience, it had significant diplomatic undertones. As Archdale explained, this was the first England team to travel to Australia since the Bodyline series, 'and I was conscious that we could help heal the bruised relationship between the two countries, and remind everyone that cricket was an enjoyable and entertaining game'.

They achieved that, but it wasn't easy. For a while they were treated as an oddity. They had to endure a patronising, chauvinistic press. Typical was the tone of *The Star*, which lampooned the fact Tests would be played at the MCG and SCG.

'A women's cricket match at the MCG — can such a thing be possible? Even in the memory of the oldest member there has never been a similar occurrence and the shock may be nearly too much for those who consider that women should keep to the gentle sports.'

But the tourists were at least praised — even if sometimes grudgingly. Following their first two practice sessions in Perth,

The West Australian said: 'Until recently, mention of a woman handling a cricket bat or bowling a ball brought a smile, almost of contempt, to the face of the average male cricketer, but those who have seen the visitors at the net have changed their minds.'

To ensure the team wasn't distracted by all the wisecracks, England needed a strong captain who had the authority and poise to handle the problems of touring. The articulate, intelligent Archdale, who knew the importance of charm, was the ideal choice.

Aged 11, in 1918, she had endured the trauma of her father, a lieutenant-colonel in the Royal Horse Artillery, being drowned at sea, and she was heavily influenced by her mother, a suffragette gaoled for smashing the windows of Whitehall with a hammer. Betty burrowed herself in study, at McGill University in Canada and London University, and sport — in particular cricket, representing her county, Kent. She described herself as a 'moderately good cricketer, quite good with a bat and okay in the field but hopeless at bowling'.

Yet she knew how to control others. On the voyage to Western Australia, via Colombo, she was nicknamed 'Hitler' by her England teammates. It had something to do with her short dark hair and forelock. Archdale thought it may have also been due to her being 'a bit dictatorial — you do as I say or else'.

She soon softened on the trip, but always held the respect of those she led. An adept spokeswoman for her sport, knowing to laugh when British newspapers such as *Evening Despatch* captioned a photograph of Archdale 'leading out her men' or when they described her as the 'Don Bradman of women's cricket'. And she knew to stand her ground when high-profile writers tried to bring her down. Even the London *Star* questioned her appearance, suggesting Archdale looked mannish as she was 'sturdy, tweed-clad, with hair cropped as close as a boy's'.

As crucial in ensuring this tour was a success was the drive of those involved in Australian women's cricket. It was a daring move by the Australian Women's Cricket Council (AWCC) to invite England, as at the time the organisation, formed only three years earlier, had only 14 shillings and sixpence in its bank account. One of the most industrious of local officials was Australian captain Margaret Peden,[43] the elder sister of Barbara and founder of the AWCC. Apart from preparing her team, she was the overworked NSW Women's Cricket Association secretary, responsible for ensuring all Sydney games, including a Test match, were run efficiently. In Test week, apart from running practice sessions and picking the Test side, she had to organise match advertisements and game arrangements.

Archdale believed women's cricket in Australia 'would probably have never got off the ground if it hadn't been for Margaret. She knew everybody, she knew all the right people.' For Margaret it was a labour of love, which included being secretary of the AWCC for well over a decade. During the 1930s, the Peden sisters ran Australia's first indoor cricket coaching school in the Salvation Army's Sydney building in Elizabeth Street. Their school had, under lights, three wickets 'specially prepared for fast, medium pace and slow bowling'.

The England team paid their own passage of £80 per person, and brought their own equipment. Australia paid for their travel, ground hire, publicity, hospitality and entertainment, but retained all match profits. The AWCC was relying on an intrigued public flocking through the gates. The gamble worked, with sizeable crowds, starting from the opening game when 3500 attended the first day of the match against Western Australia at the WACA. The crowds — the majority of which were men — did not peter out when the team headed east. The other attraction was seeing if any of the locals could beat England. It was not to be. England finished the tour unbeaten, winning the Test series 2–0 and the solitary international against New Zealand, while no state

---

43 Barbara and Margaret Peden's father was the notable legal authority Sir John Peden, Professor of Law at Sydney University and NSW Legislative Council president. He was chair of the Royal Commission on the Constitution (1927–30) and advised the Governor of NSW, Sir Phillip Game, before he dismissed the NSW Premier, Jack Lang, in 1932. A strict taskmaster, Peden's university students included H.V. Evatt, William McMahon and John Kerr, with Garfield Barwick believing the professor treated his students like children.

or country team could topple them. The majority of the games ended in draws, which often had to do with them being only of one or two days' duration.

The tourists learnt how to surf at Palm Beach, chased kangaroos and emus on a Victorian station, experienced grasshopper plagues, saw boomerang-throwing and Aboriginal singing, and suffered a bus breakdown in Deniliquin, where they experienced the rougher side of Australian life. Their bush pub accommodation was basic: 'There were only three lavatories in the yard — one marked "men", one "women" and the third "staff". They all smelt foul and I suspect were only emptied once a week.'

There was also the cultural differences. Women's cricket in England was confined to the middle and upper classes, while in Australia it was more 'lower class'. One of Australia's players was spinner Peggy Antonio, described as 'Girl Grimmett' after Clarrie Grimmett, who hailed from a Spanish–Australian family in the working-class suburb of Port Melbourne.

'The Australian accent was also a bit of a shock,' Archdale observed.

Back in the big smoke they had other pests to fight off. The team received widespread press in Sydney — not all of it encouraging. For years, women's cricket struggled to get a line in the competitive Sydney press. If it got a mention, it was often patronising. The game's biggest headline came when the NSW Women's Cricket Association decided a few years earlier to allow players to wear long, white or cream trousers. There was also great excitement just before the Brisbane Test that 'frocks had been abandoned' and Australian players would be allowed to appear in 'a new type of divided skirt similar to the pleated shorts worn by many women tennis players'.

At the time, Brian Penton was one of Sydney's leading newspaper columnists. This flamboyant, provocative writer, described by Norman Lindsay as 'the most brilliant man we have ever had in daily journalism in Australia', had a daily column for *The Daily Telegraph* called 'Sydney Spy'. It was a column of observations and opinions, often focusing on off-beat issues and subjects.

An English women's cricket team in his domain was perfect column fodder for his witticisms and smart-alec writing. Penton interviewed Archdale at the SCG before the NSW game. The following day he began his 'Sydney Spy' column with: 'A woman cricketer. Surely a contradiction in terms. There are women and there are cricketers — two quite different things.'

Underneath the headline 'Penton meets a stonewaller', the columnist outlined a frosty encounter:

'Miss Betty Archdale (the captain) took me in hand. It was plain from the start that she was not going to make any statement which could be used in evidence against her. Training and heritage well equipped her for the job of putting me down. Her mother was a suffragette and she is a lawyer.

'"Why do you play cricket?" I asked. She looked me over hostilely. "Because I like it".'

On and on, Penton continued to snap away.

'I tried flattery, then. "One has to admit it, though — you Englishwomen are wonderful. Twice as manly — I mean twice as much alive as the men. Don't you think so?"

'"Do you think so?"

'"Don't you?"

'"I haven't thought about it."

'Another cold — oh, very cold silence.

'I thought something might be done with the toreadorical method. "Anyway I think a woman's place is in the home." No response. I observed that in my opinion a woman is much better tatting and sewing on buttons than in chasing a ball round a cricket field.

'"How very interesting," Miss Archibald remarked, though for a moment, as her eye lighted with an incredulous outrage, I thought I was going to get a run out of it. But no. She tossed her head and stammered out into the garden.'

On and on. Penton eventually ended the column with:

'I tried my last googlie. A deceitful, underhand, uncricketlike, but wholly feminine subterfuge.

'"Is it true, what people say, that cricket makes women thick in the legs?"'

'"Well, it doesn't worry me, anyway," Miss Archibald retorted.

'Ah! A bite at last!

'But no — she took a deep breath, and smiled.'

Years later Archdale wrote that Penton 'these days we would call a male chauvinistic pig'. 'I can't say I liked him as he was trying to be superior and funny at our expense, but I suppose it was good journalism. It was a good try on his part, and I hardly think it did us any harm.' Just added to the crowd figures.

Penton, attending the Sydney Test, explained in 'Sydney Spy' how he ended up arguing with a female supporter who thought his opinions on women's cricket out of order.

The woman said of Penton: 'How ridiculous you are!'

'Ridiculous — yes. But a little pathetic, too, don't you think? Here we sit trying to defend the sanctities of cricket by laughing at the women who play it, by pointing out how funny they look when they run, and by asserting that some women athletes have moustaches. But in vain — alas, I know that in future, remembering how women cricketers did it, I shall no more be able to extract hearty and conceited masculine satisfaction from watching a cricketer slog a ball over the fence than I now can from watching a man do crochet.'

'"Pooh!" she said, but smiled.'

Arthur Mailey was also unconvinced. The former Test spinner covered the Sydney games for *The Sun* newspaper, and found them dull. 'With all due respect to the girls, the standard of cricket they play is not high enough to be taken seriously or appreciated by a connoisseur. They cannot field, bowl or bat nearly as well as men can', Mailey wrote.

Jack Fingleton was more sympathetic, writing that, despite the slow scoring in the second Test, 'it was worth the admission money to hear the members, binoculars slung over shoulders, assure each other with gusto that the "cricket" was worth coming to see'.

Not everyone on the SCG Hill was impressed. Archdale was stopped in her tracks when one drunk yelled out: 'You ought to be home looking after your children.'

The SCG management was reticent about the women taking over their ground. They did not use the SCG dressing rooms. Instead they changed in the Sheridan Stand.

What kept them going was the close camaraderie between the two teams. Many opponents became intense friends — in particular Archdale with 'independent types' like the Peden sisters.

As Archdale told the *Brisbane Telegraph*, men don't help themselves by 'taking their cricket too seriously'. Women understood the importance of kinship.

England returned home to media applause, with Cedric Belfrage writing in *The Daily Express*: 'Eleven sturdy British maids with eleven bats came back to London last night ... For half a year they have swept Australia and New Zealand in turn with their bats ... It's the cue for our male cricketers to blush a lovely crimson.'

The success of the 1934–35 tour, which resulted in a £1000 profit, led to Australia touring England. Margaret Peden again led the team, which arrived in Southampton in May 1937, for an intensive two-month, three-Test, 19-match tour — after two one-day games in Holland, with the Australian skipper arriving to one game riding a bicycle. The players were under strict instructions — no drinking, smoking or gambling was allowed on tour, no friend, husband or relation could accompany them. They were barred from having anything to do with the British press.

In spite of these restrictions, they still received widespread coverage back home, primarily because a notable Australian journalist, Pat Jarrett, accompanied them. Jarrett, a Victorian shotput and discus title-holder who also played women's cricket, had covered England's tour of Australia for the Melbourne *Herald* and *The Sporting Globe*. On the train trip to the first match in Perth, she astounded a group of Aboriginal people on the Nullarbor Plain by throwing a spear further than them. She had become a sports writer at 18 after writing to *The Herald*'s proprietor, Keith Murdoch, inquiring how the paper 'was coming out without me at night, I just couldn't possibly imagine'. A few weeks on she was offered a job.

She later convinced Murdoch to be the first *Herald* sportswriter to cover an overseas cricket tour. Her reports, according to Peggy Antonio, put 'women's cricket on the map in Australia'.

Soon Margaret met up with her sister Barbara, who 18 months earlier had moved to England, was on her way to being a qualified architect, and again was required to bolster the Australian middle-order batting line-up. Barbara had become teammates with Archdale at her cricket club in Kent, and they were soon upsetting the game's elders. Their stand to ignore the local Women's Cricket Association edict of wearing stockings with suspender belts, instead opting for knee-high hose in games, infuriated those running the game. It even led to headlines in Australia, with the *Daily News* in Perth reporting that Archdale had compromised by 'rolling her stockings just below the knee'.

Archdale's stand may have contributed to her being replaced as England captain for this series. She was overlooked entirely for the first two Tests — only returning for the third and last at The Oval, which ended in a draw, for a one-all series. Crowd figures were again excellent, including more than 10,000 spectators at their final game against Surrey. British media interest was also high, with several London newspapers attempting to bait the colonials, especially their 'oyster attitude' in refusing to talk to them. The ban intensified when one English newspaper quoted an unnamed Australian player as saying she enjoyed glasses of gin.

Archdale understood the Australians' anti-press stance. The players were wary of the press, describing publicity as a 'distasteful necessity'.

One of the highlights of the tour was when the wife of the Prime Minister, Stanley Baldwin, invited the Australian team to 10 Downing Street. During the function, the PM suddenly appeared. 'It was the biggest thrill we have had in England. Mr Baldwin was an umpire and knows all about the game,' Margaret said.

Betty Archdale, Barbara Peden and Pat Jarrett remained close. When Barbara married Scotsman Colin Munro at St Mary's Church in London in September 1938, Betty accompanied the bride to the church and sat in the front pew.

After their initial recruitment snub, the pair in late 1939 joined the Air Raid Precaution squad, along with notable British golfer Pam Barton. Archdale was transferred to the Women's Royal Naval Service — the WRNS or 'Wrens'. Barbara's husband had meanwhile joined the Cameronians (Scottish Rifles) and was wounded at Dunkirk, where he was captured by the Germans. The now-pregnant Peden, after discovering her husband was in a German POW camp, headed to the safer climes of Montreal, where she continued as the only female architect working at one of Canada's oldest construction firms.

In March 1941 Archdale set sail for Singapore, working as a wireless operator as well as teaching Japanese Morse code. Her key role was to listen for signals from Japanese submarines and alert British officers.

For numerous months, the life of Archdale, who was in charge of a group of wireless Wrens, was relaxed, enjoying a flourishing cricketing and social life in the British outpost. The sporting highlight was when she agreed to a men versus women exhibition match in Singapore in July. The YMCA and YWCA organised teams, and Archdale led the women, who were assumed to be mere laughing stock for the predominantly male crowd. Instead Archdale shone a beacon for women's cricket, scoring 104, before declaring at 5–184. The YMCA passed that score with three wickets to spare, but all the talk was of Archdale bludgeoning her male opponents with the bat, and then taking the wicketkeeping gloves to stump one of the men. Singapore was already aware of her cricketing prowess. Some years earlier, *The Singapore Free Press and Mercantile Advertiser* had run a feature piece on her, describing how Archdale could 'score runs with the freedom of a Jessop[44] and the artistry of Jack Hobbs'.

---

44   Aggressive England Test batsman Gilbert Jessop.

The frivolity ended in December 1941. The Japanese had the Malayan Peninsula and the supposed island fortress of Singapore in its sights. Archdale's work as a wireless telephonist intensified, including endless sleepless nights as she discovered the loss of several Allied boats. With invasion imminent, many evacuated Singapore.

Among the last English women to leave were Archdale's Wrens. A major concern was that near their wireless station were large oil containers which, if hit by Japanese planes, would have seen them all perish. In early January 1942 — five weeks before Singapore fell — Archdale's team was evacuated to Colombo.

During those final hours, Archdale was instrumental in ensuring several nurses succeeded in escaping from Singapore, 'leaving behind some tragedies and broken hearts'.

The fall of Singapore was catastrophic, described by Winston Churchill as the 'worst disaster' in British military history. More than 80,000 British, Australian and Indian soldiers became POWs. Archdale later realised she was lucky to have been given an early escape route.

In Colombo the Wrens encountered numerous air raids, prompting another transfer, this time to Mombasa in Kenya, supposedly to be closer to the Far East Fleet situated 1000 kilometres west of Ceylon. Archdale was moved to Basra in the Persian Gulf.

She was upset that another had been appointed in charge of the Wrens. Her 'nose out of joint', Archdale reacted 'badly', and was moved to the Persian Gulf to work as a secretary in the Commodore's office.

In late 1943 she returned home via train to Baghdad, bus to Damascus, truck to Haifa, train to Alexandria, and troopship to Liverpool. She spent the rest of the war at the Officer Training College at the Royal Naval College in Greenwich, where as a first officer she was in charge of planning and the timetable. Her 'zeal and wholehearted devotion to duty, including courageous work during several bombing raids', saw her in 1944 made an OBE. As Wrens colleague Phyll Puttick explained in Deirdre Macpherson's biography *Betty Archdale: The Suffragette's Daughter*: 'We owed her a great debt … She said at the time — "I got it on behalf of you all" — she was given it for bringing us safely out of Singapore.'

In June 1945, while playing in a Wrens cricket match, Archdale was told to immediately contact headquarters for her next assignment — going to Australia to take charge of Wrens personnel stationed there. Delighted to be returning to the country she fell in love with a decade earlier, she put up no resistance.

Peden, now Mrs Barbara Munro, had returned to Australia in April 1941 via Montreal, where she gave birth to her son, named Colin like his father. While working in Canada, she received a letter to return to England 'to assist in building factories in the bombed areas'.

'I could not leave my small son, so it was out of the question for me to return to London,' she told *The Sydney Morning Herald*.

By that stage, Barbara had received several letters from her imprisoned husband in a POW camp near Kassel in central Germany. It was a distressing time, but she refused to let the situation get her down. Instead she attempted to help those in a similar plight by being the founder of the Australian Prisoners of War Relatives Association (APOWRA). The aim of the Association was to provide information about Australian POWs through a monthly newsletter, give support to relatives, and liaise with the necessary welfare organisations, such as the Red Cross.

APOWRA had strong cricket undertones. While Barbara was treasurer, the honorary secretary was long-time NSW, Australian cricket official and Test team manager Syd Smith, and its headquarters was at Cricket House, in George Street, Sydney. In its first newsletter in January 1942, Smith — a short, serious man who refused to have anything to do with alcohol or cigarettes — and Mrs Munro explained that their prime aim was 'to bring comfort' to POW relatives.

'The Australians who have been captured have had a full measure of disappointment. It shows in their letters, but they don't complain. Our fellows have shown themselves coolly and calmly courageous in disappointment as in battle. We can be proud of them.'

The newsletter ran letters from prisoners, photographs from various camps, anything that promoted communication between POWs and their families. It gave advice on how to send letters, ensure food parcels get to their destination, and avoid listening to overseas radio broadcasts. While the communication lines with European POW camps were reasonable, getting any information from those in the Pacific was near impossible. The Japanese avoided any contact.

Barbara was a regular on ABC radio, in one talk stressing to her listeners the importance of 'not listening to the enemy'.

'We ask relatives to beware of propaganda in broadcasts from all enemy countries. We realise that it is expecting too much to ask that relatives should refrain altogether from listening for messages and scraps of news. When one is waiting and longing for news one grasps at each and every possible source of information, but, at the same time, will you please try never for one moment to be misled by the propaganda which accompanies any items of news from any enemy country,' Barbara told her radio audience.

The organisation sent letters to the Australian Government seeking details of the 'deaths of Australians in Burma and Thailand', and demanded that families be advised of any information the government had had on missing or dead servicemen. The names of released men should also be promptly published. Government officials at times tried to fob them off, but the Association kept bombarding them with letters. By the end of the war, their newsletter was sent to more than 23,000 members and the Association became a powerful body. The government eventually took notice and, when possible, provided information.

In April 1945 Barbara received the heartening news that her husband had been released from prison, was in reasonable shape back in England, and was trying to get to Sydney. They were eventually reunited in 1946.

Pat Jarrett's vast skills were also tested during the war. After planning to cover the 1940 Olympic Games in Finland, until they were called off due to war, she convinced Murdoch to let her travel to North America, where en route she became close to the bohemian, free-spirited Maie Casey, who was with her husband — Australian politician Richard Casey. He was heading to Washington to be in charge of the Australian legation in the United States. Mrs Casey, a manipulative figure, asked Jarrett if she would be her private secretary, and she, after Murdoch had allowed her to take up the role, reluctantly agreed to take on the role. For the next two years, Jarrett accompanied the pair as their press liaison as the Caseys met numerous important American political leaders. This was a considerable role as Australia's Prime Minister, John Curtin, came to realise in 1941 that England was focused on its own problems and would ultimately neglect Australia, so the US had to become the number one ally.

Casey's diplomatic skill and his ability to push Australia's cause with the Americans were crucial, while Jarrett's skills in schmoozing the local press ensured strong diplomatic relations. One US newspaper described Jarrett as the 'dynamic blond lady from down under' who provided a 'refreshing touch to the diplomatic scene'. She became the first overseas journalist to be admitted to the National Women's Press Club in Washington, and where possible pushed Casey's cause in the US newspapers. One lengthy article in the Melbourne *Herald* in November 1940 was Jarrett's vehicle to highly praise 'Australia's voice and eyes in the US', explaining how Casey, through his close relationship with President Franklin D. Roosevelt, was 'able to stress the real importance of Australia as the centre core of the south-western Pacific'.

She had become intimate with Casey's wife. His biographer, Diane Langmore, wrote that their 'relationship had become very close. But they were discreet about it.'

But Jarrett, despite cultivating a strong friendship with Noel Coward — a close colleague of Casey's — soon tired of the diplomatic life and, needing some space from the Ambassador's often overbearing wife, returned to Australia in February 1942.

She wanted to be a war correspondent but failed in her bid to be sent overseas to the major battlefronts. Newspaper proprietors and military leaders believed that, due to the dangers and demands of the frontline, war correspondents had to be male. She was instead confined to home matters, writing rousing articles for *The Herald* on training with the Women's Army Service Training School, and the tedium of mess duty — having to peel potatoes, turnips and onions for '180 hungry recruits'. The dateline was invariably 'Somewhere in Australia'.

She spent time with various groups, including the Women's Auxiliary Australian Air Force. Jarrett stood up for female staff, exposing discrimination and absenteeism among factory workers when their superiors showed no interest in family responsibilities.

One of her major assignments was covering Eleanor Roosevelt's visit to Australia in September 1943. She explained how, ever since the wife of the President had winked at her, she had been a Roosevelt acolyte.

'The occasion was a lunch of 300 women in Washington, at which I happened to be the only foreign newspaper woman present,' Jarrett wrote in a *Herald* profile. 'It was then that Mrs Roosevelt gave me an encouraging wink and gestured to me with her hands to rise to my feet.'

They met several times in Washington, at 'informal shopping tours, at weekly press conferences, with children rolling eggs down the lawns of the White House at Easter time; speaking before large gatherings of business men and women, and as the guest of honor at formal dinners'.

Casey was now the Governor of Bengal. At the behest of his wife, Casey wrote to Murdoch asking that Jarrett again be released to join his staff. Murdoch agreed. Jarrett immediately accepted, writing to Maie: 'I miss you more all the time but you are so tight in my heart.'

Jarrett returned to being a central figure at the Casey headquarters, again encountering unusual house guests, including the flamboyant British photographer and designer Cecil Beaton, Lord Louis Mountbatten and film stars Jackie Coogan and

Paulette Goddard. One highlight was Noel Coward's stay and his repeated performances of 'Mad Dogs and Englishmen' on the Caseys' grand piano.

Mahatma Gandhi was also a regular visitor. Jarrett described in *The Herald* that at their first meeting at Government House, 'as Mr Gandhi stepped from the back seat of a "vintage" car, I put out my hand to help him'.

'He took my arm lightly and smiled at me. Then as he stood before me, his chest bare, smooth and caramel-coloured, except for part of his dhoti which hung loosely from one shoulder he raised his hands together to his forehead in the Indian gesture of greeting. Then he put a finger to his lips. Mr Gandhi was reminding me that this was his day of silence.'

As for India, Jarrett believed it was 'a tinder box which might go up at any time'.

While in India came the chance to at last experience proper military action, when she became the first woman to visit the Burma frontline, at the personal request of Admiral Lord Louis Mountbatten, Supreme Allied Commander, South East Asia Command.

The Burma campaign had generally been ignored, particularly by the Australian press. Aware of Jarrett's strong relationship with her proprietor, Mountbatten thought giving Jarrett access would ensure what was happening in Japanese-occupied Burma would get coverage in Murdoch's *Herald*. It was a hazardous trip, with Jarrett's convoy having to find cover under a bridge from relentless machine-gun fire. But she was given access to the main military identities in Burma, including Generals William Slim and Oliver Leese, which made her the envy of other war correspondents, who were generally snubbed.

She was shown plans and diagrams revolving around the Allied plan to recapture Mandalay from the Japanese, and told to pass this information on to Murdoch. Jarrett rushed back to Melbourne, alerted Murdoch, and suddenly articles and editorials supporting the Allied campaign in Burma appeared in *The Herald*. Some of what was written was blatant propaganda, especially articles explaining how 'the RAAF was doing a wonderful job in operational and supply flying' and how 'the Australian soldier is so highly regarded by British commanders on the India–Burma front that they frequently say: "If only we had a couple of Australian divisions."'

'I met dozens of RAAF men there and they are on top of the world. They've got the Japanese on the run.'

The Allies recaptured Mandalay later that year.

Jarrett's next mission was ensuring, with Barbara Munro, that Betty Archdale, in Sydney in charge of 400 Wrens, did not go back to London. They alerted Archdale about an advertised position as principal of the Women's College at Sydney University. She applied, was appointed to the post, and held it for the next ten years. From there, Archdale became the progressive headmistress of the exclusive Sydney private girls' school Abbotsleigh. Connections again helped, as Barbara had been the head prefect during her time at the school. Archdale's mantra was: 'With education, women can do and be anything.'

Known at the school as 'Archie', she did not hide away in her office either, becoming a high-profile and often outspoken social commentator, constantly defending women's rights. She alienated some, but was mostly idolised by her Abbotsleigh students, who relished her free spirit, belief in social justice, and fearlessness. She was often caught up in controversial issues, including her early advocacy for sex education classes.

'I would not say I was a good headmistress. Abbotsleigh was an excellent school and I livened it up a bit. I made many mistakes but I think on the whole did more good than harm.'

She, along with Barbara (Peden) Munro and Pat Jarrett, was an important figurehead in the advancement of women's cricket after the war, wherever possible pushing its credentials.

An indicator of how much she was revered came in 1998 when voted by the Australian public as one of the nation's 100 Living National Treasures. The next year, she was among the first women to be made honorary life members of the MCC.

The fire in her belly never left. In her final years,[45] she constantly fired off letters to newspapers complaining about dreadful television sports commentary and the poor treatment of women's sport in the media, and demanded women's cricket be treated with respect.

Her message was often: 'On the whole, Australian women are better than the men — they are better people.'

In 1983, in a letter to *The Sydney Morning Herald*, she came to the defence of Kate Fitzpatrick, who was roundly criticised when she joined the Nine television cricket coverage.

'Cricket a man's game, forsooth. Who started round-arm bowling? Miss Christina [sic] Willes.[46] Women have played for over 200 years ... I couldn't care less whether the commentator is a man or a woman. What I want are commentators who tell me things I want to know and can't see on the screen. Apart from that I want them to stop talking. When I heard a woman was joining the commentators, my reaction was that she couldn't possibly be worse than the men. Unbelievably, she was. But the fault was not hers, but of the men who gave her nothing to do but answer silly questions, or read scores we could see for ourselves. Let's stop worrying about whether the commentator is a man or a woman and get the best.'

---

45 Betty Archdale died in Sydney on 11 January 2000, aged 92. Barbara Peden outlived her husband, and died aged 76 in Sydney in 1984. Their son, Colin Munro, became a notable rural journalist, primarily with ABC Radio. Pat Jarrett, who was Colin's godmother, became the women's editor of the *Sun News-Pictorial*. She was instrumental in renowned Australian cyclist Hubert Opperman becoming a politician, organising a 1949 meeting with Casey, then the Federal President of the Liberal Party. Opperman, not knowing Jarrett's private life, was smitten. 'Pat, an athletic blonde, threw javelins record distances, dived off Princes Bridge in *The Herald* Learn-to-Swim Week, cycled to youth hostels and wrote for the Melbourne *Herald*. She was a personality lass and had I not been so fond of my wife, I could have easily fallen for her,' Opperman wrote. Maie Casey was involved in seeing Jarrett awarded the MBE for services to journalism in 1972. Jarrett died in 1990, aged 79. She remained feisty, explaining just before her death: 'I have never been asked to march in an Anzac Day march. Men war correspondents have marched — but I think they've forgotten that there were women.'

46 Christiana Willes was reputed to have been the first to bowl in a round-arm fashion to her brother John, who played for Kent, around 1807. She had found underarm bowling difficult when wearing a hooped skirt.

Archdale, who remained a proud Brit, wanted a better deal for the Australian and English women's cricket teams.

'I was glad to hear that an Australian XI was going to England again. I hoped to be able to follow the matches in our media and to rejoice in England's victory. But hopes were dashed! Our press, TV and radio hardly mentioned the series and, to my sorrow, Australia won easily.'

Archdale, who for many years lived on a property near Galston with her actor brother Alec, wasn't a whinger. Like any excellent, progressive educator, she provided constructive ideas and answers.

One of her favoured sayings was: 'I am often wrong, but rarely negative.'

She remains a beacon of the women's summer game.

CHAPTER 13

FOR CLUB AND COUNTRY

A lusty lofted shot away from the Allan Border Oval wicket in Mosman is an imposing war memorial which lists those local citizens who lost their lives in overseas battles. The names run across the four sides of this impressive large grey stone obelisk.

The memorial's close proximity to a cricket field is not surprising, considering one of the most picturesque ovals in Sydney is centrally located in this prosperous village, and many of those who didn't come back had spent their time representing their suburb on this field. All prominent Australian cricket clubs were affected by war, but Mosman — home of numerous Test players, including Stan McCabe — has a deep tragic link. In the Great War, 52 club members served, and eight were killed, including Mosman Oval groundsman Sergeant Ernest Bennett of the 1st Tunnelling Company, who was famously engaged in burrowing under the German lines at Hill 60, Messines, detonating mines which led to thousands of enemy fatalities.

In the Second World War, 128 Mosman Cricket Club members enlisted, and ten were killed. Among those were identical twins Cecil and Fred Glover. The 23-year-old pair were posted to the 2/15th Field Regiment, 8th Division AIF, which headed to Singapore. Their letters home, now in the War Memorial in Canberra, express the mixed feelings of being in a new environment. Fred wrote to his Aunty Jean from Singapore on 23 August 1941 that he was 'quite surprised to find a beautiful harbour and such activity'.

'The wharf where we were to berth was covered with hundreds of coloured people clad in clothing of every hue. It did look a grand sight especially to one unaccustomed to black people. It's rather nice here and haven't found the climate too oppressive although a change of clothing twice daily together with three or four showers are necessary.'

Several weeks later, Fred 'was one of the lucky ones and managed to get in the regimental cricket team'.

'Yesterday we played the local club in the centre of the town. What a match. Their team included two Australians (Jack Helmrich and another), three Englishmen and three Indians. It was the first game of cricket I have played in the rain and it continued until we got their last men out at 6.30pm. We won, but not through my efforts. I did not get a bat, had the last three overs and missed but held one catch.'

Cecil was promoted, but 'don't ask me what it feels like to be a sergeant, because I couldn't tell you. We do eat in our own mess and off china plates, but with the exception of the tea, our food differs very little from the others.'

In his last letter home, dated 20 November 1941, Fred remarked: 'I don't like playing this game of soldier, but I have to.'

They were captured by the Japanese, taken to Changi, and then Borneo to construct an airfield at Sandakan. In late 1944, Cecil was killed when one of the POW camps was mistakenly bombed by the Allies. With him was fellow POW Dick Braithwaite.

'Cec became very ill and was in the hospital. I took some fruit down … I'm talking to Cec at the time when the raid started and a bomb hit the hut. As we heard it start, I flattened myself in the corner and out of the corner of my eye I saw something fly across the room. I was alright, but Cec was dead, it was his leg that I'd seen fly across the room,' Braithwaite recalled in a radio interview.

Braithwaite was given the task of telling Fred.

'Fred didn't stop crying for a week, you know, twins, they're so close aren't they. What a sad thing it was, being around Fred when he was so heart-broken and he just had no hope.'

Fred was subjected to the horrendous Sandakan Death March in 1944–45 after the Japanese abandoned the Sandakan prison camp and moved to Ranau. Of the 1000-plus prisoners on the 260-kilometre march, only six — all Australians — survived. That group included Braithwaite. Fred, however, died on the march on 18 June 1945.

Another notable cricket club that cultivated its fair share of Test players and experienced distressing wartime moments was St Kilda, in Melbourne, especially when it lost one of its most venerated all-round sportsmen in February 1943.

Stuart King was from a working-class family from the Victorian country town of Ararat. His high intelligence led to his gaining a scholarship to the prestigious Melbourne private school Xavier College, and later Melbourne University, where he studied law. King soon earnt a reputation for being 'the best' at whatever he pursued — excelling in his legal studies, at cricket as a batsman/keeper, and at Australian football as a reliable defender.

Playing for three district clubs — Melbourne, University and finally St Kilda — he made the Victorian Sheffield Shield team when 20 as a middle-order batsman, and in his second first-class game was involved in a special cricketing record that still stands. He played his first state game in December 1926 against Queensland in Melbourne, scoring a half-century. He was retained the following week for the Christmas encounter against NSW at the MCG, where for well over a day he witnessed a batting juggernaut as teammates Bill Woodfull, Bill Ponsford, Stork Hendry and Jack Ryder annihilated the visiting attack — scoring either centuries, double centuries or triple centuries. King, clearly stiff from countless hours watching his teammates having fun in the sun, eventually got to the crease at 4–631, floundered around for several overs before being stumped off Arthur Mailey for 7. At least he contributed something to Victoria's world-record score of 1107 — several runs and a second-innings catch. King played for

Victoria until 1933, his final two appearances as captain. By that time, football had taken prominence — as the previous year his broad leadership skills saw him appointed captain-coach of the St Kilda football team. However, St Kilda was riddled with internal player and administration problems, leading to a disillusioned King heading to Brighton in the second tier Victorian Football Association. After a short period as a sportswriter for *The Argus* and *Star* newspapers, he focused on his work as a solicitor, getting married and having two children.

In March 1942, King joined the 20 RAAF Squadron as an intelligence officer in northern Queensland. He wrote to his wife, Kathleen: 'It's Saturday evening and I'm going to the pictures tonight. Bud Costello and some other equally exciting feature, but there is nothing much for a man in love with his wife to do … Lots of love darling, to you and the little ones.'

On February 1943, he was part of an 11-man crew in a Catalina flying boat that at dawn left Cairns on anti-submarine patrol, heading towards Milne Bay in south-eastern New Guinea. The Catalina was scheduled to be back in Cairns by nightfall.

King, not part of the crew, had agreed to go as 'an observer'.

After several hours, the plane suddenly disappeared. A sea search found nothing. Defence authorities told the King family the aircraft 'had been on patrol duty between Cairns and New Guinea, and was returning to Cairns when a thunderstorm developed'.

'Between 10 and 10.25pm the aircraft signalled for search lights and necessary direction facilities, which were given. At 10.51pm the aircraft signalled the words "forced land for" but the message was cut off and no further signal was received. Shortly before this, the aircraft was observed circling Fitzroy Island. It rounded Cape Grafton and disappeared in a north-easterly direction from Green Island. I deeply regret to say that it is believed that the aircraft came down into the sea north-east of Green Island.'

King's family was devastated. His wife collapsed when receiving the telegram.

In 2013, wreckage of a Catalina plane similar to the one King died in was discovered by a recreational diver near the Frankland Islands, about 40 kilometres north-east of Innisfail.[47]

Less than three months on, the game was mourning two more of its first-class representatives, again resulting from air crashes. Dudley Everett, who played one game for Western Australia against the 1935–36 touring MCC, was killed while on a solo training flight outside Ameliasburgh, Canada, on 3 May 1943.

A fortnight later, Flying Officer Ken Ridings, who appeared destined to captain his South Australian Shield team and was looked upon as a potential Test early-order batsman until war intervened, was among an 11-man crew of a Short Sunderland Mark III that was shot down over the Bay of Biscay by a German fighter.

The RAAF informed Ridings's parents that it had received information from the Air Ministry in London that 'nothing was heard of or from the aircraft after taking off its base at 5.11am on the 17th May 1943 for an anti-submarine patrol'.

'A message has been intercepted from a German broadcast stating that on the 17th May 1943, German vombers [sic] on reconnaissance over the Atlantic shot down a four engine flying boat of the Sunderland type, which after combat fell into the sea and exploded.'

The body of Ken Ridings, brother of future Test selector and South Australian skipper Phil Ridings, was never found. Most of Ken's personal effects were lost, but the family at least received a

---

47 The fourth Victorian Sheffield Shield representative to die in the Second World War was the aggressive batsman Frank Sides, who, after five years with Queensland, moved to Melbourne in 1937. He played the next two seasons for Victoria. A sergeant in a commando unit, he was involved in numerous important New Guinea battles, where his job was to harass and pursue the Japanese in treacherous jungle terrain. After making several successful ambushes, and cutting off Japanese supply lines, he was killed on 25 August 1943 at Kunai Spur, Salamaua. In the Shield competition, Sides played against Queensland allrounder Glen Baker, who made 1531 runs and took 13 wickets between 1936 and 1941. A lieutenant in the Australian Advance Ordnance Depot, Baker died of scrub typhus on 15 December 1943 while serving in New Guinea. He is buried in the impressive Bomana War Cemetery in Port Moresby, while Sides is in Lae War Cemetery.

battered suitcase of his, with contents including a diary, a wool scarf, several pairs of pyjamas, a prayer book and three cocktail stirrers. It was later discovered Ridings had, just before that fatal flight, been approached to captain an RAAF team to play a Sir PF Warner XI at Lord's.[48]

John Jeffreys, who opened the batting for Western Australia in four matches between 1937 and 1940, was killed during one of the most heroic flights of the aerial battle over Germany, which led to the pilot receiving the Victoria Cross for conspicuous bravery.

Jeffreys, a 30-year-old navigator, was on a Lancaster, piloted by Scottish Flight-Lieutenant William Reid, which flew from RAF Skellingthorpe, Lincolnshire, to bomb Dusseldorf. This was Jeffreys's ninth enemy operation. After the Lancaster crossed the Dutch coast it was attacked by a Messerschmitt, which shattered Reid's windscreen, wounding him in the head, shoulders and hands. The elevator trimming tabs of the aircraft had been damaged and were difficult to control. The rear turret had been wrecked, while the communication system and compasses suddenly weren't working. Reid was in a bad way, but, discovering his crew was intact, continued on towards Dusseldorf.

The Lancaster was then attacked by a Focke-Wulf which ripped the bomber apart from stem to stern. Jeffreys had been hit and could not be revived, while Reid suffered more bullet wounds to his body. Reid's flight engineer was able to supply him with oxygen so he could somehow keep going. Reid was determined to get to Dusseldorf, having memorised the course from previous trips and pre-flight lectures. An hour later, he sighted the German city. Amazingly he released the bombs right on target.

Reid used the moon and stars to get back to England, even though a loss of blood led to him blacking out several times. Blood from a head wound was also pouring into his eyes, making vision near impossible. As an airfield in Somerset suddenly appeared, he

---

48 Mosman cricketer Clive Calvert played eight games, primarily for the RAAF at Lord's, before being killed in 1944 when as a wireless operator his plane was shot down by a German night-fighter off Denmark. Stan Sismey, who played in those games, recalled years later: 'You picked a team, said "see you next month" and you just hoped they'd all be there. Usually they were, sometimes they weren't.'

regained full control and successfully landed the bomber. Part of the plane's undercarriage collapsed when the wheels hit the ground.

On landing it was discovered Jeffreys had been dead for some time.

After attending his colleague's burial at Cambridge City Cemetery, a month later Reid received the VC. He finished the war in Stalag Luft III POW camp after a 1944 bombing raid led to his plane crashing near Rheims.

Alan Pearsall was another to join the RAAF and to be involved in the Empire Air Training Scheme, training as air crew. He was regarded as a perfect candidate, showing leadership, persistence and dedication when progressing from a Tasmanian orchard farm to play seven matches for his state. An early-order batsman, Pearsall was also a reliable medium pacer, boasting Test players Bill Brown and Ian Johnson among his six first-class victims.

A prized fullback at the Lefroy Football Club in Hobart, Pearsall was lured into playing a handful of VFL games for South Melbourne, until RAAF duties overwhelmed him in 1941.

A passionate Tasmanian — he even took a crate of the state's best apples on the boat to England — Pearsall was assigned to reconnaissance duties, which included supplying photographs for the planning for D-Day. On 8 March 1944, he flew from the RAF's Hampshire base to photograph north-east Calais. Returning to base, he was flying across the English Channel when he radioed that he was having engine problems. He was told to bail out. His body was never found.

Two months later, William Roach was relishing a break in England from flying Bristol Beaufighters in raids on German ships when he was picked to represent the RAAF in a series of one-day Services games at Lord's, organised by Plum Warner to raise funds for various war charities. Warner, the MCC's deputy secretary, knew the value of such games, believing that if the Luftwaffe could stop cricket at Lord's, it would be an invaluable propaganda tool for the enemy.

Roach was a natural choice to bolster the RAAF's middle order, accompanying a vibrant newcomer named Keith Miller.

Roach had made three appearances for Western Australia, including providing opposition to the 1934 Australian Ashes side that played a lead-up game in Perth before travelling from Fremantle to England.

The highlight for Roach was playing for the RAAF against an England XI at Lord's on 29 May, opening the batting for Australia alongside Miller, Stan Sismey and Keith Carmody against a Test-strength England outfit captained by Colonel Gubby Allen and including Flight Lieutenant Wally Hammond and Squadron Leaders Bill Edrich, Les Ames and Walter Robins. Roach's moment at the wicket was fleeting as he was bowled by Allen for seven, but he relished the interlude from endless stressful flights across Europe and enjoyed appearing in front of more than 28,000 spectators — with, in the words of *Wisden*, 'thousands left outside when the gates were closed at quarter past twelve'. At least Australian Prime Minister John Curtin, in London for war talks with Winston Churchill, and Australian Commander-in-Chief Sir Thomas Blamey, held enough sway to get into the ground in time to watch England win by six wickets and to commiserate with their fellow countrymen. Roach was deeply touched that in the dressing room he met an admired politician and leader who, like him, was a proud Western Australian.

On 8 June 1944 he was involved in a mission attacking targets in Norwegian fjords when he was shot down and killed near the Frisian Islands in the North Sea.

The intense sadness of that moment is portrayed in a photograph in the 1945 *Wisden Cricketers' Almanack*. It shows the Australian RAAF team which played on 27 May against The Rest at Lord's. Proudly standing at the far right of the top row with arms behind his body is Roach, in full creams and with RAAF cap perched on his head. The caption mentions his name, 'Flt Sgt W.A. Roach', with '(since missing, believed killed)' added. He looks so delighted to be back doing what he loved best, and being among such notable cricketers as Sismey and Carmody. Less than a fortnight later, he was a war victim. Another whose body was never found.

The Roach family, including his widow, Mignon, waited in vain for years for any news. It was not until 1949 that they received official confirmation that he had been killed.

In 1970 Mignon at least received something. Her husband's identity discs had been picked up by a Dutch net fisherman, and, as they were in surprisingly good condition after decades at the bottom of the North Sea, they were sent to his family in South Perth.

CHAPTER 14

BRADMAN AND BEYOND

Apart from being an admired journalist, cricket writer and pugnacious Test opening batsman, Jack Fingleton was a fastidious hoarder. Anything that could help him in his writing pursuits, which included columns for Australian and overseas newspapers, he would keep. During his lengthy time in the Canberra press gallery at the old Parliament House, his shoebox of an office was crammed with newspapers, files and boxes.

Fingleton kept a mountain of personal notes which provided background to many of Australian cricket's darkest secrets. One delved into Donald Bradman's Second World War service, and how it jarred with his colleagues.

After the war, there was a considerable rift between Bradman and his most popular player — Keith Miller. The issue became public when the Australian selectors — Bradman, Jack Ryder and Chappie Dwyer — excluded Miller from the team to tour South Africa in late 1949.

Numerous cricket writers struggled to comprehend why Miller had been left out at a time when, as Fingleton put it, he was 'in the top six cricketers in the world'.

Miller and Bradman had had issues during the 1948 Ashes tour. Bradman wasn't happy with Miller's carefree attitude, which included a dalliance with Princess Margaret, while his pace bowler's decision to bowl several bouncers to his Test captain during a testimonial game in 1948–49 inflamed the issue. Finally Sid Barnes, another member of the 1948 team, provided the background in his controversial *Sunday Telegraph* column. Barnes, a masterful opening bat, was a rebellious opportunist who understood publicity and controversy, and was forever trying to make a quick quid. He once even convinced his fellow teammates into buying supposedly new shirts that were old, damaged stock. This mischievous imp used a rubber stamp of his signature to avoid the stress of endlessly writing autographs while on Ashes tours. This was used on 5000 team cards, with Barnes paying a ship crew member two bottles of ginger beer to do the stamping.[49]

When returning from England in 1948, after securing numerous business deals during the Ashes tour, Barnes cleverly overcame paying custom duties on a mountain of goods he brought back by leaving the boat at Melbourne, rather than Sydney, where officials were waiting for him.

Barnes had no qualms upsetting anyone — in particular stuffy cricket officials — during his lengthy days as a punchy tabloid cricket columnist. His column was aptly named 'Like It or Lump It'.

Barnes wrote: 'Bradman, through various channels, has several times denied that any dispute with Miller was responsible for the latter's non-selection for Africa. 1948 teammates of the pair, myself included, were never taken in by such protests.'

Barnes said during the second Test at Lord's that Bradman had thrown the ball to Miller, and 'Miller, who had announced his intention of not bowling in the game because of some injury or other, kicked the ball back to the incredulous captain. I did not catch the comment which went with the action, but I'm assured that Miller curtly advised Bradman to have a go himself.

'Bradman picked up the ball and — this I did hear — replied: "You'll keep".'

---

49 Ernie Toshack, another member of the 1948 team, who had been rejected for war service due to poor health and instead worked in the Lithgow Small Arms Factory, followed Barnes's lead. He paid a ship crew member to do his autographs, until caught out by Australian team manager Keith Johnson. Johnson said to Toshack: 'I see you're spelling your name differently these days. You no longer have a "c" in your name.'

Barnes said Bradman 'was as wild as a batter-stung brumby with his star allrounder'.

Fingleton was close to both Barnes, whom he helped with the rewriting of part of his candid autobiography, and Miller. Each gave him information for his articles.[50]

Fingleton's note on his clipping of the Barnes column reads: 'Barnes, for obvious reasons, hasn't told the full story. In the dressing room that evening, Bradman grumbled apropos of Miller not bowling …

"'I don't know what's up with you chaps. I'm 40 and I can do my full day's work in the field." And Miller replied: "So would I — if I had had fibrositis during the war."'

That cut to the core of the problem, as numerous Australian cricketers were surprised by Bradman's short time in the armed forces, especially returning home in 1941 to run his stockbroking business due to illness. Several of his state and Test teammates believed he wasn't seriously ill and instead was a chronic hypochondriac. Those who served weren't overwhelmed by those who they believed had done all they could to avoid active battle. It was a cruel slur, as it appears Bradman was genuinely incapacitated during the war, but the fact that he remained well away from the frontline was often used against him by a growing army of detractors.

Bradman enrolled in the RAAF reserves in June 1940. But there were more applicants than jobs available. Test teammate Les Fleetwood-Smith made representations for his 'little mate', leading to his transfer to the Australian Army. In October 1940, Lieutenant Bradman was in Frankston, near Melbourne, where he was to be trained with Fleetwood-Smith as a physical and recreation instructor for the AIF and the Militia. The understanding was that Bradman would, on completing the course, run the AIF's physical and recreational training in Adelaide. Among the trainees at the

---

50 Barnes enlivened cricket press boxes after he retired. During the 1950–51 England tour, he sat next to Neville Cardus. 'Look here, Neville,' Barnes said. 'I've got an idea. What about me slipping a carbon paper into my copy today for you and you can do the same for me tomorrow? We both write the same sort of stuff.' It was the only time Jack Fingleton ever saw Cardus 'stumped for a word'.

Army School of Physical and Recreational Training were wrestlers Bonnie Muir and King Elliott and Wallabies winger Edwin 'Slip' Carr, who had run in the 100 metres and 200 metres events at the 1924 Paris Olympic Games.

The recruits were involved in extravagant exercises and training routines which kept them occupied for the whole day. From 9am to 4.30pm they exercised (long jump, high jump, wrestling, boxing and shot put) as well as receiving lessons on anatomy, physiology and hygiene. This was mixed up with a St John Ambulance first-aid course, which Bradman topped.

It was not all training. Bradman also played in cricket fundraisers, and was photographed playing tennis with Harry Hopman.

The Sporting Globe's Hec de Lacy headed to the camp for a feature article, admitting at first that he didn't recognise Bradman. 'He is as brown as a berry,' de Lacy wrote. 'His face is scarred by the whitish mark where the chin strap of the Australian services hat protects a narrow strip of face from sunburn. His nose is skinned by the sun and wind.'

There were signs something was wrong. He had his eyes tested in Frankston and was told they were below par. He was admitted to hospital several times with a nervous complaint — fibrositis — which Miller was referring to in the dressing rooms several years later. That still did not stop him from being involved in the Australian Fighting Forces Athletic Track Championships at the MCG in November 1940, where all proceeds went to *The Sporting Globe*'s 'Fags for Fighters Fund', which, at a time when smoking was acceptable, had 19,000 packets of cigarettes sent to 'Australia's fighting lads overseas'.

In full uniform, Bradman proudly led his army men in the march-past around the ground, where almost four years earlier he had scored a century over Gubby Allen's England tourists. He made the Declaration of Loyalty on behalf of all competitors, finishing with the words that each would follow 'the glory of the traditions of true British sport, that whether we win or lose, we will always play the game'.

He comfortably won a challenge sprint race against Fleetwood-Smith, with an attentive Prime Minister Robert Menzies standing next to the finish line. Menzies told the troops that day, which included celebrated cyclist Hubert Opperman winning the marathon footrace, that it was important to follow the example of Bradman and indulge in athletic activities. 'You should train for foot-running, because if you meet the Italians in battle they would need to be in fine form to be able to follow their opponents.'

The fibrositis continued to be a problem, with Bradman complaining of a sore shoulder and leg problems when in April 1941 he scored a century in 75 minutes against the Melbourne Metropolitan Fire Brigade in another Fags for Fighters fundraiser at the Richmond Cricket Ground. Shortly after, he was taken off the army's roster. In July 1941 he was formally invalidated out of the army.

Doubts over how serious his ailment was were raised following a short news item by Arthur Mailey in *The Daily Telegraph* in April 1942. Bradman's business partner in Adelaide, stockbroker Harry Hodgetts, had told Mailey that 'Don attends the office every day, and shows no sign of the trouble which affected him 12 months ago.'

'He did not play cricket this season, but he played golf regularly and has had an occasional game of tennis. If there is any cricket next season he will be fit enough to play,' Hodgetts told Mailey. Those envious of Bradman began to complain that, if he could work and play golf and tennis, war service shouldn't be beyond him.[51]

Bradman wrote in *Farewell to Cricket*: 'Anyone who has suffered the excruciating pain of muscular ailments will understand how

---

51 A few years later, Hodgetts, who was instrumental in getting Bradman to move from Sydney to Adelaide, was behind bars. In the biggest financial scandal in South Australian history, Hodgetts was in July 1945 declared bankrupt, with liabilities of £82,854 and 238 unsecured creditors, including Test cricketer Arthur Richardson, retired Governor-General Lord Gowrie and Bradman. Found guilty of fraud and false pretences, Hodgetts was sentenced to five years' gaol. Bradman did not endear himself to the Adelaide establishment by operating within a few days from Hodgetts's office, and with full access to Hodgetts's client list.

utterly immobilising it can be. At one point I found myself quite incapable of even lifting my right arm. It was impossible even to do my own hair. I lost all feeling in the thumb and index finger of my right hand ... They were dark days. Cricket, then or in the future, never crossed my mind.'

In Johnnie Moyes's hagiography of Bradman, he writes that the cricketer sent him a letter which read: 'I'm good only for a job as an ARP warden.'

'There was a depth of sadness behind the words,' Moyes wrote. 'The nervous tension of war, added to the strain of his cricket career, had combined to destroy. It was nature in revolt. That he would be able to play first-class cricket again seemed impossible.'

The issue was never allowed to die. In Margaret Geddes's 2003 book *Remembering Bradman*, his godson, G.R.V. (Richard) Robins, the son of England Test allrounder R.W.V. (Walter) Robins, described Bradman as a 'hypochondriac'.

'Don was always ill, and it was ridiculous,' Robins said. Bradman had been writing him letters for decades, 'always starting it off saying, "Oh, I've got bad news from Australia. I'm not too well."'

Bradman was also upset that 'there were lots of people talking behind their hands saying, "Oh bloody old Don, all he did was turn up at the recruitment place and sign a few memos going around and really didn't do anything in the war."'

Bradman's main rivals had differing wartime experiences. Bill O'Reilly was at the start of the war approaching 34, and more than two-and-a-half years older than Bradman. Shortly after starting work at the Lion Tile Company in Sydney in 1939, he undertook a physical examination 'to see what part I was to play in the War against Hitler', as he wrote in his autobiography, *Tiger*.

'The old army doctor who measured my chest said, "You'll get a trip for certain," but as I was beyond military age I imagined myself with a manual job in some obscure branch of the Australian armed forces. However the Department of War Organisation took a hand in the proceedings. The War was not expected to last long, and the Department classified Lion Tile as a protected undertaking, to be ready to resume full production as soon as the War ended. I was ordered to remain there, which I did for the next 36 years.'

His family believed he was overlooked because he supposedly had flat feet. If Tiger had been forced to serve, he would have been difficult to handle. In an interview for the National Library of Australia, he was asked by John Ringwood about his wartime memories.

As he had a wife and young family, O'Reilly had no desire to go to war. 'If I'm going to war, I'm the man who's going to decide, I couldn't give a damn what anybody else thinks, at all.'

O'Reilly's memories of the Great War and the conscription debate were vivid. He never forgot how eight of the best footballers from his small country town of Marengo, near Young, were killed. 'I thought, by God, that's war for you.'

Late in the war, O'Reilly, with close mates Jack Chegwyn, Stan McCabe and Clarrie Grimmett, played in an Invitation line-up against various Air Force teams in northern Queensland. McCabe had enlisted in January 1943, but foot problems that had marred his final seasons of cricket meant that within days of joining the army he was in its Military Orthopaedic Hospital undergoing treatment on his damaged metatarsal bones. McCabe was restricted to clerical duties at Victoria Barracks. In May 1944 he was discharged 'at own request on compassionate grounds'.

McCabe captained this ex-international Invitational team that headed north, playing on rough and ready pitches, including an Australian airstrip. For one match, airmen at Iron Range, about 300 kilometres from the tip of Cape York, cut up tent flies and sewed them together to make a 'matting' wicket. McCabe headed the batting averages, while, according to Ray Robinson, 'next to O'Reilly in the bowling averages for the tour was 52-year-old Grimmett, who bowled for two hours without a rest in one match'.

Jack Fingleton wasn't part of this tropical cricketing adventure, as he was otherwise detained. Having joined the army in November 1941, he underwent general training at Warwick

Farm. The headstrong Fingleton hated the strict discipline. In later years, whenever he drove past Warwick Farm racecourse, he blew a raspberry in the training camp's general direction. He was more interested in wooing Pip Street, daughter of the influential Sydney couple Jessie and Kenneth Street. Jack and Pip married in January 1942. Shortly after, he managed to avoid AWL charges when he went missing during the Japanese midget submarine attack on Sydney Harbour. He was supposed to be on duty at an army post in Double Bay. He was instead visiting his bride.

Fingleton was transferred to Townsville and drafted into the Press Relations unit, where he was involved in intelligence, censorship and report writing. He somehow found time to start working on his first cricket book — *Cricket Crisis: Bodyline and Other Lines*. After writing around 50,000 words, he made a dreadful novice error. He wanted his former newspaper editor, A.R.P. Palmer, to look at the manuscript. He sent it to Palmer via Army Post, but it never arrived at his Sydney office. He had also forgotten to make a carbon copy. So he had to start all over again.

That proved difficult as the army had transferred him again, this time to be press secretary to the cantankerous former prime minister Billy Hughes, now head of the United Australia Party.

Fingleton's chief assignment was to curb Hughes's persistent attacks on General Douglas MacArthur, who was in Brisbane as Supreme Commander of the Allied Forces in the South West Pacific. That proved impossible. After three months Fingleton gave up, describing Hughes as a 'complete bastard'. He was transferred back to censorship work, but was able to finish *Cricket Crisis*, which was published in 1946 to widespread acclaim. The book focused on the 1932–33 Bodyline series and Bradman's controversial central role. Fingleton cut through the core of Bradmania, revealing the truth behind the legend, including his flaws and that, far from being loved by fellow cricketers, he was disliked by some. Bradman is portrayed as a loner, suspicious of others. *Cricket Crisis* broadened the divide between Bradman and Fingleton.

As expected, Sid Barnes's war was eventful, after hooking up with one of Australia's most mischievous sportsmen — golfer

Norman von Nida. Describing himself as a mechanical fitter on his enlistment papers, Barnes joined the Armoured Division in May 1942 and was immediately granted two weeks without pay to get married. Back among the troops, Barnes was a standout.

As he wrote in his autobiography *It Isn't Cricket*, a sergeant tossed him a uniform from a pile and said: 'Try this for size, Snow.' 'He pulled it at the back while I looked at it in the front. It was a horrible fit but Troopers can be choosers. I went down town and got measured for a uniform. I suppose I was the only Trooper in His Majesty's forces with a uniform cut to measure. The boys used to whistle "Pretty Joey" to me when we were on route marches.'

When transferred from Sydney to Greta in the Hunter Valley, he became close to fellow trooper von Nida.

Von Nida taught him every shortcut. As Barnes put it: 'Norman never bothered to conceal what he thought of the army and our immediate superiors.' Even though they were supposed to be fixing tanks, none ever appeared at Greta. Instead Barnes and von Nida 'marched out of camp, over the hill, and left to settle down for a few hours under a tree, reading and playing two-up, until the time came to march back to camp for lunch'.

Army life was 'marches, parades and emu-parades'.

By September 1942, Barnes had been discharged after convincing authorities he was of greater use building tanks at a Sydney construction firm. He joined his brother Horrie in a dubious concern making and packing a mixture which would help Australia's New Guinea troops, as it supposedly killed mosquitos. Also at their Glebe shed, the pair were reconditioning drums previously used by the army. Another of their get-rich schemes was purchasing equipment from American military officers based in Sydney at the time, including motor launches, and reselling them at an exorbitant price.

Horrie worked on getting von Nida released from the army to join the business. By this stage, von Nida had become a nuisance to his superiors. He was constantly disappearing.

Several weeks before Barnes joined him in camp, he was guilty of going AWL for 36 hours, and fined £3. A week later, he couldn't be found for three days, and was fined £5.

Von Nida was court-martialled for being absent without leave for 19 days in October 1942. He explained at the court-martial, held in Tamworth, that he was angry that a friend, Private Phillips, had 'died through the inefficiency' of the commanding officer, who had demanded soldiers sleep underneath 'damp blankets'.

'My friend died through sleeping in those blankets,' von Nida said at the hearing. 'I objected to this and that helped to make me decide to get out of the Armoured Division.' Von Nida had then gone to Sydney without seeking permission.

This was scoffed at by the defending officer, Captain Cartwright, who asked von Nida if he just went to Sydney to have 'a good time'. Von Nida replied: 'I was busy. I don't smoke or drink so did not go down for a good time. I joined the army to try and get into what I thought was a fighting unit. I have been in the army for ten months and have been sitting around doing nothing.

'The inefficiency and lack of forethought on the part of my C.O. was the reason he [Phillips] died. I thought it would happen to everyone in the unit. I wanted to fight, but not die like that.'

Asked if he wanted to serve overseas, von Nida said: 'Yes.'

He was sentenced to 60 days' detention.

Von Nida joined the Barnes brothers in March 1944 when he was discharged. Soon the general public knew what they were up to when they caused a massive traffic jam at one of Sydney's busiest intersections. They were driving a truck along Broadway loaded with drums of mosquito oil, which they were taking to the wharfs. Von Nida could handle a golf club, but was poor on rope tying. While Barnes drove, von Nida's task was to tie the pile of barrels tightly onto the back of the truck. As they headed towards Central Station, the barrels fell off in all directions, hitting nearby cars. A traffic warden abused the pair, while the public, discovering who the two culprits were, barracked them:

'Why don't you get a caddy, Norman?', 'You've forgotten your creams, Sid.' As the ever-argumentative von Nida, wearing his trademark beret, argued with the warden, Barnes fled the scene with the truck. Von Nida did not talk to his partner in crime for a day or two. They remained friends, however, and went on to be involved in several other intriguing business ventures.[52]

Another Test captain, Ian Johnson, who, like Bradman, struggled to get onside with Miller and Fingleton, had a more distinguished war period. A flying instructor of high renown with more than 2000 hours piloting planes, this licensed grocer finished as an RAAF flight lieutenant in the South West Pacific. Johnson's memories of the day the Japanese surrendered were vivid. He was sitting with a colleague in a slit trench 'in the teeming rain' on Morotai, an island in eastern Indonesia. It was Friday — 'our grog day' where 'everyone was issued with two bottles of beer', Johnson wrote in his book *Cricket at the Crossroads*.

'Around 1700 hours a voice rang out over the Public Address system: "It has been reported that the Japanese have unconditionally surrendered."

'All hell broke loose. Rifles were fired in celebration. Ack-ack shells burst high above, scattering the shrapnel all around, rockets and star shells were sent screaming into the sky. The place took on the atmosphere of a major engagement and the danger was darned near as great.

'We had a single thought and grabbed our tin hats and a bottle of whisky each, and dived into the muddy bottom of a slit trench.

---

[52] Von Nida, who won 80 golf tournaments, always stood his ground — including arguing with spectators and having an on-course fight with a future US Ryder Cup player Henry Ransom. Von Nida thought Ransom had cheated during a round. Ransom punched him in the mouth, and von Nida in retaliation tried to strangle him, until a sheriff intervened. One year later, in 1949, von Nida was involved in a heavily publicised divorce court case. A private detective had nabbed him in a car with a married woman, Elva Little, at the old Avoca golf course in Randwick around midnight. The detective chased von Nida 'pantless, trousers in hand and flapping in the breeze' across the course. Von Nida's wife, Norma, who had hired the detective, was hitting Elva over the head with an umbrella. Elva and von Nida later married. Barnes was constantly in trouble with cricketing authorities, even leading to court proceedings. He had a tragic end, committing suicide in 1973.

'What was I going to do about my cricket? I didn't have a clue. I had much more definite ideas as to what I was going to do with that bottle of whisky.'

The son of a prewar Australian Test selector, Johnson debuted as an off-spinner for Victoria as a 18-year-old in 1935, a year before becoming the state's amateur squash champion. Whisky bottle emptied, cricket soon became a driving force in his life when he returned to Melbourne from Morotai, playing alongside Ben Barnett in the first Victorian postwar game. Nine years on, Johnson was Australian captain. While his record as Test skipper was commendable, involving seven wins from 17 internationals, he struggled to gain the respect of his peers, especially when chosen ahead of the more popular Miller.

Fingleton thought poorly of Johnson as a spin bowler, believing, like many, that his bowling action was suspect and that he preyed on tailenders. Teammates called Johnson 'Myxomatosis' as he always appeared to put himself on to bowl when the rabbits — the weak tailenders — were batting, improving his chances of bagging easy wickets. Many believed Johnson became Test captain ahead of Miller as he had ingratiated himself with the influential Bradman. On the 1955 tour of the West Indies, Johnson and Miller openly clashed. Miller revealed to Fingleton that he had come close to putting one on Johnson's chin during the Test series.[53]

Another Test captain — Arthur Morris — repeatedly underplayed his war experiences. He remained a private, working as a transport clerk, including with the Australian Movement Control Group in New Guinea, which involved military police wharf-side operations.

In an interview with the National Library of Australia, Morris said that as part of a four-man group which included American soldiers he received preferential treatment, including endless boxes

---

[53] During the fourth Test, a livid Miller muttered to Johnson: 'You couldn't captain a bunch of bloody schoolboys,' and threatened not to bowl again in the Test — whereupon Johnson suggested they sort it out behind the grandstand. Before the fifth Test, Miller wrote to Fingleton that Johnson had 'bullshitted his way along, which after all is what they love here, but without prejudice he's done a fine job as an ambassador'.

of cigars and quality food. It was plentiful as they were repeatedly getting rations for 20 soldiers.

Only in the final months when transferred to Lae, and put onto Australian rations, did he lose the excess weight.

Morris's greatest wartime feat was his involvement with the Combined Services rugby team alongside notable representative players Len Smith and Aub Hodgson. Following a 57–0 win over the NSW Colts, revered Australian rugby coach Johnny Wallace described Morris, introduced to the code at school, as the best footballing five-eighth in Australia.

Ray Lindwall, one of Australia's most admired postwar pacemen, similarly experienced an unexpected wartime sporting highlight. He met the celebrated American baseballer Joe DiMaggio, who had been flown in to seek revenge in an Australia–US Services baseball game in Lae.

Lindwall was in New Guinea with the Signals Corps, which involved endlessly climbing up and down telegraph poles. He set up and repaired communications lines between the troops and the command posts.

He arrived in Port Moresby at its most volatile time, with the Japanese within sight of the ramshackle seaside port. He had to remain on the boat for several more days as the situation was too dangerous. Finally he was moved to a camp outside Port Moresby, and placed on guard duty.

The first night he thought he saw thousands of Japanese advancing towards him, all shining torches.

'I didn't know what to do. If I fired they'd kill me and the other chaps in the group. So I didn't fire — just waited. And it turned out that they weren't Japanese; they were fireflies.'

Another time, there *were* Japanese, with the result that five of Lindwall's colleagues were discovered in their tent the next morning with their throats cut. Lindwall almost shot a close mate whom he mistook for the enemy.

Rats were a constant problem in camp, while in one tent they discovered several death adders and scorpions. Disease was rife, and Lindwall was struck down with dengue fever and malaria.

He was still able to play a fair amount of sport, however, including pick-up cricket matches on rough matting where, according to *The Daily Telegraph*, he scored two centuries. Whenever a rugby league game was organised, he was beckoned, as his army superiors were well aware he was a regular first-grader for the illustrious St George club in Sydney.

Morris recalled Lindwall excelling in a softball game against an American unit in Finschhafen. 'One of them made an enormous hit, and Ray flew off the ground, and made this fantastic catch. The Americans went mad about it. If he hadn't caught it, it would have been the end of the game, because the ball would have gone into the jungle, and we would have never found it.'

This moment saw Lindwall receive an invitation to play baseball for Australia against the US. When army authorities discovered Lindwall had never played the game, they made him a reserve. An Australian team had defeated the Americans a few weeks earlier, and, infuriated by that, primarily because the commanders lost a mountain of money in bets, the US Services team had brought in all the big names for the return game — including DiMaggio. It had the desired effect. The US won 13–nil, but at least Lindwall spent some time with the man who later married Marilyn Monroe. DiMaggio's war was relatively tranquil, based in Hawaii and mainly involving playing exhibition baseball games. The ever-cantankerous DiMaggio soon grew tired of the US Military exploiting his fame by continually asking him to play. He believed he should have been paid an exorbitant amount 'for all this time I lost'. Lindwall was more modest, constantly saying to his family when he returned that he was forever grateful he had made it home. Many mates didn't.

One Australian bowler whose career would have been more flourishing except for war was Victorian leg-spinner Doug Ring.[54] In 1939, following a Sheffield Shield game in Adelaide, Bradman, trapped in front of the wicket in the second innings

---

54 Another Victorian whose first-class career was cruelly cut by war was Merv Harvey, the eldest of four brothers to play for the state. When at his prime, he had to work as an air-frame fitter for the RAAF, and after the war was reduced to one Test

by the 21-year-old, according to *Smith's Weekly* told Victorian manager Ernie Dwyer: 'If I were picking an Australian Eleven for England, one of the first men on my list would be Doug Ring.'

Instead for the next few years Ring was a radar technician with an anti-aircraft regiment in Dutch New Guinea, and had to wait until 1948 to play a Test against England as part of Bradman's Invincibles. Another 1948 tourist was Bill Johnston, who like Ring was a wartime radar technician with the RAAF in Cape York and Darwin. Johnston had trained for the air crew but was not encouraged after his superiors told him they didn't have enough planes for him to smash up. Each had their moment in the sun in January 1952 when they combined in a memorable unbeaten last-wicket partnership of 38 runs that won Australia the fourth Test over the West Indies at the MCG. Ring and Johnston, who both played for the Richmond cricket club, were inspired by a voice in the outer that screamed out as they discussed tactics in the middle of the wicket, 'Eat 'em alive, Tigers.' The spectator had more faith than Victorian Cricket Association secretary Jack Ledward, who in the grandstand bumped into Johnston's mother while her son and No 11 batsman was ambling to the wicket. When asked by Johnston's mother if Australia had any hope, Ledward slowly shook his head.

As their captain, Lindsay Hassett, stood mesmerised at the dressing-room window, unaware his towel had dropped to the ground and he was in the nude, Ring went for the big hit and Johnston defended. The West Indies panicked, and after 35 minutes the pair scored the required runs, causing uproar at the ground.

Then there was Jack Iverson, who used his idle moments in New Guinea to transform himself into the most unexpected of Test spin-bowling phenomenons.

Iverson was an offbeat, awkward character. He could be gregarious but was more often intensely shy, regularly shunning

---

appearance. Mick Harvey, who later became a Test umpire, was an infantryman on the Kokoda Track. Neil Harvey was too young to serve, and after the war became Australia's premier early-order batsman. Neil always thought Merv was 'the best cricketer of us all'.

social contact. This one-time jackaroo worked to a different rhythm. Before the Second World War, he had had only a passing interest in cricket. Yet during the war years, while serving in the Middle East and then New Guinea, boredom led him to start mucking around with a table-tennis ball, working on different ways to make it spin. Posted to the Australian Anti-Aircraft Regiment as a driver/mechanic and gunner, Iverson had a rough time in the Middle East, suffering from a number of ailments including sand-fly fever and jaundice before returning to Australia in 1943. He embarked for New Guinea several months later.

Stationed at Pom Pom Park near Port Moresby Airport, there wasn't much to do. That is until a shipment from the Australian Comfort Fund including several dozen table-tennis balls arrived, inspiring Iverson and co to devise a new game while sitting around in a YMCA tent. It revolved around, in the words of Iverson in *Sporting Life* magazine, trying to 'spin the ping pong ball to beat the bat — the 12-inch ruler — and hit the pole'.

From simple pursuits came cricketing sophistication.

Iverson devised a one-off grip, holding the ball between his thumb and middle finger and then flicking it. He was soon producing deliveries and variations that spun all ways without any apparent change of action. He kept beating the ruler and hitting the pole.

Army mates convinced him he should become more interested in cricket, enticing him to play in a succession of matches in Port Moresby. He tried out his odd spring action delivery. Sometimes it worked. Often it didn't. But he knew he was onto something. From army boredom had developed an odd, but special sporting gift.

In October 1946, a year after the war ended, supposedly prompted by watching some blind cricketers playing in a local park, he wandered down to his local club to see whether his action was up to district standard. He wasn't bothered that at 31 he had never played at a reasonable level of senior club cricket. After attending two training sessions, he was picked in the Brighton third XI — VC winner Bob Grieve's club. After three games in which he took 27 wickets at 5.74, Iverson was promoted to first grade and was immediately unplayable, finishing the season by taking 9/33 off 11.4 overs against Kew — including three bowled, three lbws, a stumping, one caught behind and the other caught in the outfield. The following season he won Brighton the flag — as he was in another class with 79 wickets at 10.0, including ten in the final. It was time to go up a level.

In April 1948 the prestigious Melbourne Cricket Club approached him, and he immediately responded, moving to the district cricket ranks at the age of 33. A year on, although constantly lacking self-confidence and believing he was an outsider, he was in the Victorian team, leading the averages with 46 wickets at 16.60, and the next in the Test line-up. During the 1950–51 Test series against England he was a phenomenon, and a prime reason for Australia's 4–1 triumph. As in the Sheffield Shield competition the previous year, the touring English could not fathom Iverson. Dubbed 'The Wonder Bowler' or 'The Freak', he took 21 wickets comprising 13 different players — including Freddie Brown and Alec Bedser three times each, and Len Hutton, Trevor Bailey, Cyril Washbrook and Doug Wright twice each — over the five Tests at a mere 15.23.

After he chipped an ankle bone when tripping over a ball at net practice during the Adelaide Test, however, his effectiveness began to dim. Batsmen had worked him out. In the Sheffield Shield, NSW opponents Arthur Morris and Keith Miller took to him, sussing out that if Iverson tossed his delivery up it was invariably a topspinner, and that if he pushed it through it was the wrong 'un. Miller, standing wide of the leg stump, as did Morris, attacked Iverson's bowling during a Shield match at the SCG, repeatedly depositing him into the Ladies Stand. Iverson was in a state of shock. His secret was no more.

A short time later, a disconsolate Iverson told Victorian teammate Ian Johnson: 'I've lost it. They're playing me easily.' Then he told Lindsay Hassett and Sam Loxton to inform the selectors he was unavailable.

In November 1952, he told *The Sporting Globe*:[55] 'For some inexplicable reason, I am unable to push through with fizz and control. Rather than make a fool of myself and let the side down I advised the selectors to this effect. I've lost it, that's all.'

Under the headline '"I've lost it" says Iverson', he told journalist Ben Kerville that he had asked Hassett to closely watch his bowling during the second innings of the Sheffield Shield match between Victoria and South Australia at Adelaide Oval. Iverson's insecurities were again at play, as he was Victoria's chief first innings wicket-taker with 4-65.

Hassett 'decided to field at short fine-leg to watch my bowling from close quarters'.

'He agreed that I had slipped. If I tried to push them through a bit faster the ball dropped shortly and I was pulled to the boundary. Slowing up to concentrate on length, I was placed through the covers. I only put two fingers on the ball yet can't work out what I'm doing wrong. If I can't regain it then I'll just have to toss it,' Iverson said.

Iverson bowled five wicketless second innings overs. That was his last Sheffield Shield appearance.

There was a brief revival in which he went to India as a member of the 1953–54 Commonwealth XI headed by Ben Barnett. Then Iverson's professional life as a real estate agent took over, until in early 1961, aged 45, he reappeared in the Brighton second XI, even though sometimes he did not appear at games until mid-afternoon due to his work. Then he was a member of the 1962–63 Brighton first-grade premiership team. While admired, he was still one who kept his distance. When real estate work hadn't delayed him, he would arrive at the ground just before the start of play and after stumps would scurry off.

Numerous Test teammates later argued he didn't have a cricketing brain. Miller was one to seriously question his limited cricket knowledge, believing he did not understand intricate field placements. He was often described by his teammates as a loner.

---

55 Less than two years earlier, *The Sporting Globe* had labelled him 'Jack the Giant Killer'.

Iverson's demise was traumatic. In 1973 he shot himself. His body was found in the back shed of his Brighton home, rifle across his chest.

Gideon Haigh's acclaimed biography of Iverson entitled *Mystery Spinner* explained he suffered from depression in his final years. Haigh considered the question whether war had contributed to 'Jack's mental decline'.

'There is, after all, anecdotal evidence of some post-traumatic stress. Unfortunately for such a neat solution, Jack experienced no serious psychological impairment until at least two decades after the war,' Haigh wrote.

Colin McCool was another formidable leg-spinner to be based in New Guinea, flying RAAF transport planes, and had several narrow escapes. Compared to Iverson, he was far more settled, and knew exactly where he was heading. On his enlistment papers he wrote that he was a bus conductor. One of the laconic flying officer's most vivid memories was 'walking down the tarmac at the RAAF station at Mallala in South Australia, mulling over my new profession of flyer, when a voice sang out: "Hi, Col. How are yer?"'

In front of him was Keith Miller, 'a pick in his hand, digging slit trenches'. They became friends and committed table-tennis rivals. Just another example in which Miller, in so many ways the opposite to Bradman, was seemingly everywhere, knew all, befriended nearly all — never bothering with intentions or pretentions. His list of close and important colleagues in wartime and peacetime was endless. It was not just the Australian cricketing follower who treated him as an idol.

CHAPTER 15

THE SECRET WAR

Many who served had no interest in regurgitating war stories when back home. It was time to move on. They were also desperate to forget. Others had greater cause to refuse.

Those involved in the 'secret war' were told to keep it locked away — even if they had been involved in the most dangerous, frightening experiences that deserved retelling. It was part of their training. Confidentiality was imperative. Mission accomplished. Move on. Then again, they probably thought no one would believe them anyway.

That's why the impressive wartime feats of Bruce Dooland have hardly been noted. He was part of that secret war.

Details of Dooland's cricketing career are extensive, usually revolving around how for a time he was the world's best leg-spin bowler. After making the Test team in 1946–47 he inexplicably missed out on the 1948 Ashes tour. This convinced him to move to England, where he played league and county cricket with great success and was chosen as one of the 1955 Wisden Cricketers of the Year. He was deeply involved in the development of Richie Benaud as a bowler. His cricketing life involved numerous flourishes.

His war exploits were similarly broad, but usually passed off in one succinct sentence. It's always the same. He was on commando service to a Pacific unit. That's it. Several cricket writers referred to Dooland in their match reports as a 'former commando' —

Jack Fingleton once referring to Dooland on the cricket field as being as happy as if chasing Japanese in the war jungle. The most detail was provided in a 1948 Arthur Mailey article in *The Daily Telegraph* where he revealed that Dooland's job 'was to steal out of submarines in the dead of night, wade ashore on some unknown island, see if there were any Nips there and, if so, anticipate the strength and defences etc. It was a ticklish job.'

'Ticklish' is a gross understatement. Unbeknown to many, particularly those who admired his cricketing prowess, was that Dooland had a perilous war. He was an integral member of one of Australia's most effective Second World War commando teams, involved in heroic rescue, intelligence and sabotage missions, often working deep behind enemy lines. Dooland was at the centre of a daring campaign in which he was under constant threat of being killed by the Japanese, and for a time was believed to have either been lost to the enemy or to the perils of the sea.

What Dooland was involved in, disappearing deep into enemy territory for a month in Borneo following a daring journey involving a submarine, canoe and fishing boat, is detailed in several military books, but none refer to his cricketing background, which is not surprising considering that his sporting career blossomed after the war.

He is treated as just another daring sergeant in 'Z Special Unit', otherwise known as 'Z Force'. This group, which also included Dutch, British, New Zealanders, Timorese and Indonesians, was a specialist reconnaissance unit that operated in the South Pacific, often resorting to guerrilla warfare and harassing attacks behind Japanese lines.

To be part of this unit, one had to be brave, loyal, athletic, unemotional, knowing how to escape danger and possessing extreme self-will. They had to survive in the most inhumane of conditions. It required intense training, which Dooland gladly underwent after enlisting while still a teenager. He kept it all to himself.

For decades, those involved in Z Force were generally forbidden to talk about their wartime experiences, to the extent many wives and families had no idea what their husband or father did during the war. The men would often just say they were involved in 'special operations' and leave it at that. It had been stressed to them that they had been involved in secret military business, and it had to stay that way, in case similar actions were required in future conflicts. Some never revealed their Z Force connection, while others took 30 to 40 years before they provided some basic details.

Dooland's first-class cricketing career was supposed to start the year before he joined up, when selected as a 17-year-old to play for South Australia to play NSW in the 1940–41 season after being the standout bowler in the school ranks at Adelaide High School. He had made his grade debut for West Torrens when 16 years, 66 days old.

He was about to make his Sheffield Shield debut until his Adelaide bank employees refused him leave. War then delayed his first-class debut for five seasons.

Dooland joined up in November 1942, and was earmarked for commando training. He underwent rigorous courses at Victoria Park in Adelaide, Seymour in Victoria and Dubbo in NSW, focusing on map reading, field sketching, infantry training, camouflage and tactical work. In 1944, he was assigned for 'special duties', joining the Z Special Unit later that same year. He may have been quiet, amiable, but his military superiors had taken note of a strong inner resolve and high intelligence. He didn't get ruffled. His war records indicate he was a diligent soldier, stating in March 1945 that he 'departed for service outside Australian mandated territory'. He was headed for three months in Borneo. As Z Special Unit was a secretive group, little information is provided in official records.

The details are found in several books and reports that focus on Z Special Unit, with the prime source being *Special Operations – Australia*, the official history of the Special Operations – Australia (SOA), held by the National Archives.

The official history, documents and operational reports, which include notes written by Ivan Southall, who later became an acclaimed writer of fiction and non-fiction, reveals that Dooland was involved in the first of 12 commando insertions in the Balikpapan area of Borneo. The plan, originally known as 'Robin' but changed to 'Platypus', was for a party of Z Special Unit commandos to land near Balikpapan to 'build up an intelligence network', discover the 'layout and routine' of a POW camp north of the town, and contact natives 'for the purpose of organising armed and passive resistance movements in preparation for D Day'.

What they found would be invaluable in determining how and when the Allies would invade Balikpapan and other areas. This was a tough mission, as they would be only a few trying to discover as much as they could about a Japanese occupied area without being detected. There was no strength in numbers.

The party, headed by Major Don Stott, involved eight commandos — five New Zealanders and three Australians, including Dooland — and two Borneo natives as guides. They left Fremantle aboard the submarine USS *Perch II* in March 1945, taking a week to get to Borneo. During the trip, rubber boats were attached to the submarine's hull, along with folboats (folding kayaks), with Dooland and his colleagues practising in the open sea how to reassemble them. They also accustomed themselves to placing outboard motors onto the rafts while in rough seas.

When 50 kilometres off the coast from Balikpapan, it was decided Stott and Captain Leslie McMillan would on the evening of 20 March take off in the first folboat to work out the best place to land on the mainland. They would be followed by Dooland and Sergeant Bill Horrocks in a second folboat.

The plan was to return to the submarine that night and pick up further commandos, as well as supplies and equipment for all the commandos and their support staff, so they could head to Balikpapan the next day.

If Stott and co did not return by a specified time, the submarine would head out to sea until the following night. If there was no sign after that, the commandos would go ashore to try to find them.

There were immediate problems with the folboats. Horrocks and Dooland's outboard motor started, but Stott's wouldn't. Stott decided each would have to paddle. Soon the two boats were separated. The plan was to stay in touch via walkie-talkie.

But Horrocks could not contact either the submarine or Stott. 'We persevered with our course, and when about 400 yards from shore we grounded. At 0130 hours, we heard a Japanese voice (muffled) on the Walkie-Talkie. At 0145 hours we heard two English voices loud and clear checking frequency. It was 0200 hours when we grounded and went ashore,' Horrocks said in his official report on the Platypus operation.

Stott and McMillan were never heard of again. Horrocks and Dooland headed inland, while those on the submarine believed all four had either drowned or been captured. There had been sightings of crocodiles in the region, which would have found the commandos easy prey if their folboat had tipped over.

The rest decided to continue the mission, and in canoes fitted with outboard motors made the shore on 23 March.

Lieutenant Bob Morton, now in charge of the Platypus mission, tried to contact the other four but discovered the walkie-talkie batteries were ruined as they were corroded with acid. This main group had also been sighted by a local native, a Japanese spy. Soon they were surrounded by Japanese soldiers, but somehow most of the commandos fled into the jungle, where they survived on scraps of food. Two others were caught elsewhere, and shot.

The aim of the main group was to find their colleagues. But tropical storms and attacks by leeches and ticks made progress slow. They made friends with several natives, who had sighted Horrocks and Dooland some miles inland in dense jungle, and got a message to them, explaining where their colleagues were.

Horrocks and Dooland hacked their way through the jungle, taking a month to negotiate their way through the Japanese cordon. Helped by a sympathetic local, they had collected important intelligence about the Japanese forces in the area. Eventually on 20 April, both in a bad way with malnutrition, they found their colleagues, and with it an emotional reunion.

The official operational report said Horrocks and Dooland 'had valuable information to impart'.

With the group was a local native, who revealed his hatred towards the enemy and vowed to help the Australians, as he had been beaten up by the Japanese. He knew how to avoid them.

The only way to get off the island was to somehow find or buy from the locals a native fishing boat, known as a prahu. This was difficult, as the Japanese had confiscated or smashed them. Finally the commandos secured, after several days of 'prolonged negotiation', a four-metre fishing boat for 'the bargain price of 1400 Dutch guilders'. Aided by a stockpile of food provided by the natives, which included cooked rice, coconuts and live chickens, they headed off towards Morotai on 1 May, taking six natives with them. Only two of the commandos were fit enough to paddle the boat away from shore, while the natives refused to help. So each of the two did two-hour rowing shifts.

Somehow by daybreak they had avoided detection, were well away from shore, heading east, and hoping they would be sighted by Allied aircraft or ships. Two days later, they saw two Liberators but were too far away to get their attention, and the group's morale sunk when another passed right overhead but didn't see them. The group had a signal lamp, but it was of no use in daylight.

Luckily Bill Dwyer, one of the two capable of rowing, remembered that in his escape kit there was a small mirror, which he could use to flash at aircraft. Shortly after, they saw a Catalina about 30 kilometres away, which Dwyer flashed his mirror at. It worked. The US Navy Air Sea Rescue plane landed near them, picked them up, and took off for Morotoi. The bedraggled group decided to leave no trace behind, sinking the boat with gunshots. Dooland then sighted a familiar figure in the plane. The Catalina's navigator was former South Australian allrounder Tom O'Connell, who had played six games for the state in 1935–36. They were soon swapping cricketing stories.

There were still some testing moments before getting to their destination, as the rescue plane also had to pick up the crew of a bombed Liberator near Celebes, and with the extra weight struggled to lift itself out of the water. After about a 15-minute taxi, the plane eventually lifted, but it then had to circle Morotai as their arrival coincided with a Japanese bombing raid.

Following the Balikpapan experience, for future Australian commando raids in that area it was decided all should carry money to buy food, particularly rice, from the natives, know how to speak the local language, only have the bare essentials in their personal packs, and avoid wearing boots — after the Japanese had detected the original Platypus group through their distinctive boot marks. It was crucial to camouflage the tread and instead use a sole similar in design to the Japanese split-toe rubber sandal.

From May to June that year the Allied forces invaded Borneo. The Japanese on the island surrendered in September.

Dooland, suffering from malaria, returned to Darwin to recuperate for six weeks, before heading overseas again in October–November 1945 for an 'undisclosed mission'. It was later revealed he had been in Timor, arriving there just two days after the Japanese leaders on the island had also officially surrendered. Dooland was involved in ensuring that the Allied troops were not caught up in skirmishes with Japanese soldiers unaware that their superiors had surrendered. During this period he often had a battered tennis ball in his pocket, so that whenever possible he could ensure that he had not lost the spinning knack. That year he also married Joyce Quirk, whom he had met while at a training camp in Dubbo.

Within weeks of being discharged, Dooland revived his cricket career and was selected for South Australia's first first-class match of the season, beginning 14 December 1945 at Adelaide Oval. Despite no serious cricket for years, Dooland, who had also returned to his previous work at the Bank of Adelaide, was immediately on song, being South Australia's chief wicket-taker. Still, war hung heavily over this match, with stumps drawn 15 minutes early each day so that the NSW players could return to their hotel for dinner 'before cooking hours ceased under prevailing restrictions'. Dooland, the first to produce a postwar hat-trick when he dismissed Victorians Ken Meuleman, Ben Barnett and Percy Beames with successive deliveries, was the sixth most successful bowler of the season, with 31 wickets at 28.09.

Bradman pushed his case when determining who in 1946 would be part of the first Australian team to tour New Zealand.

Writing to fellow Test selector Chappie Dwyer, Bradman said Dooland had 'bowled beautifully' in his hat-trick match. As Bradman wouldn't be playing in Sydney, he asked Dwyer to closely watch Dooland, taking into account he was up against strong batting oppositions and was 'playing under a young inexperienced skipper' — Chester Bennett.

Although NSW won by an innings and 51 runs, Dwyer liked what he saw in Dooland's 21 overs, which included four wickets. He reported back in a private letter to Bradman: 'The highlight of the whole game was the splendid bowling of this lad.

'He confirmed the good opinion I formed of him in Melbourne. In my opinion he is one of the most outstanding prospects. He spun the ball well, bowled a little too fast I thought and could exploit his slower ball more often ... I have made up my mind that he should go into the team.'

So, less than a year after being close to death behind enemy lines, Dooland was on his way to confront the Kiwis in a far safer cricketing environment — alongside a tribe of fellow servicemen, including captain Bill Brown, Keith Miller, Sid Barnes, Lindsay Hassett, Ron Hamence, Don Tallon, Colin McCool, Ray Lindwall and Ian Johnson. After what they had endured, this five-week, five-match trip was one long, merry shindig. They admitted to having the time of their life partying their way across the North Island and South Island, finishing off with a Test against New Zealand. During the trip, Miller wanted to show off his wartime piloting skills — he asked if he could fly the Catalina which took the team across the Tasman, but was barred. He got his wish some years later when he and Johnson took spells flying a plane during the tour of West Indies in 1955, until Australian

Cricket Board officials back at home heard of it and furiously demanded it never happen again.[56]

Dooland had a relatively tame New Zealand trip, as Tiger O'Reilly was the main spinning strike bowler, finishing with five wickets from three appearances. Dooland's sporting prowess did not end there, however, as he was a standout baseball pitcher, making the South Australian and Australian teams. He is still rated among his state's mightiest pitchers. He was also a single-handicap golfer, in his final years playing off seven.

The strong belief in Dooland continued the following year when he played the third Test against England at the MCG, taking the important wickets of Wally Hammond and Cyril Washbrook. This enabled him to play the next Test on his home ground — Adelaide Oval — even though his employers provided him with no favours. The Bank of Adelaide stipulated that he would have to work until 10am in the head office. He would then sprint out the back door of the bank with his cricket gear crammed into a Gladstone bag, and hurriedly catch a tram to the ground to be there for the start of play. This time he took the first innings wickets of Washbrook, Bill Edrich and Jack Ikin, but was overlooked for the final fifth Test.

The next month he was Mentioned in Despatches for distinguished war service in the south-west Pacific region.

Dooland also played in the third Test of the lopsided 1947–48 series against India, but only secured one wicket. Before the 1948 Ashes tour, several other spinners were providing competition — in particular Doug Ring and McCool, who were chosen ahead of him. Among those surprised by Dooland's omission was Lala Amarnath, the captain of the 1947–48 Indian touring team.

While despondent to miss out on what appeared the ultimate Australian cricketing tour, a lucrative offer to play for East Lancashire in the Lancashire League came at the right time,

---

56   The team's trip back to Sydney at the end of the tour was tense, as the Royal New Zealand Air Force plane had engine failure about 300 kilometres into the trip, and was forced to return back. The replacement plane only got to Sydney just before it had run out of fuel. Sid Barnes was particularly furious, especially as on the flight to New Zealand the players had to stand.

leading to four successful years, before he joined Nottinghamshire in 1953. He was a prolific county wicket-taker, twice heading the English bowling aggregates, tallying 805 wickets over five seasons, encouraging British newspapers to describe him as 'the world's best leg-spinner'. Many years later, England allrounder Trevor Bailey argued that Dooland had been the best county bowler for three years, but then suffered as he was over-bowled.

At his peak, Dooland revitalised Nottinghamshire and was adored by *Wisden* because he had done 'much to restore right-arm leg-break and googly bowling in the strategy of the game'. By taking 368 wickets in his first two seasons, he had become 'one of the most successful bowlers of his type since A.P. Freeman retired in 1936'.

He was also willing to pass on his secrets. Dooland had learnt how to bowl the flipper from Clarrie Grimmett, his state coach straight after the war. He passed on how to bowl it to Richie Benaud.

Benaud played against Nottinghamshire on the 1956 Ashes tour, and, while having drinks after the second day's play, Dooland asked how he was progressing with several different spinning deliveries. Benaud told Dooland he had become far steadier. Then the ever-tight spinner's network came into play. As recalled in Benaud's *My Spin on Cricket*:

'Well,' Dooland said, 'I won't suggest you change that, but would you like to learn how to bowl the flipper?'

Benaud immediately said 'yes', as this was the great mystery ball — one every serious leg-spinner had to have in their repertoire. However, few knew how to bowl what is essentially a back-spinning delivery squeezed out of the front of the hand. It takes some explaining, as the ball comes out from underneath the hand with what appears to be a 'flipping' motion, involving the thumb and index finger.

Dooland recommended that Benaud get to the ground several hours before the start of the third day's play and he would, as Benaud put it, 'run through the flipper and then it would be up to me, from that point on, what I did with it'.

Dooland showed him how to bowl and disguise the delivery. Benaud admired Dooland's patience as 'what was second nature to him was something completely new to me and it would require considerable practice'.

Benaud wrote that 'it took me more than half an hour to understand completely what had to be the feel of the ball leaving the fingers, which Bruce said was by far the most important thing'.

Benaud had to practise it by himself, and not at team training sessions. Also he didn't want to bowl it in a game until he was completely confident that he could bowl it 'precisely on the spot I wanted'.

Benaud waited 18 months before bowling the flipper for the first time, during the South African tour. It worked. Against Northern Rhodesia, he took 9–16, six of which were taken with the flipper. He used it with success the next seven years.

'It was one of the most valuable lessons I was ever given and made a wonderful difference to my bowling,' Benaud wrote.

There were testing times, though. Dooland soon learnt about the English class system when he had to report to the Nottinghamshire County Club committee after a member heard him address his captain, Simpson, by his first name, 'Reg'.

The committee firmly reminded Dooland that in England an amateur captain should be addressed either as 'Skipper' or preferably 'Sir'. Dooland laughed it off, but followed protocol.

In late 1957, Dooland returned to Adelaide because he wanted his children to be educated in Australia. He was immediately back in the South Australian team, where, even though the side finished bottom of the Shield table, he was the second highest wicket-taker in the competition, with 29 at 33.17. Before he left England, numerous Fleet Streeters had predicted he would be back in the Australian Test team within months, and bowling against England's 1958–59 tourists. *The News Chronicle*'s Crawford White was among many to believe it was impossible for the Australian Test selectors not to pick him. *The Daily Herald*'s John Samuel wrote: 'Unless Australia's cricket selectors take leave of their senses, Dooland, the world's number one leg-break and googly bowler, will be launched against England in the bid to keep Australia a top cricket power.'

It didn't happen, as Dooland, now 35, retired from first-class cricket at the end of the 1957–58 season. The following season, Benaud, with the flipper now part of his repertoire, was instrumental in Australia winning the series over England 4–0, taking 31 wickets. So the Dooland presence remained, including at Adelaide grade level, playing several more seasons for the West Torrens club. According to the West Torrens District Cricket Club newsletter 'Eagle Eye', which in March 2017 provided a comprehensive profile on Dooland, his return grade appearance attracted more than 1000 spectators to Thebarton Oval, before a shoulder injury forced him to give the game away at all levels. He was rated 'arguably the most outstanding bowler ever produced' by that club.

These days, Dooland's feats are known to only a few. He is even often forgotten when the flipper is mentioned — though he was a major figure in it becoming a necessary part of a quality leg-spinner's repertoire. Shane Warne would vouch for that. His success is partly due to Dooland, who ensured the flipper lived on in Australia via Benaud and those who followed him. Even more admirable was his heroic and dangerous war service, which is unknown to virtually all.

Dooland's selfless and brave contribution to Australia, in peace and wartime, deserves greater recognition. He needs to be on a pedestal.

CHAPTER 16

THE AUSTRALIAN SERVICES TEAM

Keith Miller had a favourite photograph. It held pride of place on the lounge room wall at his Sydney Northern Beaches house for years. It wasn't of the great man playing a masterful stroke, dismissing someone, or a stunning portrait of the most debonair of all. It wasn't the classic shot of him executing a square cut at the SCG that Robert Menzies demanded be placed on the wall of his office in Canberra alongside a Tom Roberts bush landscape.

It was instead a photograph of a motley crew of cricketers walking onto a ground in England. There's a Brown's cows element to the shot. The players appear a bit disorganised and are looking in all directions. One is peering at the captain. Another is smiling. The star has his left hand in his pocket, and clearly just said something cheeky to another. One is flexing his fingers. The wicketkeeper has the pads but no gloves on. Three are wearing cricket jumpers — each a different design. The tall, skinny figure to the far left at the back of the group looks a bit detached, an almost ghostlike figure.

The shot is of the 1945 Australian Services team walking onto Bramall Lane in Sheffield, and it always kept Miller, the comrade of princes and paupers, in touch with reality. It reminded him of his favourite time playing cricket, and of the most heroic teammate of all. Hero is a word often used. But deserved in the case of this man hiding in the back left corner. Whenever asked why this was his favourite cricket photo, Miller would point to that figure.

It was Graham Williams, and for Miller what this person had endured so that he could be part of this photograph was humbling, inspiring, rousing.

It brought it all into perspective.

The previous month had provided Miller with what he termed his most emotional sporting experience. It was when Williams walked out to bat at Lord's. Just two weeks earlier he had been released from a German POW camp. He was emaciated, having lost 31 kilograms since being captured by the Germans after being shot down over Libya, spending most of his four years in captivity teaching Braille to POWs, as well as to blinded enemy soldiers.

There has never been a greater reception for an Australian No 6 batsman than on 12 May 1945 when the RAAF took on a British Empire XI at Lord's. As William was a formidable pace bowler, he had already opened the RAAF attack, with eight wicketless overs. That was some task, requiring him to drink gallons of a thick glucose drink after each over to stop himself from collapsing. In the heels of his boots were scooped-out halves of oranges to lessen the jarring of his tender feet.

One consolation was that the lunch and afternoon tea on offer were his first proper meals since 1941. He devoured them.

The crowd was aware who he was, as the London newspapers had made a special mention of the extraordinary courage of this Australian released from a German stalag and now fronting up as an allrounder.

When Williams appeared from the dressing room in his first serious game in seven years, the 15,000-strong crowd stood as one, clapping him all the way as he slowly walked to the batting crease. The batsman appeared bewildered by the reception, peering around him with a stunned look as if he could not believe where he was. In Miller's mind, it was as if he was saying to himself, 'This can't be true. I will wake up shortly.' Williams was walking as if 'in a trance'.

Miller described the crowd reception at Lord's as 'the most touching thing I have ever seen or heard, almost orchestral in its sound and feeling'.

'Whenever I think of it, tears still come to my eyes.'

They rose as one again when Williams remained unbeaten on 51, enabling the RAAF to win by six wickets.

The Australian team's wicketkeeper and one of its main organisers Stan Sismey agreed with Miller in a 1989 interview with the author that it was the most touching moment in his long sporting career.

'The crowd rose as one and gave him a magnificent reception. It was a wonder he could see anything after what he had gone through. I agree with Keith that it was the most emotional moment we have ever experienced,' Sismey said.

It happened again a week later at the same venue. The man tagged 'Flamingo' by his teammates because his legs resembled match-sticks was now opening the bowling for the Australian Services team against a Test-strength England team in the first of five Victory Tests. Now there were more than 31,000 at the ground. They watched him closely, and admired how he somehow continued to rally and regather himself, guzzling gallons of glucose drinks at the end of each over to stay upright long enough to have Len Hutton caught behind and Wally Hammond bowled. Batting at No 9, another swashbuckling half-century. Once more a standing ovation to and from the wicket. At the end of the first day, Gubby Allen dropped two £5 notes between Williams's legs, telling the exhausted bowler he could have them if he had the energy to bend over and pick them up. Williams grinned: 'Just heard my shares have gone up a bit in the past four years. Pick 'em up yourself.' The £5 notes remained on the dressing-room floor.

Miller loved talking about Williams, especially how he relished the roast lamb and jacketed potatoes on offer during the lunch break — food he often fantasised over when a POW. Miller would repeatedly tell Richie Benaud about this moment. Benaud said it was easily the most powerful Miller story he had ever told him, and the most poignant of all cricket stories. He retold it at numerous functions.

Robert Craddock of *The Courier-Mail* newspaper in 2016 described Williams's appearance at Lord's as 'one of the greatest moments in Australian cricket history … How Graham Williams was walking at all was a minor miracle.'

Williams was of sturdy Adelaide Methodist stock, one foot planted firmly in the city, one out on the land. He loved the smell, the feel of merino wool on his fingers. It was better than lanolin in keeping the hands soft, pliable. He admired the process of paddock, sheep, wool, quality cricketing pullover.

Before everything went stupid in 1939, he had been a wool classer, following his father, Spencer, a noted South Australian wool expert, into the trade. Educated at Adelaide's prestigious Prince Alfred College, he completed a wool-classing diploma at the South Australian School of Mines and Industries. He soon joined his father, manager of the wool department of Goldsbrough Mort & Co, becoming a valuer. But cricket kept dragging him back from the bush, where he was working in the shearing sheds. He was so keen to pursue a cricketing career that even when stationed at Jamestown, 200 kilometres north of Adelaide, and playing Colts cricket as a 21-year-old, he would charter an aeroplane to get to the city in time to play games. His father told *The News*, 'Graham is as keen as mustard, and would fly round the world to get a game of cricket.'

At 195 centimetres, he was one of the tallest in the South Australian grade ranks, and generated ample pace with a high, correct delivery. As the options were relatively limited in South Australia, he was soon enticed to the Sheffield Shield ranks, failing in his first game to get a wicket against Victoria in Melbourne in February 1933. He was more successful two months after the eruption of Bodyline at Adelaide Oval, when South Australia confronted the England side on the same track in their final tour match before heading to New Zealand. After the intensity of the recent Tests, England treated this game as a bit of a joke, with some players wearing silly caps — meanwhile, the Vic

Richardson-led South Australians decided on bowling retaliatory Bodyline bowling. So Williams started bowling bouncers to a packed leg-side field similar to that adopted by Douglas Jardine during the Test series to curb Bradman. Williams hit Bob Wyatt three times, but wasn't of Harold Larwood pace to make it sting. He at least finished the game with five wickets.

By wartime Williams had played 18 times for South Australia, taking 53 wickets mainly under Bradman's captaincy, but his state appearances were curbed when he was transferred to Melbourne for work. In 1938 he spent six months in England at the woollen mills of Laycock, Son and Co, playing in the local Bradford league and enjoying more five-wicket hauls.

He returned to Adelaide, joining the Civil Air Reserve in September 1939 and the RAAF as a navigator.

In June 1941, now with the 39 Royal Air Force Squadron, Williams was involved in several air missions during the Libyan campaign, photographing German camps from a Maryland bomber. On 14 June, the mission involved photographing a target at a German aerodrome in the Derna/Tobruk region. But, about 120 kilometres behind enemy lines, the bomber was shot down by German ground troops. First the Maryland's radio was shattered to pieces, so Williams could not contact the rest of his crew. Some had to evacuate by parachute and then the plane was hit six more times, forcing a crash landing. German tanks exploded the plane, after Williams and co had escaped.

Williams tried to help his wounded pilot, J.M. Coetsee of the South African Air Force, before fleeing. After walking eight kilometres, Williams was sighted by a German truck, and taken prisoner.

It was revealed that Williams's skills under pressure when the plane had been shot down were exemplary. Coetsee, who was taken prisoner, wrote to the RAAF recommending Williams for a commission, as that day his work as a navigator had been 'extremely efficient'.

'He not only carried out his work well, but was respected and thought of highly by the men of 39 Squadron,' Coetsee wrote.

Williams was imprisoned in Frankfurt, then moved to Stalag IX-C at Bad Sulza near Leipzig, and worked in several British POW hospitals before finally being taken to Stalag IX-B at Bad Soden, where he was released in March 1945 when American troops took over the camp.

Coetsee said that, as a POW, Williams 'volunteered to learn Braille and weaving and then teach blind prisoners'.

Coetsee said the report which 'came through from the camp for blind prisoners, I heard only praise and respect for him … There is much more to say for this man …'

Williams was the most generous of souls during his time in captivity. He studied the Braille system of typewriting so he could teach prisoners blinded during the war how to continue reading and writing. He also taught agriculture and economics.

His touch typing courses became very popular, with classes increasing from 12 to 30 students. Pupils were soon typing 40 words per minute.

On reaching England in April 1945, he sent a cable to his father which said simply: 'Here I am. Never felt better.' It was only then that the Williams family realised his days as a POW were over.

A few weeks later, he was a somewhat startled member of what would become one of world cricket's most special teams. The origins of this team came when Plum Warner was watching his specially selected XI — which included the Bedser twins Alec and Eric, Trevor Bailey, Gubby Allen and Bob Wyatt — play the RAAF in a one-day game at Lord's in June 1943. He was particularly taken by the dash and vim of the RAAF's Miller and Keith Carmody, and began formulating a possible Australia–England Services Victory Test series to celebrate the end of the war — whenever that may be.

No problems getting England players interested. More importantly he had to get the Australians on side. Warner knew who to lobby when the following year the Australian Prime Minister, John Curtin, was in London for the Commonwealth Prime Ministers' Conference, accompanied by General Sir Thomas Blamey. Warner, aware of Curtin's cricketing fascination, invited him to Lord's and gave him the silver service treatment. Curtin was in the Pavilion at the start of the 1944 cricket season to watch the Civil Defence Services play the Army. Around the same time, he emphasised the importance cricket played in both countries.

On 10 May 1944 Curtin used a lunchtime speech at Mansion House to explain how important cricket was to his nation. 'Lord's is to Australia what it is to this country. We would refuse to contemplate a world in which there would be a jurisdiction over Lord's which would prohibit the playing of Test matches. We are helping to defend this historic city of London and those 22 yards of turf,' Curtin said.[57]

No wonder the PM enjoyed a standing ovation.

Curtin was back at Lord's two weeks later with Stanley Bruce, former PM and now High Commissioner in London, to watch Australia beat The Rest on the third-last ball of the match. Warner again used the opportunity to convince Curtin of the importance of an Australian Services team. The PM didn't need much sweet-talking. He had made it clear he wanted regular cricket to restart as soon as peace was achieved, as did Blamey. Curtin, whose Labor Party colleague Bert Evatt was another cricket obsessive, realised the game could provide unity, hope and relief. It just required some clever manipulation to bring this team together. It involved melding together the successful RAAF team that had been appearing at Lord's for the previous two seasons with the AIF side that had been playing with success in North Africa.

Suddenly excellent Australian cricketers were being transferred to an 'AIF Reception Group'. This group, organised by Blamey, was to establish a reception centre at Eastbourne to prepare for the repatriation of 6000 Australian POWs about to arrive in England from Europe. Those transferred soon realised something was afoot. On arrival, they were told they were to be part of an Australian cricket team.

---

57 Curtin's full speech is in *Men and Women of Australia! Our Greatest Modern Speeches*, by Michael Fullilove.

This proposal had countless positives, especially in overcoming the problem of finding something to do with the many Australian servicemen stuck in Europe due to a drastic lack of transport. It would also help buoy the spirits of a battered home country. An Australia–England Test cricket series was the perfect elixir.

In the background, the now Major Bert Oldfield, serving in his second war, this time in the Army Amenities Fund, had been instructed to do what he could to resurrect the same type of Services team he had been involved in in 1919–20. He had to find suitable Australian Army cricketers — the only proviso being that they had served in the Middle East or New Guinea. Among the army personnel soon on their way to Eastbourne were Lindsay Hassett, Cec Pepper and Richard Smallpeice 'Dick' Whitington.

The leader of these weathered men was the impish, forever-mischievous Hassett — the only one in this group to have experienced Test cricket. Ray Robinson had him right in his celebrated book on Australian Test leaders, *On Top Down Under* — the Hassett chapter is titled 'Puck in Flannels'.

Only 168 centimetres tall, Hassett, one of nine children, overshadowed the majority in the departments of rat cunning, raw wit, wisdom, street knowledge and intelligence. As a batsman he was a purist, playing his shots with elegance and ease, ensuring this Geelong College student was a member of the 1938 Australian Ashes team, where captain Don Bradman praised him for being 'a masterful player in a crisis'.

The next crisis was a global war, and again Hassett was hard to pin down. He had little regard for authority. He was forever the acidic smart-alec. Yet, as Miller often said, Hassett could claim more friends in all walks of life than any other cricketer.

Enlisting as a gunner in the 2/2 Anti-Aircraft Regiment, his ambivalent attitude was apparent from day one. He was sent in late 1939 for general training to the Puckapunyal camp in central Victoria. On arrival, Hassett noticed that his long-time mate George Schofield was on his way to a nearby pub. Hassett dropped his bags and joined George for a rowdy afternoon in the saloon bar.

Within a year, his war papers were revealing that he was often in trouble — once for 'conduct to the prejudice of good order and military discipline', followed by paying a 15 shilling fine for 'without order from his superior officer leaving his post'.

Not even boarding the *Mauretania*, which took Australian troops to the Middle East, could calm him. Within days he was fined £5 for not appearing at parade. When the ship stopped in Fremantle he missed a fire drill, as he was on a pub crawl. Another £20 fine, and leave cut by 28 days.

The cheekiness continued in the war zone. Hassett found an impressive-looking private men's club in Haifa which had a sign that said 'Officer's Only'. He convinced soldier mates to come with him that night, making out they were officers to gain entry. It worked. While at the elegant main bar, ordering beers all round, a provost marshal realised they were fakes and kicked them out. The provost marshal said he would report them to Hassett's battery, but by the time he did they were long gone.

As his cricketing presence was well known, Hassett was soon selected for military matches. Again he stood for no nonsense.

Once he was confronted by an over-officious commander who thought he was a handy cricketer. Grabbing Hassett's firearm in Haifa, the commander said: 'If you took the trouble to clean your rifle, Gunner Hassett, you might manage to become a good soldier in a long war.'

Hassett gave him the once-over and replied: 'If you cleaned and oiled your bat for twenty years, sir, you'd still never score a run.'

He was the master of the one-liner, telling his cricketing colleagues when bumping into a sheikh surrounded by his 199 wives: 'One more and he's entitled to a new ball.'

He also seemed to be everywhere — bobbing up in numerous localities. Hassett returned home to get married, before heading to New Guinea, where he was struck down by malaria. After stints of extra fire picket duty when caught playing poker at his post, and another AWL charge added to the list when in Sydney he disappeared to visit his old Test mate Stan McCabe, he was then in northern Queensland when his commanding officer called him over.

Hassett was asked if he had asked for a transfer. When replying 'No', he was told the CO had received a signal from Melbourne that he had to go to the United Kingdom.

'I'll have to give a very good excuse if you don't go. I'll give you half an hour to think about it.'

Hassett decided the UK sounded better than New Guinea. Back in Europe he received hints he was about to be handed a special role. He was being considered as captain of the Australian contingent, even though recent military intelligence generated some doubts. In a special leadership test, he finished only 47th in the class with a mark of 60.8 per cent. At least his assessor believed he was 'industrious and painstaking, rather quiet, but good sense of humour and popular'.

Some days later he was handed 'the best darned job anybody had in the army'.

Accompanying him to the AIF Reception camp was the aptly named Pepper. This rambunctious character knew how to spice up proceedings. Cecil Pepper was of NSW country stock, rude, raw and often rowdy. Growing up in Parkes in the NSW Central West, Pepper was a promising tennis player, a single-figure golfer and a notorious ladies' man. Starting his working life as a striker at the local blacksmith and coach-builder, he had a crude tongue. Profanities dominated his conversation. He won over women of all ages by being a brash extrovert. But he was best known as the town's young cricketing colossus.

In the local inter-town competition, Pepper was the renowned big hitter and baffling spin bowler who could turn the ball both ways. He hit the biggest six at Parkes's Woodward Park, with the ball bouncing down a street and finishing almost 200 metres away. One game, he scored a century in 27 minutes. In another, he had two hat-tricks in the one innings. For decades, his unbeaten innings of 258 was the record for most runs in a Parkes competition match. In Tamworth one day, he belted a ball 170 metres into the newly opened town swimming pool. He was also the Parkes district's undisputed champion in both tennis and ice skating.

The Petersham club lured him to Sydney in 1936, where he learnt more bad habits living with Sid Barnes. Two years later, when 22, Pepper was in the NSW team for the start of the 1938–39 season as the team allrounder, often accompanying Bill O'Reilly as his spin twin.

But what made Pepper stand out was his spectacular innings in the first match of the 1939–40 Sheffield Shield season when NSW played Queensland at the Gabba. He produced an hour of outlandish batting, hitting seven sixes and eight fours. There was even a lost ball when one Pepper six ended up in the top of the outer members' reserve. Several others landed in nearby Stanley Street when Pepper took a liking to the leg-spin bowling of Queensland's Bill Tallon (brother of Don), who was renowned for his stuttering and endless swearing. This encounter led to one of Australian cricket's most-told stories.

Tallon said after being continually belted by Pepper that he was the only cricketer to ever 'get a f-f-f-ucking s-s-s-s sunburnt roof to my f-f-f-ucking mouth'.

To add to the pain, one of Pepper's huge hits was dropped by a fielder on the boundary.

'H-h-h-hard luck son,' stuttered Tallon. 'B-b-b-but don't w-w-w-worry. Anyone would d-d-drop a b-b-b-bloody ball covered in f-f-fucking snow.'

Pepper's time in the Middle East and New Guinea, which involved stints as a military policeman and the 2/3 Australian Field Company in the Middle East and New Guinea was generally hazard free. He even had time to marry Maurine Ford in 1943 at the Imperial Hotel in Wagga Wagga, where she was working at the time. While in the Middle East, he became one of the AIF's most reliable players, hitting a century in 24 minutes on a soft Palestine wicket. He followed that up when preparing for New Guinea in northern Queensland in 1943 with a century in less than half an hour in Charters Towers. Ten sixes and several lost balls were part of the package.

By Pepper's side as they strode towards Eastbourne was Whitington, another first-class cricketer who as one of Australia's most prolific, controversial and erratic cricket writers was instrumental in ensuring the feats of these wartime players were not forgotten.

The Whitingtons were a notable South Australian family, featuring solicitors, journalists, businessmen, political correspondents, authors, accountants, musicians and arch-deacons.

The family's best cricketer enjoyed being a bit of a troublemaker. Attending Scotch College before studying law at Adelaide University, this tall, somewhat defensive opening batsman made the South Australian Sheffield Shield team in 1932–33, where he enjoyed the captaincy of the worldly Vic Richardson. He wasn't so enamoured with Richardson's successor — Bradman. They tussled for decades. Whitington became one of Bradman's harshest critics.

He was also soon at odds with cricketing administrators. After a South Australia–NSW game in Sydney, Whitington became ill with tonsillitis. He was supposed to play in a two-day match with his colleagues in Broken Hill on the way home to Adelaide, but obtained permission from a Sydney doctor to return directly to Adelaide so he could be admitted to hospital.

Whitington decided to save the South Australian Cricket Association 'considerable expense' by taking his £3 allowance for the last three days of the tour and paying his own medical expenses. SACA wasn't impressed with that, demanding the £3, and was also angered that Whitington later complained of how he had been treated.

He was an Adelaide social butterfly, with his marriage to Peggy Dale in December 1939 making headlines in *The News*, as did details of their 'most attractive flat at Belair, just opposite the water tower', where there was a marvellous 'panorama of the city, with its myriad of twinkling lights at night'.

This marriage didn't twinkle for too long. Joining the 2/27th Battalion in April 1940, Whitington served in the Middle East, but also appeared to have done intelligence work during a lengthy

Western Australian stint. While in Perth, he met Jean Drake-Brockman, a socialite from a well-known Western Australian grazing family, and in June 1944 they married — he and Peggy having divorced in 1942. Adding to the confusion, his war papers state that he was also married to an Alison Margaret Whitington. Cricket provided a relief for the ever-entangled R.S.W.

At Eastbourne, Whitington met up with numerous RAAF cricketing notables, including NSW wicketkeeper Stan Sismey.

'Stan the Stoic' was born in Junee and educated in Goulburn, before moving to Sydney and playing for the Western Suburbs club. Just before the war, he took over from Frank Easton as NSW wicketkeeper. Test representation was a serious possibility, but he had to delay that to join the RAAF.

As with many Australian pilots, Sismey received advanced training in Canada. He then joined the crew of a Catalina flying boat, which was shot down by Vichy French forces 35 kilometres north of Algiers. The crew, of which Sismey was the co-pilot, was forced to land in the sea, and escaped before the Catalina sunk. For many hours, the crew waited for someone to pluck them out of the water, believing they would be picked up by the enemy and placed in an internment camp on the African coast. But a British destroyer, HMS *Ithuriel*, picked up their SOS signal, and the crew, including an unconscious Sismey with shrapnel through his back and right shoulder, was on its way to Gibraltar.

On the danger list for a week, Sismey, with fragments still in his body that regularly and painfully came to the surface, cutting through his skin, gradually recovered and was transferred to Britain, where within four months he was flying again, primarily as an instructor. And he still had time to play in Services matches in England.

With him was Ross Stanford, one of Australia's most courageous fighter pilots, who was also a childhood cricketing prodigy. The son of Adelaide market gardeners, Stanford in 1931 received worldwide publicity when as a 14-year-old he scored 416 not out for Lockleys Primary School against Richmond Primary. This was recognised as a world record for the highest score by a schoolboy.

Stanford's first-class debut was less celebratory. In March 1936 he waited for an eternity to play his initial Sheffield Shield innings as the South Australian captain, Bradman, was annihilating an average Tasmanian bowling attack at Adelaide Oval. As Bradman progressed to a triple century, Stanford finally got to the wicket with South Australia at 4–533. His first shot went into the covers, and he scurried down the pitch to be easily run out for nought.

That was Stanford's one and only Shield appearance before the war.

After enlisting in the RAAF, Stanford joined the RAF's No 617 Squadron, where he was involved in 23 operational trips. This was followed by 24 missions with the Special Duties (Dambusters) squadron, where he was awarded the Distinguished Flying Cross. Stanford was involved in numerous crucial operations, including acting as a decoy during the D-Day invasion of Normandy, as well as bombing railway tunnels in the days after the landing. He had some narrow escapes, such as when his bomber lost two engines and all hydraulics on a trip to a rocket site in the Pas-de-Calais area. He was also part of the first squadron to drop the 12,000 lb 'Tallboy' bombs. Whenever Stanford could, he played cricket, becoming a close ally of Sismey's.

Sismey had taken over the RAAF cricket team's leadership from Keith Carmody, after Carmody's arrival was delayed due to the trials of suddenly becoming a POW.

Carmody was from a tough background. He grew up in one of Sydney's now prestigious suburbs, Mosman, in the 1930s, but at the time it was an area badly affected by the effects of the world depression. The Carmody family, which ran a small boot and shoe shop, struggled to survive. Not helping was that several members of the family, including Keith's father, drank away most of their earnings. To escape, Keith headed to cricket training at the nearby Mosman Oval, now named Allan Border Oval. This lad, who had learnt to play hitting a ball on a string hanging from a peach tree, would in time develop into one of the deepest and clearest thinkers of the game.

He made his first-class debut for NSW on the same day that Cec Pepper was belting balls out of the Gabba ground, but his appearance was less spectacular. He was bowled for a duck. After four more appearances for NSW, Carmody, who had qualified as an accountant, joined the Air Force Reserve and went to North America for training, becoming a pilot officer in October 1942, receiving his 'wings' from the celebrated Canadian Great War pilot Billy Bishop.

Carmody transferred to England as a flying officer, joined 461 Squadron RAAF, where he made his first flight in June 1943. When not in the air, he was often persuaded to play for the RAAF cricket side. He was soon a central cog of that team, while also captaining a Dominions XI that included Keith Miller and West Indian Learie Constantine at Lord's in August. That winter he also played rugby in the Cumberland district.

In 1944 Carmody was at the centre of one of world cricket's most important conversations when he explained for the first time his innovation — the umbrella field. In the bar at the Strand Palace Hotel in London, where the RAAF cricketers were staying, Carmody told fellow New South Welshmen Stan Sismey and Mick Roper about his idea of a cordon of fielders behind the wicket — five in the slips on the off side and three on the legside — to take any batsman's edge. Carmody told his teammates how he had been infuriated by so many batsmen's 'snicks' going through the slips cordon for easy runs. He showed them his diagrams of the umbrella field, and it was soon adopted.

Returning to flying duties, on 13 June Carmody was above the Dutch coast on anti-E-boat patrol covering the sea approaches to Great Britain when hit by enemy fire while attacking an armed trawler. Carmody alerted the other crews that he had suffered engine damage and 'would have to ditch', then disappeared. The rest of the formation went searching for Carmody's Beaufighter, but soon left the enemy area. Carmody's crew was reported as 'missing'.

Carmody and his navigator, Bill Bullen, had to crash land after the plane was hit with flak. As oil poured from the starboard engine, Carmody, who suffered facial injuries when thrown forward and hitting the gun sights, successfully ditched the wrecked aircraft. He escaped quickly enough to salvage and get into a rescue dinghy. Twenty-three hours later he and Bullen were found by a German R Boat and interrogated. After five days locked in a room without ventilation, Carmody was taken to Stalag Luft III at Sagan, 150 kilometres south-east of Berlin.

To overcome the drudgery of POW life, Carmody organised softball and baseball matches, but most crucially became the overseer of cricket games, a role which, apart from involving coaching, playing and organising, included being the curator of a rough and ready camp wicket. Soon Australia–England Test matches were being played on Carmody's pitch, where he enjoyed several sizeable innings in the middle order. This was something for him to look forward to, especially as he was constantly placed on latrine duty.

Carmody kept getting moved around, including to the Luckenwalde prison camp, where he was kept with 16,000 prisoners from nine different countries, struggling with lack of food, substandard amenities and frostbite. Adding to the turmoil were the repeated marches, some as long as 250 kilometres, in blizzards. This, and the depression of numerous stretches in solitary confinement, took its toll on Carmody. He was constantly fighting the black dog.

Gradually life improved when the Allies in 1945 gained the ascendency over the Germans. Food provisions picked up. Then, in April, a Russian tank burst through the Luckenwalde camp's barbed wire, and they were rescued.

Weeks of exasperation followed as Carmody was detained by the Russians in a concentration camp, where he fretted over the possibility of being sent to Siberia, until eventually in May, with the aid of American forces, he was back in London. On seeing his Australian mates in England he became very emotional, explaining that he felt 'a bit round the bend'. From then on, Carmody was known by his mates as 'Bendy'.

CHAPTER 17

THE MOST TESTING OF TOURS

Mateship was crucial to Keith Ross Miller. He never forgot a name or face. He cherished those he knew he could rely on if there was trouble in the trenches.

There are endless examples of how seriously this intensely loved figure believed in camaraderie, such as when he decided to join the air force. At the start of the war, Miller was reasonably well known around Melbourne. He was in the Victorian Sheffield Shield team as a batsman, but more importantly, in a VFL-drenched city, was a promising footballer with St Kilda.

Miller knew how to look after himself. As Collingwood captain Lou 'Louie the Lip' Richards said of the Saints defender: 'Keith would knock your head off at the drop of a hat.'

But Miller didn't ask for any special treatment when joining the army motor transport division in 1940. He was soon in trouble, fined ten shillings for 'using indecent language to a superior officer'.

At least he enjoyed some aspects of army camp, especially as it was based at Caulfield Racecourse, which appealed to his lifelong love of betting on the horses. He was allowed to sneak off some days, hop over the fence, and put bets on for various soldiers, including his commanding sergeant. It didn't help their meagre finances. They usually lost.

With his mate John Hosking he decided to join the navy as 'a stoker'. Miller was accepted, but Hosking wasn't. Miller was furious, and decided to walk away from the navy and instead join the Royal Australian Air Force. He later said it was among the best decisions he had made in his life.

What also convinced Miller to join the air force was the exploits of his close Melbourne High School mate and mentor Keith 'Bluey' Truscott. Truscott was Miller's school captain before becoming a member of the Melbourne 1939 and 1940 VFL premiership-winning line-up. Miller was won over by Truscott 'sneaking in a bottle of beer to school, often in front of the headmaster'.

Truscott became Australia's second-highest Australian Second World War ace. Within three months, Truscott had destroyed at least 11 German aircrafts, boasting a Distinguished Flying Cross for courage and determination.

Miller went to Victor Harbor in South Australia for training, determined not to be an air gunner, because he hated being in a confined space. His mark was high enough for him to be a pilot. There was also the prestige of having achieved 'your wings'.

In early 1943 he was on his way to North America, where during a two-month spell at the Miles Standish training base near Boston training as a fighter Mosquito pilot, he saw snow for the first time in his life, discovered martinis and met his future wife — Peg Wagner.

Miller proposed to Peg, she accepted, and, as he departed for Scotland on the *Queen Elizabeth*, promised to return. That sea cruise was notable for a bored Miller discovering another lustful experience — gambling games such as crown and anchor, two-up and poker to while away the time and fill his pockets. Shortly after transferring to Bournemouth, which he classed as 'one of the most beautiful cities' in England, Miller was devastated to discover that Truscott was gone. He had been in a Kittyhawk off the Western Australian coast escorting a Catalina flying boat when he crashed into the sea.

Then Miller escaped death. With a group of locals and trainee pilots who had travelled from North America with him, he had discovered several cosy pubs in Bournemouth that became their second home. One Saturday he was invited to London to play for the RAAF cricket team, led by Keith Carmody, at the Dulwich College ground.

On the way home he discovered a German bomber had attacked Bournemouth, hitting a church spire, which had fallen onto a pub. It was the same pub his mates had gone to for a roast lunch, and if he wasn't playing cricket he would have been with them. Seven of his mates were killed.

The next day, at rollcall, he was marked as missing, as the authorities thought Miller was among those dead. Miller had to scream out 'present' to convince them he was still alive. For years, he kept thinking about that moment, and how cricket had done him a favour.

He repeatedly described it as 'the fortunes of war'. Others called it 'Miller's Luck'.

Not long afterwards he was supposed to be at a London theatre but got waylaid in a West End pub. When the drinking session eventually finished, he discovered the theatre had been destroyed by a V-1 flying bomb.

The RAAF cricket appearances continued, including visits to Lord's, which he thought was 'a crummy little ground', and an initial encounter with Denis Compton.

In a game between an England XI and Dominions, Miller was fifth change bowler, and Compton turned to keeper Stan Sismey and asked: 'What does this fellow do?'

'He's not really a bowler at all,' Sismey replied. 'He just chances his arm.' After flicking his hair back, Miller came bounding in and bounced one past Compton's brow. Compton said it was the fastest ball he had faced since batting against Ernie McCormick during the 1938 Ashes series.

Miller was also chancing his arm with authority, having to do hard labour for several weeks at the RAF camp after threatening to belt an over-bloated British officer who baited him with stupid remarks. Miller detested the British class system — how it protected the incompetent, and how upper-class twits looked down on the colonials.

There were other mishaps, including flying a Beaufighter on a night exercise when suddenly the instruments stopped working. He negotiated the plane home, reporting the aircraft to mechanics as unserviceable. An hour later another pilot, Jock Meek, flew the same plane, but just after becoming airborne informed base there was something wrong with the instruments. He was directed back to base, but crashed at the end of the runway and was killed.

After one operation in France, Miller misjudged the landing and almost ended up in the hangar. There was a similar close escape when after attacking a German field, one of the Mills bombs had not dropped during the flight, and luckily did not explode when he landed the plane. He could have easily been blown up. More 'Miller's Luck'.

Another time a joy flight on a trainer plane made of laminated wood went awry when, after Miller had attempted stunts above the aerodrome, one wing nearly hit the ground and flames started to spit out of the starboard engine. He was forced to belly-land the plane, which was 'a write-off'. As the ground crew rushed to see if Miller was fine, he replied: 'Nearly stumps drawn that time, gents.' An hour later he was playing soccer with his mates. But the 'jolting and careering' while landing the damaged plane had injured his back. This ailment never went away for the rest of his sporting career.

Maybe his slapdash attitude, which saw one colleague argue that every Miller landing 'was a close shave', is why he wasn't involved in any serious manoeuvres until April–May 1945. Then he was involved in two dangerous missions — an attack on a German stronghold in Denmark, and attacks on two aerodromes, Jagel, on the German mainland, and Westerland, on the island of Sylt in the North Sea.

The constant near misses did affect him, especially when told another pilot and close mate, Bill Newton, had suffered a terrible fate in New Guinea. Newton, a promising St Kilda pace bowler, played one game for the Victorian Second XI at the MCG in January 1939 alongside Miller against NSW. Newton took three wickets in the match, including those of future Test keeper

Ron Saggers and a young Arthur Morris, batting at No 8. Miller described Newton as 'a big, handsome strapping bloke'.

Miller had also played with Newton in the Victorian Cricket Association (VCA) team. Newton gained notoriety when, before a 1938 match against Melbourne, he said he would dismiss Bill Ponsford, and cheaply. He put up a wager of five shillings. Miller had him on. Newton won the money. He had Ponsford caught behind for four.

Newton flew Boston light bombers, and from his completed 52 operational sorties was known as 'The Firebug' for leaving big fires behind him.

In March 1943 Newton was attacking the Japanese near Salamaua in New Guinea when he dived through intense shellfire. Although constantly hit, Newton kept his course, destroying buildings and fuel installations. Although his plane was badly damaged, he flew it back to base.

The following day Newton targeted another building in the area. However, this time his aircraft burst into flames. Newton turned the aircraft away, landing it in the sea so his crew could escape. Newton's escape hatch did not open, but he was eventually able to prise his way out. He had trouble inflating his dinghy, but somehow swam to shore. Captured by the Japanese, after being subjected to continual torture and interrogation for 11 days, Newton was beheaded. His body was recovered when Australian troops recaptured Salamaua several months later. Newton was posthumously awarded the Victoria Cross.

Miller was devastated by Newton's death. He would later tell people that the often-published photograph of an Australian soldier about to be beheaded by a Japanese executioner was of Newton. It wasn't.

He also had to overcome the shock of arriving at one RAAF game in London to discover that Ken Ridings, who was supposed to be his captain, had just been killed.

Maybe that's why he had to be pushed hard to talk about his war reminiscences. He knew there were greater heroes than him. He would constantly say his war was modest.

Miller had to be coaxed into discussing his war years, and when he did it was more to highlight the courage of others. He was reviving their memories, not his own.

But Miller relished talking about the Australian Services team. Those months were deeply cherished. He repeatedly described, including during interviews with the author, the Victory Tests as the most exciting, entertaining and best quality cricket he played in. This was because it was again peacetime, and everyone was involved for the right reason — revelling in playing cricket again.

He thought the resumption of Test cricket led to a negative 'dog eat dog' attitude, and he disliked those who took it far too seriously. As far as Miller was concerned, Bradman was in that category.

Whitington, who for some time was Miller's ghost-writer, described the Victory series as 'the happiest, friendliest, yet one of the most exciting and eventful ever played between England and Australia'.

Crucial to the Victory Tests success was Miller's involvement. He gave it a broad sex appeal — presenting an attractive, alluring figure which everyone was intrigued by and wanted to witness in person. He was the crowd attraction. Females, as well as men, swooned.

The concept was well organised. Plum Warner, with help from Sismey, oversaw the England side of the operation, while Australia wisely appointed Keith Johnson team manager and organiser. Johnson had deep cricketing roots, hailing from the Mosman club in Sydney, and for several years was a NSW delegate on the Australian Board of Control. A welfare officer for the RAAF, he was seconded to take over the Services team. It was a masterstroke, with *Wisden Cricketers' Almanack* later praising Johnson for his astute handling of the players' match schedule.

Even more important was who would be captain. There was strong support for Sismey or Carmody, but Hassett, due to his Test status, was given the job. Miller admitted there was originally resentment among the RAAF contingent, which provided the most members to the Services team, about Hassett's appointment, believing Carmody should have been chosen. However, Carmody, still overcoming the psychological traumas of being a POW, never objected to Hassett being the skipper. The players knew Hassett had not pursued the captaincy, so he soon gained their respect. Carmody was instead a team selector, alongside Hassett, Sismey, Whitington and Mick Roper — smartly melding the army representatives with those from the air force.

Adding to the Hassett debate was that as a warrant officer class II he was outranked by everyone else in the team. Hassett was offered a commission when appointed Services captain but, despite General Sir Thomas Blamey's backing, refused the promotion as he did not believe it was appropriate to his military duties.[58] That again impressed the RAAF contingent, even though officials at its London head office continued to apply pressure, believing Carmody should take over after the second Victory Test.

Arthur Morris, Ray Lindwall, Ian Johnson, Colin McCool and Bill Brown were considered, but overlooked as they were involved in fighting on the other side of the globe.

Their 'medicine man' — Larry Maddison — was an intriguing addition. One of the Rats of Tobruk, Mentioned in Despatches at El Alamein, he was a part-time wrestler. Maddison's war experiences were chequered, constantly in trouble for missing patrols, disappearing from camps and causing a disturbance. A knockabout, he was approached to be the team's physical fitness advisor and masseur.

'So I said: "That'll be alright. How long is it gonna be?" They said: "Not long." I was still with them 14 months later,' Maddison said in an oral interview which is in the Australian War Memorial archives.

After the army, being surrounded by cricketers was a relief. 'It wasn't regimented. There were no orders. Hassett never said: "Right you do this?" Or somebody said: "You do that." It was a sporting venture,' he said.

'And we were well looked after. There was not an abundance of food in England. They were still on rations. We were lucky because ... when we were with the AIF Reception Unit, our

---

58 Blamey also threw Hassett one time when he asked the skipper: 'Are you a bowler or wicketkeeper?'

canteens were supplied with comfort fund stuff, so we had wine and tinned ham and all that sort of stuff.'

Maddison's massage table was in constant use during the Victory series, working on players from both teams, with England's Len Hutton and Wally Hammond regular clients.

Maddison came up with a smart idea of adding protection to Sismey's batting gloves after he had hurt his thumb while batting during one of the Victory Tests. Maddison placed two bottle tops along the front of the thumb of the glove and another on the tip, binding them with adhesive plaster.

'I had been hit hard on the thumb, but it was important that I batted,' Sismey told the author. 'So we taped two or three bottle tops to my thumb, and I went out to bat. It didn't work, as I was out shortly after.'

It wasn't the only problem Sismey had to overcome during the series. He sometimes left the field when pieces of shrapnel worked their way to the skin surface, causing huge abscesses that had to be surgically removed.

The Services team members weren't exactly treated as special citizens either, getting no more than their usual army or RAAF pay. Unlike the 1919–20 AIF team, each member of which received a lump sum of £150 and an occasional share of gate takings, the Services side captain received just 12 shillings a day.

They were up against a considerable opposition. England fielded ten Test players — Bill Edrich, Cyril Washbrook, Wally Hammond, Len Hutton, Laurie Fishlock, Doug Wright, Les Ames, Alf Gover, Errol Holmes and Walter Robins and many who made the Test side after the war — Jack Robertson, Billy Griffith, Dick Pollard, George Pope, Donald Carr and John Dewes. But the Australian authorities refused to go as far as giving these matches Test status.

That Australia drew the series 2–all was testimony to the skill and camaraderie among the visitors. 'We were never overawed,' Sismey told the author.

Whitington wouldn't go that far, admitting that in the Australian players' hearts was 'a deep and haunting misgiving that they might all make fools of themselves'.

Then again, they all got on well, because at most grounds the teams shared the dressing rooms, leading to lifelong friendships. Obtaining cricket gear proved difficult due to rationing, and on numerous occasions players would walk onto the field without any socks.

But some received preferential treatment. Miller became great mates with Jack O'Shea, the Lord's dressing room attendant, who secured for him a special corner, and more importantly a little known shower he could use. Miller had no interest in frolicking in the Lord's bathtub.

The First Victory Test at Lord's was special for Graham Williams getting another standing ovation and scoring a half-century. The crowd, which included its fair share of Australian soldiers proudly wearing their AIF or RAAF regalia, began queueing outside the ground before 5am. As soon as the gates were opened, they rushed to take positions around a ground that they had only read about. Like the players, the Australian spectators were in a state of wonderment. A few weeks ago they were fighting. Now they were applauding their cricketing heroes — most importantly from their own ranks. They celebrated hard, with the members' bar running out of beer as Miller scored a century, which ultimately saw them winning by six wickets.

The Cricketer magazine, explaining that the £1935 made from gate takings would be divided between the Red Cross and RAAF funds, said it 'was as good a game of cricket as ever was played'. C.B. Fry was 'surprised and disappointed to notice how little prominence was given to this truly sporting and truly dramatic event in our great London press'.

Londoners knew all about it, though, with 66,560 paying a shilling each to see Miller and co.

For the second Victory Test, at Bramall Lane in Sheffield, German POWs cleaned up the premises, and again the teams shared a dressing room as the pavilion had been taken over by government officials.

It was Hammond's turn to score a century, while Miller tried to provoke Hutton with a rising delivery that hit him and ricocheted to fine leg. Hutton struggled to get to the other end, and Miller could have run him out. Instead he went over and rubbed Hutton where he had been hit. That didn't stop some in the crowd moaning: 'Come on Larwood.'

He had already stirred up Hutton before the innings when sighting the England opener in the dressing room combing his hair, saying: 'Good, Len. If you can't be a batsman at least try and look like one.'

The English spectators also kept their players on edge. Cec Pepper produced a beautiful cover drive which Surrey captain Errol Holmes, with a spiffing cream cravat around his throat, let through his legs.

A crusty Yorkshireman yelled: 'What's that around the neck? … Cravat or noose? Whatever it is, sir, tighten it.'

Australia lost by 41 runs.

In the Lord's broadcasting booth for the next two Victory Tests was one of Australia's most remarkable war correspondents, Chester Wilmot. Wilmot's war had been frenetic, covering North African battles, the disastrous Greek campaign, the Kokoda Track, and the Normandy landing. His fearless writing and broadcasting for the ABC and BBC received worldwide praise.

Chester also loved cricket. It was a family trait, as his father, R.W.E. 'Bung' Wilmot, was for half a century a sportswriter and athletics editor for *The Argus* and *The Australasian* newspapers in Melbourne. He covered overseas Australian cricket tours and wrote the book *Defending the Ashes*.

Wilmot's role in covering the cricket deeply irritated his arch-enemy, General Sir Thomas Blamey. The pair were involved in a long feud after Wilmot attempted to expose Blamey over numerous questionable wartime acts. Wilmot thought Blamey an incompetent crook. In retaliation, Blamey attempted to cancel Wilmot's war accreditation.

Wilmot ignored him and gladly took up the ten guineas a day on offer to provide cricket reports for BBC radio and a later summary for Australia. He told the audience on the opening day that despite the 'threat of thunder … it hadn't deterred the enthusiast'.

'Before 11.30 there must have been 15,000 people waiting at Lord's, and they included many thousands of Australian airmen and troops — most of the Diggers are ex-prisoners of war, who're waiting to go home,' Wilmot began in his daily report.

Wilmot gave a detailed report of what had happened during the day's play. This time it was Hutton who received all the plaudits for a first-innings century, but Australia rallied to win by four wickets. But the toll of age and war began to show. Hammond couldn't bat in the second innings due to lumbago, and Miller's bowling was restricted by a back complaint resulting from his recent failed daredevil flight. Masseur Maddison was suddenly in hot demand.

In between the Tests, the players were involved in countless matches and Miller was still making the occasional flight, but all assembled almost three weeks later for the fourth Victory match in early August, again at Lord's. In the interim, Winston Churchill's Conservative Party lost the general election, with the public believing Labor would bring an end to austerity and decades of gloom. A brighter, more utilitarian society was the prime hope.

The dignitaries, including the new Prime Minister, Clement Attlee, and the country's most revered soldier, Bernard 'Monty' Montgomery, were guests in the MCC president's box, but their viewing was interrupted by rain. It didn't deter the 35,000, sitting ten to 12 deep inside the fence, who gladly sat in the constant drizzle. Wilmot broadcast that the crowd experienced 'almost a tropical squall. One flash of lightning seemed to strike at the wicket itself and the claps of thunder reminded us of the cricket played last year in the days of the buzz bomb.'

Several cricket writers were close to being knocked out when huge pieces of plaster fell from the ceiling of the press box. Miller and Washbrook scored centuries, but again the good spirit between the two teams came to the fore.

Sismey, while wicketkeeping, left the field to have stitches inserted in a wound after getting hit under the chin. Jim Workman, who often opened for the Services team but had never kept before, was handed the gloves, and struggled. Carmody, who had some keeping experience, was 12th man.

Hammond, the England captain, approached Hassett and said that he would allow Carmody to keep wickets. Hassett was surprised, as he thought the laws of cricket forbade such a replacement, but gratefully took up the offer. This was one of many examples of the strong camaraderie between the two teams.

Carmody kept for the rest of the game, which ended in a draw.

The series finished at Old Trafford, where once again German POWs, paid three farthings an hour, transformed a war-battered ground into something substantial by the time the players arrived in late August. A German signwriter fixed up the scoreboard.

Before the final Victory Test, Sismey had time to get married to his Scottish fiancée, Elma McLachlan, a WAAF. Earlier in the tour they had been introduced to each other by Miller.

Miller told Sismey: 'Look after her. Hope you do better than me!'

Carmody was Sismey's best man.

Again thousands missed out on getting into the ground, but those who did, including a group of five-shilling fans who refused to move from a more expensive area of the ground, gorged themselves on pork pies, beer, beer and more beer.

The highlight was Bob Cristofani showing off his considerable all-round skills. His impressive leg-spinning capabilities had some in NSW before the war describing him as the next Grimmett. Old Trafford discovered his talents when the RAAF pilot officer took five England first innings wickets, including Hammond and Washbrook. Batting at No 8 in the second innings, he found an able ally in Graham Williams, combining in a 95-run ninth-wicket partnership. Williams, still requiring glucose drinks to keep him going during the day, was the minor partner, scoring 12. Cristofani flashed away and scored to all parts of the boundary.

On the other side of the world, English cricket writer E.W. Swanton had just been released from a POW camp and 'taken my first walk for three and a half years as a free man'.

'We found ourselves in a Thai village on the edge of the jungle. In the little café our hosts politely turned on the English programme. Yes, we were at Old Trafford, and a gentleman called

Cristofani was getting a hundred ...' Swanton wrote in the 1946 *Wisden*.

Cristofani's gallant unbeaten 110 wasn't enough to stop England from winning by six wickets. R.C. Robertson-Glasgow said in *The Observer* that, while England won, 'the match belonged to Cristofani'.

Whitington believed Cristofani's innings was one even Victor Trumper would have been proud of.

For this drawn series, Miller led the Australian batting average with 443 runs at 63.28. Cristofani, apart from his batting feats, was the most successful bowler, with 14 wickets at 15.21. By winning half of their matches over a four-month period, the players thought their job was done. Now it was time to get home and see loved ones.

No — the military and Australian governmental powers had other ideas. They wanted to squeeze as much as they could from these money-spinners. Miller, along with Jack Pettiford, Pepper, Cristofani, Williams and Reg Ellis were picked to play in a Dominions team, alongside New Zealander Martin Donnelly, flamboyant West Indian Learie Constantine and South African Desmond Fell against England.

What made this game special was that on the morning of the match Hassett withdrew as he wanted the captaincy to go to Constantine as it was to be his last first-class match. To hand the leadership to a black player ahead of numerous notable white cricketers was a radical, historic step. It was only two years after Constantine had been barred from staying at a London hotel near Lord's by a hotel manager who said that being 'a nigger' (the term used by that hotel manager) would offend other guests.[59]

Warner, as Dominions manager, made the captaincy decision. As Constantine was the most senior international cricketer in the team, Warner thought him the obvious choice, but thought it better to pass it by the rest of the team. Miller's positive

---

59 Constantine had booked rooms and paid a deposit; he sued Imperial Hotels Ltd for breach of contract and won.

support was critical in ensuring Constantine led the team out on the field.

Miller became even more of a cricketing matinee idol by belting 185 in 165 minutes, including seven sixes, one of which lodged in the small roof of the broadcasting box above the England players' dressing room. Constantine followed Miller's example and, urged on by the crowd, hit two sixes during their 91-run partnership in 35 minutes. The game was an unqualified triumph.

The 1946 *Wisden Cricketers' Almanack* described a match where the Dominions scored the required runs with eight minutes to spare as 'one of the finest ever seen'. While Miller was the undisputed king of Lord's, scoring 548 runs in eight innings, twice not out, including three centuries and an average of 91.33, the Australian Services squad had emerged as memorable ambassadors and promoters of their craft.

Now they would be stretched to the limits. They had to fly the flag in India and Ceylon.

Bert Evatt, an even bigger cricket fan than Curtin, as evidenced by his long involvement in NSW cricket administration, was the chief instigator of the tour being extended. After being approached by Indian government officials, Evatt contacted Lieutenant General Edward Smart, Australia's representative on the Imperial War Council, about the positives of the team stopping off in India and Ceylon. Smart met with Blamey, and they convinced the Minister for the Army and later Prime Minister, Frank Forde, to 'issue directions that the team should be kept together and moved to Australia as a unit'.

The only problem was that the players weren't consulted. They had heard a whisper of an invitation from South Africa to tour their country on the way home, but were relieved that was knocked back. Not all were enthused to be heading to India and beyond, but at least realised it was one step closer to eventually getting home.

There was brief respite on the ship, before discovering the Indian cricket authorities had organised the most demanding schedule — nine matches, including three unofficial Tests — in 44 days. The players would remain on normal Service wages, but during the 29 days of play they 'may be paid £1 per diem to meet additional personal expenses'.

The Australian Army issued each player with the edict: 'This tour is being arranged as a goodwill gesture — also to foster good cricket relations with India. All ranks are asked to remember they are the representatives of Australia, and it is expected that their conduct at all times will be exemplary.'

Sismey was 'responsible for discipline and administration throughout the tour'. He had to report to Sir Iven Mackay, the Australian High Commissioner in India, and keep him 'informed of the movements of the Services team'. All profits had to be handed over to Mackay.

After a grand welcome in Bombay in October from Prince Kumar Shri Duleepsinhji — who played 12 Tests for England between the wars and was now head of the local cricket association — the tour, which revolved around a ridiculous travel schedule, began to derail. It involved countless long, uncomfortable train journeys so that they could play in Lahore, New Delhi, Bombay, Poona, Calcutta and Madras. Now they wouldn't be getting home until at least the New Year.

Suddenly travelling to South Africa sounded far more tantalising. Tempers soon rose, especially when their Bombay-to-Lahore train trip took 42-and-a-half hours. Then there was a 12-hour trip to New Delhi on a crowded, noisy, dirty train in which the players sat wherever they could after their original carriage was damaged when a shunting engine ran into it. They were kept awake all trip due to a zealous driver who merrily tooted his whistle every time he sighted a cow near the tracks. There were thousands of cows near the tracks.

At least there was a welcoming face at the other end — meeting them at New Delhi was Vic Richardson, in Whitington's words 'iron fit and deeply tanned by the joint effect of [anti-malarial] Atebrin and sunshine'.

On another train trip they endured an invasion of monkeys, while there were problems with dysentery and appalling hometown umpiring. A seething Cristofani walked off after one dreadful decision when Imtiaz Ahmed refused to leave the crease after edging the ball to second slip. Hassett had to coax Cristofani back onto the field. Later the fast-medium bowler Mick Roper openly accused the umpires of cheating. This outburst led to the umpire demanding Roper be immediately taken out of the attack. Hassett didn't mind. Roper needed a rest anyway. Shortly after, Roper was taken to hospital with a high temperature. Adding to the distress was that several players struggled to cope with the confronting environment, the squalor, the slums and the endless crowds.

While a flock of vultures flew above the pavilion, Miller, suffering with the runs, had to counter a swarm of huge wasps. Hassett told a furiously waving Miller: 'They must be females.'

Miller grinned for a second before bolting off for another toilet stop.

The Australians remonstrated when several Indian teams adopted bodyline tactics and fields, as well as when Indian XI captain Vijay Merchant opted for painfully negative fields in Bombay, placing nine fielders on the off side and bowling almost half a metre outside off stump.

At least there were occasional moments of gaiety, including luncheon breaks enlivened by Sikh military bands playing marching songs while striding around the ground. Inside the pavilion, the players were entertained by an Indian orchestra playing 'Lili Marlene' and 'Begin the Beguine'. Elsewhere violinists and percussionists would play Chopin, Tchaikovsky and Beethoven.

Hassett and Pepper discovered the danger of loose lips when an Indian reporter printed inflammatory remarks they had made about the umpiring in Lahore. Hassett had also upset India's key player, Mushtaq Ali, by describing him as 'an ugly batsman'.

The pair cleverly bobbed and weaved their way out of that dilemma, arguing the reporter had made up countless quotes attributed to them.

At least they were able to get their side of the story out, as accompanying them for most of the trip was Bill Marien, a *Sydney*

Morning Herald war correspondent. For the *SMH*'s Central Pacific correspondent, this was a welcome relief, as he had for months been an eyewitness to numerous dangerous battles, including at Timor and New Guinea, before being with the US Third Fleet when it retook the Philippines, covering the landings at Okinawa and Iwo Jima, as well as the Japanese surrender. A passionate follower of the Randwick rugby club, Marien had been an ABC war correspondent between 1942 and 1944.

Sometimes Marien's cricket copy was a little astray, or his Indian telex operator was at fault, as suddenly Whitington had a new Christian name in some *SMH* reports — Mick, rather than Dick.

When reporting the first day of the match against West Zone, Marien opted for R.S. Whitington. He was impressed with R.S.'s courage in opening the innings: 'Early in the game, R.S. Whitington had to lie down beside the wicket for a few moments. He was suffering from a "hangover" after an attack of dengue. After five minutes he resumed batting confidently.' R.S. made 23.

Marien delighted in telling Miller and co gripping war battles, particularly as he knew several of their cricketing mates who had been involved in South Pacific skirmishes.

One compelling story Marien did not know about was how close the series was to being postponed due to an attempted midtour coup.

Roper, an RAAF flight pilot who often opened the bowling, was sick of the train travel and told Hassett and manager Johnson they had to go by air. No ifs or buts. He was ignored. Roper called a meeting of his fellow RAAF men and said it was time for drastic action. Either travel by air, or call the rest of the tour off. Also Roper wanted Hassett replaced as captain by Carmody.[60]

---

60 Roper was involved in controversy earlier in the tour when bowling to Gubby Allen. The England batsman chopped the ball into the ground near his crease. The ball rolled towards the stumps. Believing the ball was dead, Allen picked it up and threw it to Roper. Roper appealed to the umpire, believing Allen had been bowled. Allen was dismissed for handling the ball. An infuriated Allen walked off, and even though asked to continue his innings by Miller and Carmody, refused. 'The Australians subsequently stated that they had called me back but the only one who came near me was Keith Miller and he was not captain,' Allen said.

The crisis was averted when Carmody refused to stand against Hassett, and Sismey organised a RAAF freighter plane for their next leg. However, they soon regretted this when the plane which took them from Bombay to Calcutta flew into a violent electrical storm. The only person to enjoy the flight was Miller. The rest were in the brace position, trying to stop themselves from being sick. Delhi belly was bad enough, but this …

At the other end, after the usual official dinners and endless meeting of dignitaries, they were caught up in several political mess-ups. Arriving in Calcutta at the end of a five-day garbage strike, they discovered the dictatorial Australian Board of Control had added more matches to their Australian schedule. Several Australian state associations had approached the Board arguing that Services matches should be central attractions of their 1945–46 season.

The forthright president of the Victorian Cricket Association, Dr Reg Morton, contacted Blamey, calling on him to ensure the team be kept together 'to play one match in each state during the current season'.

Board secretary Bill Jeanes wrote to Forde, arguing: 'First-class cricket, as doubtless you know, has not been played in Australia for several years and it is felt that matches against the services side which has played so well in England would do much to re-establish first-class cricket in Australia, in preparation for the continuation of the Test matches against England.'

Oldfield was also working in the background to make certain it happened, leading to a rift between him and several Services players, who believed he was 'grandstanding'. They scoffed at the irony of Oldfield being appointed as a liaison officer for the Australian leg when one hadn't been required for the more intricate trip through the United Kingdom, India and Ceylon.

Six matches in Australia were scheduled. The players were furious. Roper organised another protest meeting and received unanimous support from his teammates. They weren't going to cop such treatment.

Marien was alerted. The main sport story in the 10 December 1945 edition of the *SMH* was headlined: 'Cricketers say home tour "unreasonable".'

Marien wrote from Madras that the Services cricketers had asked manager Keith Johnson to cable the Australian Board of Control 'pointing out that, in their opinion, the scheduled tour of Australia is unreasonable and drastic'.

'The players objected strongly to the fact that in Perth they are called upon to play on Christmas Day, and that the Adelaide, Melbourne, Sydney and Brisbane games are of four days duration instead of three. The men feel that they have already played more continuous cricket than any other combination previously, that the Indian tour has been more than strenuous, that if the Indian tour is followed by an equally laborious Australian tour, their cricket will suffer as well as their health,' Marien wrote.

In the United Kingdom they had played match after match between May and October, 'including one period in Scotland when they played eight games in different centres on eight consecutive days'.

'Here, too, the cricket has been most strenuous, and the men are certain that the Australian Board of Control has not fully realised just how much strenuous cricket has been played, with very little chance of relaxation away from the game. Already, many of the team are obviously stale.'

The players had approached Johnson in the dressing room during the Madras 'Test', following a protest meeting.

Johnson sent the cable to the ABC, but the complaints were ignored.

Then there was the subject of their own personal safety in India. The push for Indian independence was intensifying, and the Australian players were warned of possible riots while playing at Eden Gardens, especially as England batsman Denis Compton, stationed with the British Army in India, was in the opposing East Zone team.

After lighting fires outside the ground and in the stands, rioters invaded the pitch. In two lines they marched towards Compton as he approached his century. Sismey told the author that the riot leader said: 'You play very fine innings for us Mr Compton, but you must go. Five of our friends have been shot by the British police.'

Compton pointed towards Hassett. 'You'd better speak to Mr Hassett. He's the captain. He's in charge of the field.'

Hassett was standing next to the masseur, Maddison, who, sensing trouble, had run onto the field to provide physical support. Hassett greeted the riot leader with a broad smile.

'You wouldn't happen to have a cigarette, would you, old boy?'

That calmed the situation. The protesters went through their pockets for cigarettes and matches. Eventually the mob dispersed, and the game continued. From that day onward, whenever Miller saw Compton his greeting was: 'You very good batsman Mr Compton ... but you must go.'

The stay in Calcutta was also notable for Hassett buying a green parrot at a streetside market. Hassett brought the parrot back to the team hotel, where he proudly displayed it on his arm.

Unbeknown to Hassett, the parrot was sedated. Next morning there were screams for help from Hassett's room when the now volatile parrot, undrugged and nasty, was attacking him. The parrot soon disappeared.

In another match, Hassett was speechless when again encountered by rioters. Several thousand anti-British-rule protesters hopped the fence and surrounded Vijay Merchant, telling him: 'Mr Merchant, if this game goes on, we'll burn your house down.' They confronted an official: 'Mr Leslie, we'll burn your house down.'

Next was Hassett. 'And Mr Hassett, if you had a house here, we'd burn that down, too!'

After a quick visit to Ceylon, where even though most were suffering from dysentery they enjoyed an easy win in Colombo, an exhausted band was at last on its way home — for some their first glimpse of Australia in five years. Again it wasn't luxury travelling to Perth. Miller convinced an Australian pilot to take them home in a battered York bomber which had its fair share of bullet holes. The players had to sit on a ledge along the side of the plane. As disconcerting was Miller arriving with six black trunks. Worried it would overweigh the plane, the crew told Miller that he had to leave most of it behind, until he informed them that the trunks were all empty — as they were family gifts.

By this time a completely exhausted and sick-of-cricket entourage, who had not been in their home country for three, four or five years, was easy prey for Australian opponents eager to put them in their place. Miller could not bowl at full stretch as his boots had fallen apart and were being held together by plaster, string and adhesive tape. With it came some pathetic media comments, as well as controversy.

The players had no interest in being friendly with a severe Australian Board of Control especially after it had issued a statement saying the tour program was 'framed after consultations with Major WA Oldfield and representatives of the Services in Australia'.

Sismey wrote: 'At no time had any contact been made with the team itself — rather the team was presented with a "fait-accompli".'

He was also angry authorities had no interest in arranging an incoming voyage for his Scottish wife, who had been left behind for several months. When she did arrive, Mrs Sismey discovered Australia was in many ways like the country she had just left. Rationing of food, including meat and petrol, was in force, there was a housing shortage, and many were on the poverty line.

Adding to the Service players' ire when they arrived in Perth via Cocos Island was that Oldfield was there to greet them. He was soon telling them Bill O'Reilly was bowling like a demon, Bradman was back, Ray Lindwall, who they were going to play against in Sydney, was the fastest bowler going around, and Sid Barnes was scoring a mountain of runs in Sydney grade cricket.

Then the final indignity.

'They've given you a whole day off tomorrow,' Oldfield said to Hassett. The skipper just glared. The only other consolation was that games were cut back from four to three days, and a proposed match against the ACT had been called off.

Sismey said the team was soon infuriated with press criticism that the Services players had become too militant, were whingers, and 'other members of the Services not in the happy position of being cricketers, are still in uniform overseas with no idea of when they will return to Australia'.

It was a cruel way for gallant ex-servicemen to be treated. Little wonder there were sparks when the team had its second game in South Australia and came up against Bradman — another eager to put these players in their place.

Sismey explained many years later to *SMH* sportswriter Phil Wilkins: 'I played against Don in 1939–40, and then he disappeared. Six years later, he reappeared and I'm playing against him again, and he made another century. I remember it clearly. Don made 112 against our Australian Services XI and he was a sick man in all the war years, but he walked out there and batted just like Bradman always batted ... getting runs, hundreds of them.'

It was a Bradman century which the Services believed he didn't deserve. Hometown umpiring once again worked in The Don's favour. But this time it unfairly led to the dramatic upheaval of another cricketer's career and future.

Cec Pepper was one of the Services' most volatile characters. He didn't like Bradman, thinking he was a strutter. Like many of his servicemen colleagues, Pepper was sceptical about Bradman's early departure from the war, especially when he used the moment to improve his business career.

On New Year's Eve, Pepper was bowling to the 37-year-old Bradman at Adelaide Oval when he was in single figures. He tried a few stock leg breaks first up, which Bradman watched warily. Pepper tried his trick ball — the flipper. Bradman misjudged it, with the ball hitting his back pad, right in front of the stumps. Pepper turned and appealed to local umpire Jack Scott. Scott showed no interest. Pepper was aghast.

A few balls later, he tried the flipper once more, and again trapped Bradman in front. Again Pepper appealed. Sismey, the fairest of wicketkeepers, was convinced Bradman was out. Yet again the same response from Scott.

Pepper had had enough, yelling at Scott: 'What do you have to do to get the little bastard out? You're a fucking cheat.'

Bradman heard every word and, as Pepper walked to slip at the end of the over, he approached Scott and said: 'Do we have to put up with this sort of thing, Jack?'

Scott, who worked for the South Australian Cricket Association, had no option but to report Pepper. Pepper knew, due to Bradman's overwhelming influence in Australian cricket, that his cricketing future in this part of the world was effectively over.

The tour finally ended in late January in Tasmania, with a draw that ended the Australian leg with two losses and six draws in their six games. With it came more despairing moments. The team had grown accustomed to pot shots, some more stinging than others. The Sydney *Truth* newspaper delighted in baiting them with such headlines as 'Services Gave Sorry Performances. Bananalanders Made Visitors Look Silly'. Their batting performance in Sydney was described as 'the poorest ... that has been seen on the Cricket Ground for some years'. They regularly read how they were 'write-offs' or over-rated.

When they played Victoria, the *SMH* provided a brief, bitter report, finishing with: 'Their [Services] general bearing yesterday suggested that they had had too much cricket and were sick of the game. There was no evidence of a strong desire to overtake Victoria's huge score.'

What especially hurt was those who should have known better, such as fellow serviceman Sid Barnes, who tried to bring them down with caustic comments. In his autobiography Barnes wrote that the Services team had returned to Australia 'with a big reputation'. 'They were supposed to be full of brilliance and were thought to be on the verge of revolutionising the game back in Australia. They were greatly overboomed.'

Even Neville Cardus, who was in Sydney from 1940 to 1947 primarily as a music critic for the Melbourne *Herald* and *The Sydney Morning Herald*, couldn't resist a dig. In a letter to the *SMH* in January 1946, shortly after the NSW–Services match had finished in a conclusive home victory, Cardus criticised Australian cricketers for complaining about being 'overworked on the field'. They also found 'batting and bowling and all-round play too heavy a strain upon the frail frames of children still only in their twenties'.

Australian players had it easy compared to their English counterparts. 'If Keith Miller, O'Reilly, Lindwall and others were English professionals they would be expected to bowl at least 1000 overs during a four-month season — as well as be ready for tours overseas at the end of it,' Cardus wrote.

This slap infuriated numerous readers. George Garnsey, a former NSW player who became state coach, was furious Services players had been targeted, especially as 'many of the team have participated in active service over Germany, one at least becoming a prisoner'.

'The severe strain of these activities on the mental and physical energies of the participants must be great, and may account for some of the tiredness at which Mr Cardus scoffs. In any case, these lads left a remote part of the Empire to risk their lives for the mother country in the hour of her direst need,' Garnsey wrote.

New Zealand journalist Clarke Bickley[61] added: 'The Australian Services team has been rushed by air from country to country, and even from city to city, with few or no physically and mentally revitalising rest periods.'

'The Services players are tired out,' Bickley wrote.

Cardus tried to backtrack, writing another letter explaining that his previous one 'was a criticism in general and made no allusion to the AIF cricket team'.

But he couldn't resist. 'Never before in the history of the game have cricketers been so well paid and their physical comforts so well looked after. Yet we hear more and more of players leaving the field through "strains" and what-not; and bowlers are "rested" after each has sent down half a dozen or so overs.'

---

61 In 1937, Bickley, the chief reporter for the *Dominion Post* in Wellington, covered the New Zealand cricket team's tour of England. He even played in one tour match against Scotland in Dunfermline, batting at No 10, finishing unbeaten on six. He was later editor of the *Wanganui Herald* and after the war worked for the *SMH*.

Bickley responded by writing that Cardus should not have singled out Miller, Lindwall and O'Reilly. 'Bill O'Reilly, mind you, who bowled 56 overs in one innings of one Test and 85 overs in one innings of another Test in England in 1938. What frailty!'[62]

Considering that over a nine-month period, in often trying conditions and with little rest, Services teams played 64 matches in four vastly different countries, won 26 and only lost 13, this team deserved in Barnes's words to be 'overboomed'. There were numerous excellent individual performances, with Miller and Hassett often holding the batting line-up, while leg-spinner Reg Ellis was a prolific wicket-taker.

During the final match against Tasmania, Whitington wrote an article for *The Mercury*, arguing it was unfair to compare the Services side with the First AIF team. The AIF had the luxury of Jack Gregory, 'probably the greatest all-round player of the century', and five weeks' rest between the England and South African legs, and another five between South Africa and Australia.

'The Services have not finished in a similar blaze of glory,' wrote Whitington, 'first because they have no Gregory and secondly because following their tour of England and their 6,000 mile tour of India, they started their Australian tour of six matches (First AIF played three) after only six days rest instead of five weeks rest.'

Although for justifiable reasons the team petered out in the final stretch, their value to the Australian game should not be underestimated. Mocked ... never.

---

62 Cardus antagonised music followers in his *SMH* columns, especially when discussing the use of the German language during the war. He criticised those who wanted to stop German songs, and upset others for being overly critical of his music reviews. Even one Senator complained in Parliament: 'How much longer are the people of Australia to be pestered with Neville Cardus?' When he left, Cardus wrote to a friend: 'I am sick of Australia ... I have not heard ONE witty remark from an Australian in five and a half years. Dein bin ich, Vater! — rette mich! (Thine am I, father! Rescue me!)'

CHAPTER 18

THE AFTERMATH

Don Bradman understood the link. He believed Australia's two most formidable cricket sides were the 1921 and 1948 teams. That had a great deal to do with each being dominated by those who had recently sacrificed their all in global battles.

Bradman explained: 'Men's finest achievements are when motivated by idealism which sometimes even transcends the rational.'

Yet, after the Second World War it took a while for the sturdy servicemen to take over. The ill-fortunes of the Australian leg of the 1945–46 Services team resulted in backlash. Only two — Miller and Hassett — were selected for the first Australian touring team after the war when a 13-man squad, led by Bill Brown, travelled to New Zealand in March–April 1946.

The original plan was for the Services team to continue on and play in New Zealand, but after witnessing a side on its last legs the authorities at last realised they could not push them any further. Instead a full Australian team was selected, with the prime aim being to test the players' form and fitness before the Ashes series against England later that year.

One to cruelly miss out was Cec Pepper. His spat with Bradman had worked against him. Despite constant suggestions that The Don had demanded he not be picked for the short New Zealand tour as punishment for his abusive language in Adelaide,

Pepper was ultimately discarded by another Australian selector, Chappie Dwyer.

Jack Scott had made a report on the Pepper incident which was referred to the NSW Cricket Association and his own employer — the South Australian Cricket Association. Pepper had made a reply, supposedly written and posted by Whitington, but officials said they never received it. Australian Services manager Keith Johnson tried to save Pepper but failed.

Bradman, who did not tour New Zealand due to health and financial issues, wrote a letter to Dwyer that although dated 25 January 1945 was clearly one year later. On the subject of Pepper's Australian selection, Bradman wrote: 'Rumoured that QCA[63] has also reported him for misconduct in Q v Services match. Try and check on this because as I have previously indicated, I think this position a key one in our selection.' In this letter, Bradman also complained he had 'very bad recurrence in the back'.

On 6 February 1946 Bradman wrote to Dwyer that he was keen on Bruce Dooland 'for I feel that he has great possibilities for the future ... Pepper seems to me the obvious choice for the other bowler, whilst if we are to send 13 men, it looks as though McCool warrants selection for his all-round performances and should be named as 13th.'

Dwyer replied on 8 February, explaining that the NSWCA executive had considered a report from its South Australian counterparts and that NSW selectors were told not to consider Pepper 'until such time as he explains, to their satisfaction, his conduct in South Australia ... In view of the above, I think we should forget this man for New Zealand, even to the risk of losing him to England.'

And they lost him to England.

In a letter a few months later, Dwyer wrote to Bradman: 'As you know Pepper left Sydney a short time after the team went to New Zealand. I think Australia has lost a particularly good player, in fact an outstanding player and one who would have

---

63 Queensland Cricket Association.

been a great help to us next season, but I have no regrets in this matter as I think he would have let us in for a lot of bother by his foolishness.'

Pepper took up a lucrative £1000 offer to play for the Rochdale club in the Lancashire League, transforming himself into one of the most flamboyant characters on the English cricketing scene. He achieved the double of 1000 runs and 100 wickets three times for various clubs in the Central Lancashire League, but his cantankerous behaviour continued to be an issue, including leaving a Commonwealth XI tour of the subcontinent in 1949 early because he thought the local umpires were cheats.

From 1964 to 1979, he was one of the most popular English county umpires. Yet there was a sense of sadness, as countless teammates of high authority believed he would have been an outstanding Australian Test player — even if uncontrollable.

Instead he is remembered for endless anecdotes. He was accused of being the first master of cricket sledging. To one batsman, who had absolutely no idea when facing Pepper's wide array of spinning deliveries, he yelled at the end of the over: 'You can open your fucking eyes now, mate, I'm finished.'

During another Central Lancashire match, he appealed loudly. The umpire replied: 'Not out. It would have missed leg stump.'

'You're quite right,' Pepper countered. 'It would have missed leg stump. It would not have hit off stump either. It would have hit fucking middle stump.'

One-time Indian batsman Vijay Manjrekar wore a loud checked blazer to a game. Pepper bluntly asked him: 'Hey Manjy, did you pull that coat off a bloody horse?'

Numerous notables, including Miller, Whitington and Jack Fingleton, never forgave Bradman for forcing Pepper out of Australian cricket. Miller, who believed Pepper was the best allrounder in the world, said in his book *Cricket Crossfire* that after the incident with Bradman and Scott in Adelaide, the Test skipper should have shown some sympathy.

'I saw the [Scott] report and it finished Pepper,' Miller wrote. 'He should have been a cast-iron certainty but was not picked for the tour of New Zealand, which took place immediately afterwards. Pepper replied he had "had his chips" as we used to say in the Services. I think Bradman should have intervened on Pepper's behalf. He could have done so very easily. Surely, he had the power to save Pepper? As it was, a potentially great player was lost to Australia.'

Bob Cristofani and Jack Pettiford were other Services players who headed to the Leagues but they had more subdued lives compared to Pepper's. Pettiford had six seasons with the Kent county club as an allrounder. Cristofani's troublesome knee forced him to retire, and he later became Australian Trade Commissioner in London.

Keith Carmody's postwar life went on an unpredictable and ultimately traumatic path. The Services players discovered Carmody's life as a POW had affected him. He struggled to concentrate and his mind would wander. He had lost some of his flashiness. Innings would end prematurely as Carmody appeared distracted, combining brilliant shots with 'blind swipes'.

Carmody returned to the NSW team but soon was offside with state and Test selectors. Chappy Dwyer wrote in a letter to Bradman that Carmody had been in the Cricketers' Club of NSW complaining that the Australian selectors were out of touch, and didn't realise that their best player was Miller. Carmody was apparently abused by a club member, but continued criticising the selectors.

It was no surprise Carmody was easily lured to Western Australia, which had been at last admitted to the Sheffield Shield in 1947–48, to be the state team's inaugural captain/coach. He was an immediate success, with WA winning the title in its first Sheffield Shield season, when they were added on a restricted basis. The team took advantage of a system in which WA played four matches compared to the other states' seven and won through a superior win/loss ratio, which took priority over actual points.

But then things began to fray. Some teammates found him helpful, others distant and uncommunicative. Several were convinced he was a cricket psychologist. A cricket whisperer.

Carmody's umbrella field was an immediate success for WA, but some, like Ken Meuleman, believed it wasn't his invention but had been instead used before the war in the Melbourne grade ranks. Carmody began to bicker with the Western Australian Cricket Association over financial issues, eventually resigning as captain and state coach in late 1950.

Carmody's fame might have faded, but he was still admired by many. In 1952 Miller nominated Carmody the captain he would most like to play with, because he had a 'happy knack of getting the best out of players'.[64]

Carmody returned to Sydney a decade later, where it was evident he was troubled with depression. He became a close drinking mate of actor John Meillon. For a short period he was NSW coach, before he died in 1977.

Stan Sismey found another wicketkeeper in his way after the war, with NSW preferring Ron Saggers. But he kept persevering, playing 12 more games for the state before moving for work purposes to Scotland, where he played one game for their national team, against Yorkshire in Glasgow in 1952.

Sismey, who became a respected and astute NSW selector for 20 years, always stood his ground. When he was chairman of the NSW selection panel, Bradman wanted NSW opening bowler Alan Davidson rested from a Sheffield Shield match to be fit for an upcoming Test.

Sismey told *SMH* sportswriter Phil Wilkins that he approached Bradman and said: 'I hear you're suggesting we rest Davidson, Don.'

Bradman snapped back with: 'It's not a suggestion. It's a request.'

A request Sismey refused.

Several gave the game away straight after the Services tour, or only had the occasional game. Reg Ellis played one more match

---

64 Miller named a hypothetical XI he would 'really like to play for'. The team was Carmody (capt), Ray Lindwall, Neil Harvey, Bill Johnson, Don Tallon, Denis Compton, Bill Edrich, Doug Wright, Dudley Nourse, Tufty Mann, Frank Worrell and Everton Weekes.

for South Australia before retiring, while Ross Stanford had several first-class seasons in Adelaide. Mick Roper, suffering with appendicitis, gave it away after the Services tour, while masseur Maddison went on to work with VFL clubs and the Australian Davis Cup side.

Graham Williams opted against the India/Ceylon leg of the Services tour, but came back for the South Australian match at Adelaide Oval, taking Bradman's wicket after The Don had scored a first innings century. That was Williams's farewell game, and he soon returned to his peacetime job on the wool staff of Goldsbrough Mort & Co, where in 1946 he was transferred from Melbourne. The same year, Williams was awarded the MBE 'in recognition of his splendid services while a prisoner of war'. Memories of his feats and bravery soon faded until revived by Miller's persistence in reminding all in numerous interviews of what an important Australian Services teammate he was. One of Williams's last noble war gestures was ensuring a Russian pilot — First Lieutenant Vladimir Rhusemoff — Raz for short — became a temporary Australian. Williams met Raz, who was severely burnt in an air crash and required skin grafts, while a POW, and they became close friends. When they were released, Williams called upon the Australian Red Cross to adopt Raz so that he received the same comforts he and other Australian POWs were receiving. Williams was a constant visitor as Raz recovered in an English hospital. This mighty cricketing Samaritan died in Adelaide in 1978, aged 67.

Hassett's and Miller's cricketing careers flourished. Hassett became Test captain; Miller should have. By the time of the 1948 Ashes tour, the ranks revolved around hardened ex-servicemen.

Miller's relationship with Bradman, while respectful, was cool. The mighty allrounder wasn't happy that after the war Bradman told his Australian teammates in the dressing rooms one day they had to treat Test cricket as if it was war. This infuriated Miller. As he explained in his National Library of Australia interview, the players wanted to relax and enjoy sport, and did not appreciate Bradman's remarks, 'who I might add had been in the war for about five minutes'.

'He got out with a bad back injury, supposedly, and therefore he was invalided out of the Army, and the strange thing that happened, as soon as the war was over and the Australian Services side were coming home, Bradman's back mended rather rapidly and he played against us and made 112.'

Miller added that bowling bouncers at Bradman during an exhibition match also worked against him. 'I suppose you shouldn't throw peanuts or rotten eggs at the headmaster,' Miller said. 'He was Mr Cricket. He controlled [Australian] cricket wholly and solely.'

As for Miller's long-time teammate and journalistic partner Dick Whitington, his life went on strange trajectories. Whitington opted against pursuing law after the war, and became a sports journalist with Sydney's *Sun* newspaper, before later joining *The Daily Telegraph* and spent several years working in South Africa.

He collaborated with Miller in newspaper and magazine pieces. In tandem they wrote six books, even though Miller often joked he had never read any of them. They were primarily Whitington's work, using Miller's name for sales and promotional purposes. Miller did provide a great deal of information and background on numerous issues, ensuring the books were lively, even if at times a little loose with the facts. John Arlott described one as having a 'Runyonesque narrative'. The pair had regular bust-ups, usually over book-writing and royalty contracts, but both retained a strong animosity towards Bradman.

Whitington repeatedly wrote scathing articles about Bradman, as well as using Miller's books to criticise his former state teammate.

In 1947 Whitington argued that Bradman should retire because his priorities were all wrong. Covering the India–Western Australia game in Perth, Whitington began one *Sun* report by stating that the teams 'played cricket late yesterday in weather which would have found Bradman back in his office, buying and selling shares'.

'People will tell you I am biased against Bradman,' Whitington wrote. 'Believe them if you like, but I cannot forget five NSW sheep farmers who went 400 miles to Sydney to see Bradman in the Fifth Test last March. They paid more than 10/- each for reserved seats and sat on the asphalt footpath outside Sydney Cricket Ground while Bradman dallied over his lunch and was long overdue carrying out his promised inspection of the wicket.

'Bradman is incomparably the greatest batsman I have ever seen, which makes it all the harder to understand why he has so rarely since his early years set an example of the true spirit of cricket. Twenty years of cricket do not seem to have taught Bradman the real British Empire meaning of the word. For sheer love of the game, he would make an even greater contribution by announcing his retirement.'

Less than a fortnight later, Whitington wrote that Bradman had rudely informed the Indian Test team that South Australia had declared its first innings through a message made on the Adelaide Oval public address system.

During the 1946–47 series against England, 'Hammond, manager [Major Rupert] Howard and their team learnt from the press that Bradman had decided to bat on. The press learnt from one of the umpires and two SCG members whom Bradman informed of his decision after spending nearly three-quarters of an hour inspecting the wicket and even the sightboard with the curators.'

Whitington persistently criticised Bradman as a Test selector, especially after Miller was omitted from the Australian squad which toured South Africa in 1949–50.

Dwyer was incensed with the constant criticisms, writing to Bradman in 1951 that one Whitington piece was 'the filthiest article that I have ever read in a newspaper written by a so-called sporting journalist'.

Bradman replied that he was not taking it personally, 'because I have been putting up with such personal insults for years'.

'The article Whitington wrote about me years ago was a reflection on my personal character and probably libellous.'

He also pondered why Whitington's employers paid him, and that with Miller he had 'an unholy alliance ... that brings him lsd (pounds, shillings and pence)'.

Whitington's private life became a mess. This somewhat distinguished-looking gentleman was a philanderer. In 1956 he hit the headlines during 'dramatic divorce proceedings' after the judge, Justice Dovey, refused to suppress the name of the woman charged with misconduct with Whitington. Jean Whitington, previously Drake-Brockman, won her divorce case after it was revealed that her husband had been having an affair with a South Australian woman, Helen Matheson. Whitington had told Jean in 1953 that he would leave her 'in the best interests of the whole family', including two children.

The divorce papers reveal the relationship had been shaky for many years, with Whitington's wife refusing to live with him from around 1949, but that they spent time together for the sake of the children. Then he left her. This was followed by a lengthy court battle over alimony after she took custody of the children, and remarried.

Paying for his sons' Sydney private school education caused financial distress to Whitington, who revealed that virtually all of his limited income from writing, publishing and subediting was used to pay a mountain of bills. After a stint late-night subediting for Consolidated Press newspapers, Whitington for a time was unemployed, before joining the Department of Trade and Industry in Melbourne. His income continually fluctuated. This was a key reason why he was so prolific, writing more than 20 books, including a biography of his boss, Sir Frank Packer. He needed royalty cheques to keep himself afloat. The standard of Whitington's books wavered, and his reputation for being somewhat slapdash with his facts ultimately worked against him.

Whitington attempted on numerous occasions to ensure the memory of the Services team did not fade. In his biography of Hassett, entitled *The Quiet Australian*, he began one chapter with: 'I have waited twenty-three years in vain for a cricket-writer to chronicle the Victory Tests of 1945.'

The next 65 pages focused on that subject, even if sometimes the link to Hassett was faint and instead revolved around Whitington's personal anecdotes.

At least Whitington, a flawed character who died with few assets in 1984 aged 71, succeeded in that area. In spite of numerous participants believing otherwise, the Australian Services team has not been forgotten.

PART FOUR
VIETNAM WAR

CHAPTER 19

TONY DELL

Tony Dell was born on one of world history's most infamous dates — 6 August 1945, the day an American B-29 dropped the world's first deployed nuclear bomb, on Hiroshima.

Considering how a later war — the messy Vietnam campaign — had such a cataclysmic effect on this Australian Test representative, one would have assumed the unfortunate Hiroshima link be constantly used as a connection for this battle-damaged victim.

It's not, because in all the record books, even in the Cricket Bible — *Wisden Cricketers' Almanack* — his birthdate is different. Each one of these states that the Queensland paceman was born on 6 August 1947.

Why the discrepancy?

Simple. A young player took the advice of his streetwise skipper. When he was about to make the Test team in 1970–71, his Queensland Sheffield Shield captain, Sam Trimble, told him the easiest way to prolong a career was to manipulate your birthdate. No one would check.

'Sammy told me to make it 1947. So I did,' he said in an interview with the author.

Dell chopped two years off his age, telling all he was of 1947 heritage. Trimble was right. No one checked.

Dell is not the first Australian Test player to tell white lies about his age. 'Chuck' Fleetwood-Smith, the most deranged spin bowler Australian cricket ever fielded, did exactly the same thing. But that was part of an elaborate ruse cooked up by his landed gentry rural family to make him more acceptable to the 1930s Melbourne cricketing elite.

In Dell's case, a bid to make himself more appealing to Test selectors as a promising 23-year-old rather than a mature, possibly past-his-best 25-year-old was one of many twists in an extraordinarily mixed life that involves every emotion. Few Australian sportsmen have experienced the high level of success and depths of despair that Dell has over the past half-century. As he puts it — he's had his head among the stars, and been on 'the bones of my arse'.

Born in Hampshire, England, Dell arrived in Brisbane as a 14-year-old after his father, who served in the British Navy during the Second World War, was transferred to Queensland.

Rugby union was more of an interest than cricket for the tall teenager. He was big, gangly, towering over all, and during his teenage years at Anglican Church Grammar School in Brisbane found himself in the school rugby pack, usually as a second rower. Rugby remained such a compelling interest that some years later he played for The Rest against Queensland in a selection trial.

However, his father could see a cricketing future for Tony, organising personal pace-bowling training from Ray Lindwall. Around the time his school days ended, he was playing A-grade cricket with Eastern Suburbs, where his near-two-metre height, a lumbering action and an ability to swing and seam a ball with a high, angular left-arm action made him an immediate irritant. National Service thwarted his plans. While numerous notable Queensland identities, such as Tom Veivers, kept telling him he had the ability to make the state team, he had been called up in 1965.

'Tom had just come back from an Australian tour to South Africa, and was telling me I was a better bowler than Jimmy Hubble who was on that trip. I kept getting told this type of stuff by Shield players, and I'd be taking 60 wickets in grade cricket, but still wouldn't get picked in the Queensland team.

'Some thought I wasn't fit enough. Then I got called up for National Service, and the first thing I thought was: "Awww shit, I'm never going to play Shield cricket",' he told the author.

Dell used every excuse to get out of National Service. The army authorities refused to give him any leeway. He compromised by doing six months' training at Singleton before relocating to Enoggera, so he could play Brisbane club cricket on the weekend.

'I did three months of recruit training and three months core training, which was twice as hard, and then came back and in my first club match, I bowled all afternoon and took seven wickets. After that I went back to army training.'

He agreed to be part of the 2nd Battalion, Royal Australian Regiment, 'even though I knew they were the next to go to Vietnam'.

He even waved off an opportunity to walk away.

'We went to a jungle training centre in Canungra, and I fell down the side of a cliff. I suffered a greenstick fracture of my leg which saw me choofed off to hospital. This kept me sidelined for some time. So when we were almost due to go to Vietnam, I was called in with about half a dozen others and was told: "You're a National Serviceman. You didn't complete Canungra. So you don't have to go."

'Still I had this feeling that I had done all this work, so why not go? You felt you had to put all this training to use. Whether it was brainwashing or not from those above, I don't really know. But I went.'

His time in Vietnam with the 2RAR between May 1967 and March 1968 was traumatic. He witnessed horrendous, often nightmarish battle scenes he would never be able to forget.

'When I look back, it was Boy's Own stuff. I was a testosterone filled 21-year-old playing real war games, firing real bullets and getting shot at. It was a dirty jungle war. I saw atrocities, and experienced abject fear. You were seeing Viet Cong with their heads blown off, and all that sort of shit.

'We were on search and destroy missions in the jungle for three or four weeks at a time, going through villages, and witnessed horrible things. But you were so focused that when you'd come back into camp again, you couldn't wait to get out there again. You're fit and young, and that's the way it was. You did what you were told. I had no idea where we were going, or where we were on the map in relation to Nui Dat.[65] We just did what we had to do. You'd be jumping into a helicopter, with your legs dangling over the side, not strapped in or anything, and you'd be looking straight down at the ground below, wondering why you weren't falling out. All these odd memories.'

There were moments of abject terror, especially when close to the enemy, or forced to hide from the Viet Cong during the Tet Offensive. If he coughed or made any sound in the jungle undergrowth, he and all his mates would be killed. He didn't look upon himself as a 'gung-ho' soldier but as someone who at an immature age constantly feared he was about to die in a foreign land.

Released from the army, with no fanfare he went home to Brisbane, and 'no one wanted to talk to me about it'.

'Maybe if my family had started talking, or asking about what I had experienced in Vietnam, things might have been different. But nothing … no counselling or anything. I might as well have been down the shop getting a bottle of milk.'

Within a week, he was back at work with a Brisbane advertising agency. Due to the intense public opposition towards the Vietnam War, he had to keep quiet about where he had been. He had to bottle it all up. Vietnam War soldiers returned home not as heroes but as social outcasts, to the extent they were told for their own safety not to wear their military uniform. The stigma hurt, especially for those who had no option but to serve, and were then forced to fit back into society.

As Dell put it: 'They teach you to kill, but they don't unteach you.

---

65 Nui Dat was the 1st Australian Task Force base.

'I came home in one piece, got discharged, but I wasn't telling anyone where I'd been. The 1968–69 cricket season started, and life supposedly continued on as it had been before I left for Vietnam. It was almost as if nothing had happened.'

But on the cricket field there were significant differences.

'People would say before I went to Vietnam I was a gentle giant. That's what the papers used to describe me as. But when I came back I think I was a lot more aggressive. I was abusing umpires, abusing my own fielders if someone let a ball through and so on.'

He also had extraordinary stamina. The combination transformed Dell into a serious first-class cricket candidate.

In early November 1968 he was picked in the Queensland Colts team to play at the SCG against a formidable NSW Colts line-up which included Bruce Francis, David Colley, Kerry O'Keeffe and Gary Gilmour.

Dell was handed the new ball and it was never taken off him, bowling without change for 30.7 of Queensland's 61.7 overs, in which NSW was dismissed for 195. He finished with four wickets.

Queensland had appointed England's Tom Graveney to be their captain-coach. 'I bowled to him in the nets, got some around his throat, and he said: "I want you in the side."

'That was the start. It was still a surprise I was picked, but Queensland were looking for someone as Peter Allan had retired. In the first few matches, I didn't get any wickets, but they kept picking me.'

Queensland was certainly persevering, as Dell, who made his debut at the start of the 1970–71 Shield season, was wicketless until his fourth state game. He had bowled 78 eight-ball overs and had had 167 runs taken off him when he confronted Victoria at the MCG in December 1970 and finally snared someone. Victorian opener Ken Eastwood dabbed at a seamer, and the edge went straight to Queensland wicketkeeper John Maclean. The drought was over. Then wickets became prolific.

The turning point was against South Australia at the Gabba in January 1971. Bowling unchanged in the South Australian second innings, Dell took 6/76, his dismissals including Ashley

Woodcock, John Causby and Ken Cunningham. He didn't snare either South Australia's prized South African batting import, Barry Richards, or its captain, Ian Chappell, but they took note.

'In that Brisbane game, I had Barry and Ian dropped off consecutive balls. Then Barry came out and said I was the one he least liked facing in Shield cricket.'

Richards was quoted in an article saying that Dell was the quickest bowler he had faced in Australia: 'His first five or six overs are as good as I've seen, and his bumper can be frightening.'

Ray Illingworth's England team was touring Australia and, due to a washout of the Melbourne Test, an extra Test was added — with the seventh Test to be played in Sydney in February 1971. It was one of the most volatile internationals of all time. The build-up was dramatic, highlighted by Bill Lawry being sacked — the first Australian captain to be dropped mid-series — and replaced by Chappell.

For the final Test, the Australian selectors wanted pace bowlers to match the venom of England's John Snow, who had been instrumental in England taking a 1–0 lead after the fourth Test in Sydney. They had introduced the raw Dennis Lillee for the sixth Test, and dropped several spinners, including John Gleeson and Ashley Mallett. Dell, after just eight first-class matches, was the big experiment.

It was a bold selection, laughed at by the touring English press. The whole attack, which also included O'Keeffe and Terry Jenner, had taken only seven Test wickets. It was the least experienced Australian contingent since seven players made their debut in the March 1946 Test against New Zealand in Wellington — the first international after the war.

Some were staggered by Dell's selection, including Richie Benaud, who believed the selectors should have brought back Graham McKenzie to accompany Lillee. *The Times*'s John Woodcock said the Lillee–Dell combination was 'reckoned at the time to be the weakest opening attack ever to represent Australia'. The Brisbane newspapers were more positive, headlining his Test selection with: 'Ring a bell for Tony Dell'.

The raw pair were up to it. Dell could not have experienced a more eventful Test debut. The match went from one drama to the next, with Jenner felled by a Snow bouncer, Snow having a scuffle with a spectator that led to an infuriated Illingworth leading his team off the field, and the tourists almost forfeiting the game when for a short period they refused to return to the field. Illingworth was also constantly arguing with the umpires over whether Snow was guilty of intimidatory bowling. No Australia–England Test match had been this provocative since the 1932–33 Bodyline series.

Dell's memories of that Test? The Jenner incident in which the Australian leg-spinner ducked into a rising Snow delivery that saw him collapse onto the pitch remains vivid.

'A No 8 batsman trying to hook John Snow was pretty stupid. But that was TJ. My most lingering memory of that Test was being so nervous before the start of the game. Eighty per cent of my first three overs all went down the legside. I was bowling these big swingers, but somehow I couldn't get it off middle and leg.'

He eventually found his rhythm and accuracy, having John Edrich caught and bowling Basil D'Oliveira in the first innings. He dismissed Alan Knott, John Snow and Derek Underwood in the second for impressive Test figures of 5/97 off 42.7 overs.

'Ian Chappell always tells me that I out-bowled Dennis [Lillee] in that Test. The only problem was I only got one more Test and Dennis got about 300 more Test wickets.'

Dell had to wait almost three years for his next Test appearance. Why such an extensive delay?

'I had this long run-up … and people like Sam Trimble were telling me to cut it down, and be more economical. So I spent a winter working on a shorter run-up. It was the worst advice I was ever given. I was this young rookie and I thought all these people knew what they were talking about, but all it did was slow me down. Just the effort of trying to bowl quicker saw me strain a muscle and it wasn't until halfway through the season, I went back to the old run and was a lot more effective. But my time had passed.'

During this period, the Australian selectors opted for a 'hit and miss' policy, trying a vast array of pacemen, including Alan 'Froggy' Thomson, Alan Connolly, Ross Duncan, David Colley, Bob Massie, Jeff Hammond, Geoff Dymock and Alan Hurst before realising that Dennis Lillee and Jeff Thomson was the obvious standout partnership.

After being overlooked for the 1971–72 Rest of the World series, and seeing Colley and Hammond preferred for the back-up bowling spot in the 1972 Ashes tour, Dell was suddenly in demand when New Zealand arrived in Australia for a three-Test series that began in late December 1973. A fortnight before the Test series began, the Kiwis found Dell near unplayable on a juiced-up Gabba wicket. A Queensland victory by an innings and two runs resulted from Dell's startling match figures of 12/63 off 25.3 overs.

'At the time I had a good job in advertising, and cricket was just a pastime, a way of having fun. Then I got two lots of six-fors for Queensland, and was picked in a squad of 12 for the first two Tests. They played me instead of Max Walker in Melbourne. Then Max got the green top in Sydney the next week, and I was 12th man. I think if I played that Sydney Test I might have got a heap of wickets, but who knows?'

Dell took one Melbourne wicket, but during the Sydney Test, where he was drinks waiter, he realised it was time to move on.

'What you learn in the army is that the sectional platoon is only as strong as its weakest member. Work was now more important and I felt guilty about pissing off and playing cricket, while people filled in for me at work. I said to [selector] Sam Loxton: "I don't want to play anymore." I was 30. There was going to be a tour of New Zealand, and I was going to be away from my job. Deep down I felt guilty about that. I didn't really want to go.'

Test cricket was off the agenda, and it was assumed so too state cricket. However, Greg Chappell, now in charge of the Queensland team, convinced him to continue to play Shield cricket, with the lure being that he would accompany Thomson, who had moved from NSW.

'That was an offer I couldn't refuse.'

The pair took 93 wickets for Queensland in 1974–75. Thomson was top of the national averages with 62 wickets at 19.37, and Dell 11th with 31 at 27.35, with Queensland finishing just behind Western Australia on the Shield table. At the end of that season, he gave it away.

For a while, Dell was a highly successful director with one of Brisbane's leading advertising agencies. But his life was not as settled as it appeared. He couldn't sleep at night. He couldn't eradicate the Vietnam horror scenes from his mind. He suffered from night sweats. He hated being among crowds. If he went to a restaurant, he would have to sit with his back to the wall, usually facing the front door. He avoided small talk. He was often uncommunicative, keeping all his anxieties to himself. He admitted to being 'anti-social'. He would suffer from erratic mood swings, subjecting others to unexplainable violent outbursts. He had also married and started a young family.

To stop thinking about Vietnam, he became a workaholic. By absorbing himself in his career he didn't have time to think about the messy past. However, becoming more difficult to work with, he was sacked from several high positions at advertising agencies. One reason was that he was 'too hard on others'.

The 1990s recession led to a business collapse, and he lost everything. Now deep in debt, he struggled to be a coherent father, and his family moved away. His marriage ended. For a time he was estranged from his three children. He describes the 90s as a 'forgettable, nightmarish experience'.

After moving from 'rental to rental', he ended up in the early 2000s living in his mother's garage at Caloundra. He had fallen through cricket's cracks.

In 2007, Australia's only surviving Test cricketer to be involved in frontline battle received a telephone call.

'That year, due to my involvement with Vietnam and cricket, I was invited to an International Defence cricket challenge in Canberra. At the end of it, a couple of retired colonels asked me if I still had my medals. I said my kids probably tore them apart when they were growing up. They said I had to go and get replacements. I kept stalling, but eventually went to a Vietnam veterans drop-in centre on the Sunshine Coast to pick up my medals. We didn't talk about the medals. All they wanted to talk about is cricket, and half an hour later they said I had PTSD. I said to them: "Bullshit." I didn't believe them.

'They asked me some pertinent questions, and I gave them all the right answers. By then I was on the bones of my arse, and living in my mum's garage. My family had gone. They said they could get me a pension. I thought "good". So they sent me off to be officially diagnosed, and from there I was able to get help, because what happened in Vietnam was the cause of my PTSD.'

Consultations with psychiatrists confirmed he was suffering with stress disorder, and he was also encouraged to talk about his Vietnam experiences.

'It did take a while to overcome that hurdle.'

Some of his Test teammates were even unaware he had been to Vietnam. It was for so long a taboo subject.

In 2009 Dell was asked to speak at the International Defence Cricket Challenge awards night, where he received a standing ovation from the 400 servicemen and women in attendance. This encouraged him to go the next step by organising a foundation aimed at helping veterans overcome their personal difficulties when returning from battle. He founded the support group Stand Tall for PTS (StandTall4PTS). The 'D' for 'Disorder' was dropped to remove any stigma associated with this mental condition. The logo for Stand Tall for PTS is a lightning bolt — symbolising the impact traumatic events can have on a person's mental state. Stand Tall for PTS, which has been endorsed by numerous notable figures, including retired Chief of the Defence Force Angus Houston, was the official charity partner of the 2015 Prime Minister's XI match against England in Canberra.

The Chappells — Ian and Greg — also remain close to their scarred teammate.

When interviewed for this book, Dell had just completed a three-week road trip, promoted as the Lightning Bolt 2 Invictus convoy, through Queensland, NSW, Victoria and the ACT, visiting numerous cities and country towns with army personnel, firefighters and even a British actor, Tim Marriott, who presented a confronting one-man theatrical show called 'Shell Shock' about the experiences of a soldier who had served in Afghanistan and Iraq before suffering with PTSD. The aim of the Lightning Bolt convoy was to improve public awareness of how widespread PTSD is and to provide help and support. It was exhausting, and rewarding. Dell does it all on adrenaline, and belief. This is not a top-to-bottom, bottom-to-top story. Life remains tough.

'I've still got nothing. My only income is the pension. I have no assets. No nothing. It's all gone. But I've learnt to manage it all. I never feel depressed. I never feel sorry for myself. I do have outbursts. I've had some on this trip. But I correct it straight away. I take the adage: "I'm okay. It's the rest of the world which is out of kilter."

'That's the way you feel. You get told you're a prick but you don't know why. My wife who is now deceased used to say that I was no different to my father. My dad was in World War II in the British Navy, but he never, ever talked about it. I thought about that, and she was dead-right, he was the same as me. He suffered because he didn't talk about it.

'I still only sleep about two hours a night. At one stage during this convoy trip, I only slept two hours in 60. I just lie in bed, or get up and go for a walk. You try to think of stuff that is going to help you sleep, but it doesn't seem to come. I just can't fall asleep. At home I will get up, get on the computer, have a warm bath, do something. I do fall asleep but no longer than a few hours. I can take the most powerful sleeping pill and still only sleep an hour and a half. You have to live with it.'

It must be taxing for Dell to be continually asked to tell his harrowing story. But he does so willingly, because such a blunt public admission 'might hopefully help others get over a situation similar to what I've gone through'. He looks upon it as part of his therapy.

His is a courageous and admirable pursuit. More power to Tony Dell.

EPILOGUE

The sentiment was on the mark. But, in this relentless marketing mumbo-jumbo spin-doctor age, the delivery was astray.

It wasn't surprising that a re-enactment of the C.E.W. Bean photograph at Shell Green 86 years on by the Australian cricket team caused uproar.

Australian cricket prides itself on its thick, often oozing nationalistic streak. The Australian anthem is struck up before every Test, and the cricketers then stride onto the ground between fluttering Australian flags, many lovingly caressing the fabric on their way to fielding positions or the batting crease. Their dressing room ditty 'Under the Southern Cross I Stand', based on an old Second World War Digger drinking song, drips with crude, jingoistic Australian dinky-di-ism.

This is an organisation which knows how to push the national cause with a sometimes antagonistic edge, and fastidiously promote its successes, such as the embarrassingly rude inflatable four fingers victory sign that was placed on the official dais after Australia won the 2017–18 Ashes series 4–0.

Little wonder that when Australian captain Steve Waugh — who, unlike numerous Test players, has a deep appreciation of history and tradition — showed interest in having his team respect the past by travelling to the Dardanelles on their way to England for the 2001 Ashes tour it received overwhelming support from the game's administrators. Apart from giving thanks to those who sacrificed their all for Australia, it would act as a critical motivational spur before the most important cricket series of all.

The idea to go to Gallipoli and Shell Green to re-enact the 1915 Bean cricket match photograph came after a conversation between Waugh and Peter Cosgrove, then the head of the Australian Army.

Waugh explained in Gallipoli, where the team visited numerous important battle sites and laid wreaths at war memorials along the peninsula, that his discussion with Cosgrove had revolved around similarities between cricket and army, including camaraderie, discipline and commitment.

He wrote in his 2005 autobiography *Out of My Comfort Zone* that the Gallipoli visit was a 'true bonding experience' and 'had a profound effect on most of the squad'.

'In the limited-overs tournament (which preceded the Ashes Tests) we put to good use the increased unity we had gained from Gallipoli and dominated our matches. We elevated the aggressiveness in our play and tried to consume our opposition as quickly and ruthlessly as possible,' Waugh wrote.

A few days after Gallipoli, each squad member was asked what the experience meant to them.

Waugh wrote: 'Like many, I was moved by the words of [team physiotherapist] Patrick Farhart, who is of Lebanese descent. He said that for the first time in his life, even though he'd been born in Australia, he felt 100 per cent Australian as he stood among the trenches at the Nek. [Team coach] John Buchanan had worn his father's war medals to Gallipoli, but didn't know why. "I felt compelled to ring my (18-year-old) son, Michael, and tell him how much I love him, as you never know what might happen tomorrow," he told us. "We don't spend enough time telling our family how much we love them."'

In his autobiography *True Colours*, Adam Gilchrist recalls that on the bus trip to Gallipoli a Turkish guide became very emotional when explaining the relationship with Australia and the mutual respect that was generated from their Great War encounter.

EPILOGUE

'Coming first thing in the morning, my reaction was "give us a break" and "she's getting a bit carried away". I was soon to change my tune,' Gilchrist wrote.

On the bus trip back to Istanbul some hours later, overwhelmed by what he had seen and learnt that day, he choked up.

What caused consternation was the cricket match re-enactment. They found the exact spot, now overgrown with thick bush. Waugh took the batting role of Macarthur-Onslow, Gilchrist positioned himself as keeper, and Glenn McGrath was the anonymous bowler. Others, wearing either baggy greens or Anzac slouch hats, moved into the same fielding positions.

When the photograph appeared in the media, it led to indignation from cricket followers and historians who believed Waugh's men were milking soft publicity from what was an Australian military disaster. The only success of the Gallipoli campaign was the Australian evacuation. Many thought wearing slouch hats was mocking their predecessors. Some historians believed it was an act of subterfuge and a feeble attempt to inspire a team, in a climate of match-fixing accusations, with the resolute Anzac spirit. Cricket Australia officials even contacted historians complaining that they had been offended by being criticised.

Waugh said some years later: 'When we re-enacted the photo it was great fun, and a good way to pay respect to our past. I think it was where the spirit of Australia came from, and you can see the sacrifices the diggers made at Gallipoli. It was really almost the birth of our nation. It was where we got our character, our spirit. What we are today is born out of Gallipoli.'

Gilchrist made mention of the drama in *True Colours*.

'We toured around Anzac Cove and all the memorials. We'd been presented with slouch hats by the Australian Army, which I believe caused controversy back home. The line was: "Cricket doesn't hand out baggy green caps to anyone, so why should the Army hand out slouch hats?"'

During a short ABC *Grandstand* documentary about the re-enactment, Ricky Ponting said: 'It was really important for all of us that day to put ourselves in the position of those who were actually there fighting that battle. We tried to imagine what it was like for Australian soldiers who gave their lives for us.

'We copped a bit of criticism as a result. It wasn't so much for that photo. We had our baggy greens on in that photo, but at different times we had been given slouch hats to wear in the trenches as well. That was the one thing that really got people a little bit offside with what we were doing. They felt it wasn't for us to be doing that. Looking back now, that's probably pretty fair criticism. But it wasn't as if we went there with the plan to be in the trenches with the slouch hats. They were presented to us there and then — probably more for media reasons than anything else to make it really like as if we were there as Australians almost going into battle. So I can realise why people got upset about it. But we did what we did and thoroughly enjoyed our experience there. What was rammed home to us on that trip was just what the Anzac spirit was really all about.'

Ponting wrote in his autobiography *At the Close of Play* that the Gallipoli trip made him proud to be Australian. A few weeks after the trip he went to a Taunton tattooist to have the stars of the Southern Cross 'permanently inked on my lower back'.

The Australian team wanted to go back to Gallipoli in 2005, but Cricket Australia refused, citing budgetary reasons. Instead the players went to Fromelles and numerous Western Front sites, but, in Gilchrist's words, while 'very interesting, it did feel like we were trying to recapture a past experience through imitation'.

A lesson is gradually being learnt. Remembering and honouring the past is crucial — especially as the links between Australian cricket and war are diverse, complicated and often unexplained — but it has to be done with humble respect, and not with promotional or success-driven undertones. To truly honour those countless Australian cricketers whose lives were marred by war, it must involve difficult journeys well away from the tourist routes.

This includes making the effort to trek to where Tibby Cotter fell; find out exactly where Ross Gregory was buried; visit J.J. Ferris's grave in Durban; comprehend what Norman Callaway might have been; explore the Burma–Thailand Railway, where numerous cricketers suffered dreadfully or were buried; applaud the incredible human spirit and sacrifice of Ben Barnett, Ern Toovey and co; admire the valour of Bruce Dooland; negotiate the Kokoda Track; understand the relevance of Japanese and German POW camps; go to the Australian burial sites along the Western Front; find the cricketers buried and honoured around that most special of French rural towns, Villers-Bretonneux, which to this day with dignity treasures Australia's war efforts and where on one grave the fallen's parents paid to have inscribed *'Another life lost / hearts broken for what'*; appreciate their involvement in battles all over the world; applaud the women cricketers who played a crucial role in the Second World War campaign; construct a statue for Graham Williams at Adelaide Oval; publicise those who made enormous sacrifices; and make more of a statement about the many in creams who never came back, or just disappeared.

They deserve it.

BIBLIOGRAPHY

Newspapers and periodicals

The Advertiser
The Age
The Argus
Athletic News (UK)
The Australasian
Australian Statesman and Mining
    Standard
Brisbane Courier
The Brisbane Truth
Cairns Post
The Courier-Mail
The Cricketer (UK)
The Cricket Field
The Cumberland Argus and Fruitgrowers'
    Advocate
The Daily Herald (UK)
Daily News
The Daily Telegraph
The Daily Telegraph (UK)
The Evening News
The Herald
The Leader
The Mercury
The Mirror of Australia
Morning Bulletin
The Morvada
Narandera Argus and Riverina
    Advertiser
The Natal Mercury
The News Chronicle (UK)
The Preston Leader
The Referee (Sydney)
The Referee (UK)
The Riverine Grazier
Smith's Weekly
Sporting Life
Swan Hill Guardian and Lake Boga
    Advocate
The Singapore Free Press and Mercantile
    Advertiser
The Sporting Globe
The Star
The Sydney Morning Herald
The Sunday Telegraph
The Sydney Sportsman
Sydney Sun
The Times (UK)
The Torch Bearer (the magazine of
    The Sydney Church of England
    Grammar School)
The Weekly Times
The West Australian

Western Mail
The Winner
Wisden Cricketers' Almanack
The Yorkshire Post (UK)

Books

Adam-Smith, Patsy, *Australian Prisoners of War*, The Five Mile Press, 2014

Allen, Peter, *The Invincibles: The Legend of Bradman's 1948 Australians*, ABC Books, 1998

Baker, Jeannine, *Australian Women War Reporters: Boer War to Vietnam*, New South, 2015

Barker, Anthony J., *The WACA: An Australian Cricket Success Story*, Allen & Unwin, 1998

Barker, Tony, *Keith Carmody: Keith Miller's Favourite Captain*, ACS Publications, 2012

Barnes, Sid, *It Isn't Cricket*, Collins, 1953

Batchelder, Alf, *Only Yesterday: Don Bradman at the Melbourne Cricket Ground*, Australian Scholastic Publishing, 2007

Bean, C.E.W., *The Official History of Australia in the War of 1914–1918*, Vol I, The Story of Anzac, Angus & Robertson, 1942

Bean, C.E.W., *The Official History of Australia in the War of 1914–1918*, Vol II, The Story of Anzac, Angus & Robertson, 1935

Bean, C.E.W., *The Official History of Australia in the War of 1914–1918*, Vol III, The AIF in France 1916, Angus & Robertson, 1938

Bean, C.E.W., *The Official History of Australia in the War of 1914–18*, Vol IV, The AIF in France 1917, Angus & Robertson, 1933

Benaud, Richie, *Anything but an Autobiography*, Hodder & Stoughton, 1998

Benaud, Richie, *My Spin on Cricket*, Hodder & Stoughton, 2005

Blackburn, Kevin, *The Sportsmen of Changi*, NewSouth Publishing, 2012

Blackburn, Kevin, *War, Sport and the Anzac Tradition*, Palgrave Macmillan, 2016

Bonnell, Max, *Lucky: The Life of H.L. 'Bert' Collins: Cricketer, Soldier, Gambler*, Cricketbooks.com.au, 2015

Bonnell, Max, *Something Uncommon in the Flight: The Life of J.J. Ferris*, Roger Page Cricket Books, 2013

Bonnell, Max and Rodgers, James, *Golden Blues: Sydney University Cricket — 150 Years of the Club and its Players*, Darlington Press, 2014

Bonnell, Max and Sproul, Andrew, *Tibby Cotter: Fast Bowler, Larrikin, Anzac*, Walla Walla Press, 2012

Bose, Mihir, *Keith Miller: A Cricketing Biography*, Allen & Unwin, 1980

Bowerman, Martin, *One Test*, GTI Media, 2006

Bradman, Don, *Farewell to Cricket*, Hodder & Stoughton, 1950

Braithwaite, Richard Wallace, *Fighting Monsters: An Intimate History of the Sandakan Tragedy*, Australian Scholarly Publishing, 2016

Brear, James, *Cricket's Unsung Legend: The Jimmy Matthews Story*, Cricketbooks.com.au, 2012

Bridge, Carl (ed.), *A Delicate Mission: The Washington Diaries of R.G. Casey, 1940–42*, National Library of Australia, 2008

Brune, Peter, *Descent into Hell: The Fall of Singapore — Pudu and Changi — The Thai–Burma Railway*, Allen & Unwin, 2014

Buckridge, Patrick, *The Scandalous Penton: A Biography of Brian Penton*, University of Queensland Press, 1994

Cardwell, Ronald, *The AIF Cricket Team*, R. Cardwell, 1980

Carlton, Mike, *Cruiser: The Life and Loss of HMAS Perth and Her Crew*, William Heinemann, 2010

Carmody, Keith, *Keith Carmody on Cricket*, n.p., Perth, 1948

Cashman, Richard; Franks, Warwick; Maxwell, Jim; Stoddart, Brian; Weaver Amanda; and Webster, Ray (eds), *The Oxford Companion to Australian Cricket*, Oxford University Press, 1996

Cashman, Richard and Weaver, Amanda, *Wicket Women: Cricket and Women in Australia*, NSW University Press, 1991

Cliff, Paul (ed.), *A Sporting Nation: Celebrating Australia's Sporting Life*, National Library of Australia, 1999

Clowes, Colin, *150 Years of NSW First-Class Cricket*, Allen & Unwin, 2007

Coleman, Robert, *Seasons in the Sun: The Story of the Victorian Cricket Association*, Hargreen Publishing Company, 1993

Coulthard-Clark, Chris, *The Encyclopaedia of Australia's Battles*, Allen & Unwin, 2001

Courtney, G.B., *Silent Feet: The History of 'Z' Special Operations 1942–1945*, Slouch Hat Publications, 2002

Cramer, Richard Ben, *Joe DiMaggio: The Hero's Life*, Simon & Schuster, 2000

Cullen, Barbara, *Harder than Football*, Slattery Media Group, 2015

Dapin, Mark, *The Nashos' War*, Penguin Viking, 2014

Dawson, Madge and Rodi, Heather (eds), *Against the Odds: Fifteen Professional Women Reflect on their Lives and Careers*, Hale & Iremonger, 1984

Dennis, Peter; Grey Jeffrey; Morris, Ewan; and Prior, Robin, *The Oxford Companion to Australian Military History*, Oxford University Press, 1997

Derriman, Philip, *True to the Blue: A History of the New South Wales Cricket Association*, Richard Smart Publishing, 1985

Feuer, A.B., *Australian Commandos: Their Secret War against the Japanese in WWII*, Stackpole Books, 2006

Fingleton, Jack, *Masters of Cricket: From Trumper to May*, Pavilion Books Limited, 1990

Forbes, Cameron, *Hellfire: The Story of Australia, Japan and the Prisoners of War*, Pan Macmillan, 2005

Franki, George, *Far from Mosman Oval: Members of Mosman Cricket Club Who Served in War and Those Who Did Not Return for a Second Innings*, Mosman Cricket Club, 2014

Frindall, Bill, *England Test Cricketers: The Complete Record from 1877*, Willow Books, 1989

Frindall, Bill, *The Wisden Book of Test Cricket 1876–77 to 1977–78*, Queen Anne Press, 1979

Frith, David, *Bodyline Autopsy*, ABC Books, 2002

Frith, David, *By His Own Hand: A Study of Cricket's Suicides*, ABC Books, 1990

Frith, David, *Frith on Cricket: Half a Century of Writing*, Great Northern Books, 2010

Frith, David, *Frith's Encounters*, Von Krumm Publishing, 2014

Frith, David, *The Ross Gregory Story*, Lothian Books, 2003

Fullilove, Michael, *Men and Women of Australia! Our Greatest Modern Speeches*, Penguin Viking, 2014

Geddes, Margaret, *Remembering Bradman: Sir Donald Bradman as Recalled by Those Whose Lives He Touched*, Penguin Viking, 2003

Gilchrist, Adam, *True Colours: My Life*, Pan Macmillan, 2008

Greenwood, Michael, *The Grinsted Cup: A Cricket Tradition*, Macquarie Publishing, 1985

Growden, Greg, *Bowled by a Bullet: The Tragic Life of Claude Tozer*, The Cricket Publishing Company, 2015

Growden, Greg, *Gold, Mud 'N' Guts: The Incredible Tom Richards, Footballer, War Hero, Olympian*, ABC Books, 2001

Growden, Greg, *Jack Fingleton: The Man Who Stood up to Bradman*, Allen & Unwin, 2008

Growden Greg (ed.), *My Sporting Hero*, Random House, 2004

Growden, Greg, *The Snowy Baker Story*, Random House, 2003

Growden, Greg, *A Wayward Genius: The Fleetwood-Smith Story*, ABC Books, 1991

Haigh, Gideon, *The Big Ship: Warwick Armstrong and the Making of Modern Cricket*, Text Publishing, 2001

Haigh, Gideon, *Mystery Spinner: The Story of Jack Iverson*, Text Publishing, 1999

Haigh, Gideon, *The Summer Game*, Text Publishing, 1997

Haigh, Gideon and Frith, David, *Inside Story: Unlocking Australian Cricket's Archives*, News Custom Publishing, 2007

Ham, Paul, *Sandakan: The Untold Story of the Sandakan Death Marches*, William Heinemann, 2012

Hansen, Brian, *The Blue Boys: The History of the Carlton Football Club from 1864*, Brian Hansen Publications, 2002

Harte, Chris, *The History of the South Australian Cricket Association*, Sports Marketing Australia

Harte, Chris and Whimpress, Bernard, *A History of Australian Cricket*, Andre Deutsch, 2003

Hill, Tony, *Voices from the Air: The ABC War Correspondents Who Told the Stories of Australians in the Second World War*, ABC Books, 2016

Holmesby, Russell and Main, Jim, *Encyclopedia of AFL Footballers: Every AFL/VFL Player since 1897*, Bas Publishing, 2018

Hudson, W.J., *Casey*, Oxford University Press, 1986

Jenkins, David and Cardwell, Ronald, *No Dazzling Deeds with Bat or Ball: A Centenary History of the NSW Cricket Umpires and Scorers Association 1913–2013*, The Cricket Publishing Company, 2013

Jenkins, Peter, *Wallaby Gold: The History of Australian Rugby*, Allen & Unwin, 2003

Johnson, Ian, *Cricket at the Crossroads*, Cassell & Company, 1957

King, David, *A Famous Old Club: A History of the Brighton Cricket Club*, Brighton Cricket Club, 2017

Knox, Malcolm, *Bradman's War: How the 1948 Invincibles Turned the Cricket Pitch into a Battlefield*, Penguin Viking, 2012

Knox, Malcolm, *The Captains*, Hardie Grant, 2010

Knox, Malcolm, *The Keepers: The Players at the Heart of Australian Cricket*, Penguin Viking, 2015

Knox, Malcolm, *Never a Gentleman's Game: Blood, Boycott and Bullyboys*, Hardie Grant, 2012

Langmore, Diane, *Glittering Surfaces. A Life of Maie Casey*, Allen & Unwin, 1997

Lindwall, Ray, *Flying Stumps*, Stanley Paul, 1954

Lloyd, Peter, *A Sporting World*, WHIM Press, 2017

Macarthur, Brian, *Surviving the Sword: Prisoners of the Japanese 1942–45*, Abacus, 2005

Macartney, C.G., *My Cricketing Days*, William Heinemann Ltd, 1930

Macdonald, Donald, *How We Kept the Flag Flying: The Story of the Siege of Ladysmith*, Ward, Lock & Co, 1900

Macpherson, Dierdre, *Betty Archdale: The Suffragette's Daughter*, Rosenberg, 2002

Madden, Michael C., *The Victoria Cross: Australia Remembers*, Big Sky Publishing, 2017

Main, Jim and Allen, David, *Fallen: The Ultimate Heroes*, Crown Content, 2002

Mallett, Ashley, *One of a Kind: The Doug Walters Story*, Allen & Unwin, 2008

Marr, David, *My Country: Stories, Essays & Speeches*, Black Inc, 2018

McCool, Colin, *Cricket is a Game*, Stanley Paul, 1961

McCrery, Nigel, *The Coming Storm: Test and First-Class Cricketers Killed in World War Two*, Pan and Sword Military, 2017

McCrery, Nigel, *Final Wicket: Test & First-Class Cricketers Killed in the Great War*, Pan and Sword Military, 2015

McDonald, Neil, with Brune, Peter, *Valiant for Truth: The Life of Chester Wilmot, War Correspondent*, New South, 2016
McHarg, Jack, *Arthur Morris: An Elegant Genius*, ABC Books, 1995
McHarg, Jack, *Lindsay Hassett: One of a Kind*, Simon & Schuster, 1998
McHarg, Jack, *Stan McCabe: The Man and his Cricket*, Collins Australia, 1987
Midwinter, Eric, *The Lost Seasons: Cricket in Wartime 1939–45*, Methuen, 1987
Miller, Keith, *Cricket Crossfire*, Oldbourne Press, 1956
Miller, Keith and Whitington, R.S., *Cricket Caravan*, Latimer House, 1950
Miller, Keith and Whitington, R.S., *Cricket Typhoon*, Macdonald, 1955
Miller, Keith and Whitington, R.S., *Straight Hit*, Latimer House, 1952
Mills, Roy, *Doctor's Diary and Memoirs: Pond's Party, F Force, Thai–Burma Railway*, R.M. Mills, 1994
Moyes, A.G., *Bradman*, Angus & Robertson, 1948
Mullins, Patrick, *Tiberius with a Telephone: The Life and Times of William McMahon*, Scribe, 2018
Oakman, Daniel, *Oppy: The Life of Sir Hubert Opperman*, Melbourne Books, 2000
O'Brien, Christopher, *Cardus Uncovered: Neville Cardus — The Truth, the Untruth and the Higher Truth*, Whitehorse Range Publishing, 2018
Oldfield, W.A., *Behind the Wicket: My Cricketing Reminiscences*, Hutchinson, 1938
Opperman, Hubert, *Pedals, Politics and People*, Haldane Publishing Co, 1977
O'Reilly, Bill, *Tiger: 60 Years of Cricket*, Collins, 1985
Palenski, Ron, *c Tindill b Cowie: The Story of Bradman & New Zealand*, New Zealand Sports Hall of Fame, 2015
Pearson, Harry, *Connie: The Marvellous Life of Learie Constantine*, Little, Brown & Co, 2017
Perry, Roland, *Don Bradman: The Definitive Biography*, Hachette Australia, 2014
Perry, Roland, *Miller's Luck: The Life and Loves of Keith Miller, Australia's Greatest All-rounder*, Allen & Unwin, 2005
Piesse, Ken, *The Greatest Game: Timeless Tales from the Greats of Aussie Rules*, Viking, 2006
Piesse, Ken, *Great Australian Cricket Stories*, Five Mile Press, 2010
Piesse, Ken, *Pep: The Story of Cec Pepper, the Best Cricketer Never to Represent Australia*, Ken Piesse, 2018
Pollard, Jack, *Australian Cricket: The Game and the Players*, Hodder & Stoughton, 1982
Pollard, Jack, *The Bradman Years: Australian Cricket 1918–1948*, Angus & Robertson, 1988
Ponting, Ricky, *Ponting: At the Close of Play*, HarperCollins, 2014
Reece, Craig, *Patriotic Cricketers: From Creams to Khaki*, Bill Ram Cricket Publications, 2018

Renshaw, Andrew (ed.), *Wisden on the Great War: The Lives of Cricket's Fallen 1914–1918*, John Wisden, 2014

Richardson, Nick, *The Game of their Lives*, Pan Macmillan, 2016

Ringwood, John, *Ray Lindwall: Cricket Legend*, Kangaroo Press, 1995

Robinson, Ray and Haigh, Gideon, *On Top Down Under: Australia's Cricket Captains*, Wakefield Press, 1996

Rosenwater, Irving, *Sir Donald Bradman: A Biography*, B.T. Batsford Ltd, 1978

Rowe, Mark, *The Luckiest Men Alive: Australians in Bomber Command in Britain in World War II*, Mark Rowe, 2003

Rowe, Mark, *The Victory Tests: England v Australia 1945*, SportsBooks, 2010

Rowlands, Robin, *A River Kwai Story: The Songkrai Tribunal*, Allen & Unwin, 2007

Roy, S.K. (ed.), *Australian Cricket Tours to India*, Illustrated News, 1947

Saunders, Kay, *Notorious Australian Women*, ABC Books, 2011

Scott, John, *Caught in Court*, Andre Deutsch, 1989

Sismey, S.G., *History of the 1945 Australian Services Cricket Team*, S.G. Sismey and G.C. Pinder, 1994

Smith, Rick, *Cricket's Enigma: The Sid Barnes Story*, ABC Books, 1999

Smyth, Rob (ed.), *Benaud in Wisden*, Bloomsbury, 2015

Spurling, Kathryn, *Cruel Conflict: The Triumph and Tragedy of HMAS Perth*, New Holland, 2008

Stephenson, Paul, *A Cricket Club at War*, The Cricket Publishing Company, 2017

Swanton, E.W., *Gubby Allen: Man of Cricket*, Hutchinson Stanley Paul, 1985

Tasker, Norman and Heads, Ian (eds), *Richie: The Man Behind the Legend*, Stoke Hill Press, 2015

Tate, Audrey, *Fair Comment: The Life of Pat Jarrett 1911–90*, Melbourne University Press, 1996

Von Nida, Norman, with Robertson, Ben, *The Von: Stories and Suggestions from Australian Golf's Little Master*, University of Queensland Press, 2014

Wall, Don, *Heroes of F Force*, D. Wall, 1993

Wallish, E.A. 'Ned', *The Great Laurie Nash*, Ryan Publishing, 1998

Walters, Doug, as told to Ken Laws, *The Doug Walters Story*, Rigby, 1981

Walters, Stephen, *A Forgotten Adventure: Australia's Elite Cricketers in New Zealand 1946 — And the Belated Birth of Antipodean Test Cricket*, The Cricket Publishing Company, 2018

Waugh, Steve, *Out of My Comfort Zone: An Autobiography*, Penguin, 2005

Weate, Mark, *Bill Newton V.C.: The Short Life of a RAAF Hero*, Australian Military History Publications, 1999

Webster, Ray, *First-Class Cricket in Australia*, Vol 1, *1850–51 to 1941–42*, Ray Webster, 1991

Webster, Ray, *First-Class Cricket in Australia*, Vol 2, *1945–46 to 1976–77*, Ray Webster, 1997

BIBLIOGRAPHY

Whiting, Brendan, *Ship of Courage: The Epic Story of HMAS Perth and Her Crew*, Allen & Unwin, 1994

Whitington, R.S., *Keith Miller: The Golden Nugget*, Rigby, 1981

Whitington, R.S., *The Quiet Australian: The Lindsay Hassett Story*, Heinemann, 1969

Whitington, R.S., *Sir Frank: The Frank Packer Story*, Cassell Australia, 1971

Wilde, Simon, *England: The Biography — The Story of English Cricket 1877–2018*, Simon & Schuster, 2018

Woodward, Ian, *Cricket, Not War: The Australian Services XI and the 'Victory Tests' of 1945*, SMK Enterprises, 1994

Private letters, accounts, club and official reports

J.C. Davis, Davis Sporting Collection. Parts I and II (State Library of NSW)

E.A. 'Chappie' Dwyer, correspondence with Don Bradman, 1938, 1945–57, undated (State Library of NSW)

'Eagle Eye' West Torrens District Cricket Club newsletter

Jack Fingleton papers, 1902–1981 (State Library of NSW)

Glover family war letters (Australian War Memorial)

Robert Grieves, Account of Battle of Messines by Robert Grieves (Australian War Memorial)

Keith Miller interviewed by Neil Bennetts (sound recording) (National Library of Australia)

Larry Maddison oral interview (Australian War Memorial)

Robert J. Massie papers (Australian War Memorial)

Arthur Morris interviewed by John Ringwood (sound recording) (National Library of Australia)

New South Wales Cricket Association reports, documents and papers (NSWCA)

Bill O'Reilly interviewed by John Ringwood (sound recording) (National Library of Australia)

The Official History of the Operations and Administration of Special Operations Australia (SOA) (National Archives of Australia)

Ernest A. Toovey, For the Duration: HMAS *Perth* — The Ship That Died Fighting (unpublished)

War Crimes Tribunal hearing transcripts (Australian War Memorial)

INDEX

Note: Page numbers followed by 'n' indicate references to footnotes.

Abbotsleigh School 197
ABC Radio 193, 265
Adamson, Charles 108n
Adelaide and Suburban competition 48
Adelaide Cricket Club 48
Adelaide Oval 144, 236, 253, 277
The Advertiser 48–9, 51, 158
AFL 156
Against the Odds (Archdale) 181
The Age 95, 110, 152–3, 158
Ahmed, Imtiaz 271
AIF *see* Australian Army
Alexandria 55, 68, 147
Ali, Mushtaq 271
Allan Border Oval, Mosman 200, 253
Allan, Peter 297
Allen, Gubby 153, 157, 160, 207, 242, 245, 272–3n
Amarnath, Lala 236
Ameliasburgh 204
Ames, L.E.G. 'Les' 153, 207, 263
Anderson, Charles 172
Andrews, Tommy 28n, 133
Antonio, Peggy 185, 189
The Anzac Book (Bean) 68
Anzac Cove 57, 101, 307
Aoki, Toshio 177
Archdale, Betty 181–92, 197–9

The Argus 19–20, 23, 147, 265
Arlott, John 287
Armstrong, Warwick 28, 30, 32, 45, 67, 72–3, 87, 94, 130, 136
Army School of Physical and Recreational Training 212
Ascanius (ship) 49, 129
At the Close of Play (Ponting) 308
Atatürk, Kemal 36
Atherton, Mike 85
Athletic News 97
Atkinson, Jim 'Snowy' 156
Attlee, Clement 266
The Australasian 105, 142, 149, 265
Australia
 proposed South African tour cancelled (1914) 28–9
 vs Great Britain (1886) 13
 vs Great Britain (1887) 13
 vs Great Britain (1889) 13–14
 vs Great Britain (1903–04) 98
 vs Great Britain (1905) 96
 vs Great Britain (1907) 99
 vs Great Britain (1911–12) 30, 100
 vs Great Britain (1920–21) 43
 vs Great Britain (1926) 136
 vs Great Britain (1930) 174

 vs Great Britain (1932-33) 62–4
 vs Great Britain (1932–33) 156–7
 vs Great Britain (1934) 165, 207
 vs Great Britain (1934–35) 184–5
 vs Great Britain (1936–37) 152–4
 vs Great Britain (1937) 188–9
 vs Great Britain (1938) 159, 165–6, 174, 247, 258
 vs Great Britain (1948) 209–10, 223
 vs Great Britain (1950–51) 225
 vs Great Britain (1956) 236–7
 vs Great Britain (1958–59) 239
 vs Great Britain (1965–66) 5
 vs Great Britain (1968) 7
 vs Great Britain (1971) 7, 298–9
 vs Great Britain (2017–18) 305
 vs India (1947–48) 236
 vs New Zealand (1913) 53–4
 vs New Zealand (1934) 182
 vs New Zealand (1946) 235, 281–2
 vs New Zealand (1973) 300

INDEX

vs Rest of the World (1971–72) 300
vs Rhodesia (1957) 238
vs South Africa (1910) 53
vs South Africa (1931–32) 156
vs South Africa (1932) 143
vs South Africa (1949) 209
vs South Africa (1951) 288
vs South Africa (1957) 238
vs South Africa (1966–67) 5
vs Surrey (1910) 53
vs The Rest (1908) 72
vs The Rest (1909) 109
vs The Rest (1944) 246
vs West Indies (1952) 223
vs West Indies (1954–55) 220, 235–6
Australia/South Africa Services team 38
Australian Army
  1st Australian Field Artillery 69
  1st Australian Imperial Force 55
  1st Tunnelling Company 200
  2/2 Anti-Aircraft Regiment 247
  2/3 Australian Field Company 250
  2/8 Field Ambulance Australian Army Medical Corps 175
  2/15th Field Regiment, 8th Division AIF 200
  2/16th Australian Infantry Battalion 143
  2/27th Battalion 251
  2/48th Infantry Battalion 145
  2nd Australian Casualty Clearing Station 70
  2nd Battalion, Royal Australian Regiment 295
  3rd Australian General Hospital 41
  3rd Division AIF vs British Southern Command 74
  3rd Pioneer Battalion 121, 123
  4th Australian Light Horse Field Ambulance 103
  4th Division 89
  4th Field Artillery Brigade 73
  8th Division Signals 167
  9th Australian Field Artillery 68
  9th Battery 69
  12th Australian Light Horse Regiment 101–3
  12th Reinforcements, 14th Battalion 115
  15th Battalion AIF 82n
  15th Field Ambulance 113
  17th Battalion 116
  19th Battalion 84–5
  20th Australian Infantry Brigade 147
  21st Battalion 74
  24th Battalion 66
  33rd Battalion 37
  34th Battalion 107
  37th Battalion 88
  40th Infantry AIF Battalion 70
  47th Battalion, Citizen Military Forces 163n
  102 Howitzer Battery, 2nd Brigade 111
  AIF Reception Group 246–7, 249, 262
  AIF Services Team vs British Services Team (1941) 147
  AIF Sports Control Board 39, 116–17
  AIF touring team (1919–20) 112–38, 263, 280
  Armoured Division 217
  Army Amenities Fund 247
  Australia/South Africa Services team vs British Army 38
  Australian Anti-Aircraft Regiment 224
  Australian Armed Services vs The Rest (1941) 167
  Australian Army Medical Corps 54
  Australian Imperial Force 7th Light Horse 58
  Australian Movement Control Group 220
  Australian Services team (1945) 240–2, 246–7, 261–81, 286, 289–90
  C Company, 10th battalion 47
  First Field Ambulance 40
  Internationals–AIF match (1925) 93–4
  Original AIF Team (1939) 138
  Press Relations Unit 216
  Royal Australian Army Medical Corps 150
  Signal Corps 221
  US Services team vs Australia (baseball) 222
  vs British Army (1916) 124
  vs British Army (1917) 115
  vs Royal Air Force (1941) 161
Australian Board of Control for International Cricket 7, 22, 28–30, 34, 64, 97, 115–16, 129, 151n, 154, 261, 273–4, 276
Australian Comforts Fund 136, 224
Australian Cricket Board 7n
Australian Fighting Forces Athletic Training Championships 212
The Australian Imperial Force in Sinai and Palestine (Gullett) 102
Australian Prisoners of War Relatives Association 192–3
Australian Rules 55
Australian Services team (1945) 240–2, 246–7, 261–81, 286, 289–90
Australian/South African Services Team (1917) 127
Australian Statesman and Mining Standard 33
Australian War Crimes Board of Inquiry 164, 176
Australian War Memorial 170, 200, 262
Australian Women's Cricket Council 183–4

Bachman, Kasper 48
Backman, Annie 51

Backman, Charles James 47–51
Backman, Edward John 51
Badcock, Jack 158
Baggott, Bertha 149
Baggott, Jack 149
Bailey, Trevor 225, 237, 245
Baillie, E.H.M. 15, 162
Baker, Glen 204n
Baker, Reginald 'Snowy' 141
Baldwin, Stanley 189
Balikpapan 231
Bannerman, Charles 83
Bapaume 60, 75
Barassi, Ron 1
Barbour, Eric 28n, 38, 98, 113–16
Barbour, George 98
Bardsley, Warren 28n, 31, 83, 98–9, 134
Bardsley, William 31
Baring, Frank 28n
Barnes, Horrie 217
Barnes, Sydney 48, 210–11, 216–19, 235, 236n, 250, 276, 278, 280
Barnett, Benjamin Arthur 76n, 160, 164–70, 173, 175–9, 220, 235, 309
Barnett, Charlie 154, 157
Barnett, Ross 178
Bartlett, Ashmead 32
Barton, Victor 14
Barwick, Garfield 184n
baseball 222
Basra 191
Batavia Railway Station 171
Battle of Aubers Ridge 111
Battle of Bullecourt 108n
Battle of Fromelles 61
Battle of Lone Pine 36, 40
Battle of Messines 88–90, 107, 126, 200
Battle of Passchendaele 105
Battle of Sunda Strait 170
Bay of Biscay 204
BBC 265
Beames, Percy 235
Bean, C.E.W. 57–64, 68, 90, 92, 305
Bean, Ernie 93
Bean, John 59
Bean, Montague 59
Beans, Ernie 32
Beasley, Jack 104
Beaton, Cecil 195
Beaurepaire, Frank 122, 125

Bedser, Alec 225, 245
Bedser, Eric 245
Beersheba 96, 102, 104–5
Beersheba War Cemetery 105
Behind the Wicket (Oldfield) 114
Beldam, George 51
Belfrage, Cedric 188
Belgium 71
Belvidere Cricket Club 13
Benaud, Richie 228, 237–9, 242–3, 298
Bennett, Chester 235
Bennett, Ernest 200
Bennett, Gordon 146
Betty Archdale: The Suffragette's Daughter (Macpherson) 192
Bickley, Clarke 279–80
Big Six cricket dispute (1912) 30–1
Birdwood, William 118–19, 128–9
Birkett, Annie 106
Bishop, Billy 254
Blackham, Jack 87
Blamey, Sir Thomas 57, 146–7, 207, 245, 262, 265, 269, 273
Bodyline series 18, 62–4, 138, 156–7, 182, 216, 243–4
Boer War 11–23
    First Boer War (1880–81) 16–17
    Second Boer War (1899–1902) 17–21
Boers 16–17, 21
Bohemians cricket team 137
Bomana War Cemetery 204n
Bombay 270
Bonnell, Max 12, 18
Borneo 229–31, 234
Bournemouth 257–8
Bowman, Mary 92
boxing 142
Boyle, Harry 13
Brabant, Sir Edward 11n
Bradman, Sir Donald
    in the 1936-37 Test 152–5, 157–8
    in the 1946 Test 288
    in the 1947 Test 287–8
    in Arthur Mailey's Bohemians 137
    batting partnership with Moyle 174

on Ben Barnett 166
Bodyline controversy 62, 216, 244
Cec Pepper controversy 277–8, 282–4
dismissed by Gregory 152
dismissed by Thorn 149
dismissed by Williams 286
Donald Macdonald on 22
on Doug Ring 222–3
furious with Grimmett 159
given benefit of doubt by Scott 152
hits a century in 80 minutes 145
hits triple century against Tasmania 253
on idealism 281
Invincibles squad (1948) 174n, 223
Jack Fingleton on 216
on Lindsay Hassett 247
Moyes' friendship with 35n
plays Australian Services Team 276–8
plays for NSW in Sheffield Shield 165
Richard Robins on 214
rift with Keith Miller 209–11, 261, 286–7
as a selector 157, 175, 235, 285
suffers from fibrositis 213–14
uninterested in Malaya offer 178
war service 211–13, 286–7
Whitington tussles with 251, 287–8
Braithwaite, Dick 201–2
The Brighter Side of Cricket (Robertson-Glasgow) 148n
Brighton Cricket Club 88, 92–3, 95, 224–6
Brisbane Courier 53, 70
Brisbane Telegraph 188
Brisbane Truth 99–100
British Army
    3rd Division AIF vs British Southern Command 74
    107th Royal Horse Artillery 147

INDEX

AIF Services Team vs British Services Team (1941) 147
Air Raid Precaution squad 190
Australian Armed Services vs The Rest (1941) 167
Brabant's Horse 11, 17
Cameronians (Scottish Rifles) 190
  Imperial Light Horse 20
  Royal Scot Fusiliers 108n
  snubs Archdale and Peden 181–2
  vs Australia/South Africa Services team 38
  vs Australian Army (1916) 124
  vs Australian Army (1917) 115
  vs Civil Defence Services (1944) 246
British Empire XI vs RAAF 241–2
Broadmeadow Military Camp 54, 73
Broodseinde Ridge 74
Brooks, Tom 5
Brown, Bill 175, 206, 235, 262, 281
Brown, Freddie 225
Bruce, Stanley 246
Brunswick Cricket Club 147
Buchanan, John 306
Buchanan, Michael 306
Bull, Eric 117
Bullecourt 77, 84, 108n
Bullen, Bill 254–5
Buller, Redvers 19–20
Burma 146, 161, 196
Burma–Thailand Railway 148, 164, 168–9, 172, 178, 309
Burn, Kenny 13–14
Butler, Lionel 'Leo' 67
Byng, Julian 'Bingo' 17

Cade, Private 50
Café Monico 129
Cairns 203
Cairns Post 148
Calcutta 273–5
Callaway, Ernest 79–80
Callaway, James 79
Callaway, Norman 4, 77–86, 308–9
Callaway, Tom 79
Calvert, Clive 205n

Cameron, Ernie 118
'Camp Murphy' 145
Campbell, Gordon 114
Canungra 295
Cape Town 16
Cardus, Neville 158, 166, 211n, 278–80
Carkeek, Barlow 28n
Carlton Cricket Ground 175
Carlton Football Club 55
Carmody, Keith 'Bendy' 207, 245, 253–5, 258, 261–2, 266–7, 272, 284–6, 285n
Carr, Donald 263
Carr, Edwin 'Slip' 212
Carter, Hanson 30, 83, 87, 94, 133–4
Cartwright, Captain 218
Casey, Maie 194–5, 198n
Casey, Richard 194–5, 198n
Causby, John 298
Central Lancashire League 283
Ceylon 269, 275
Changi 150, 167–8, 171–3, 201
Changi Gaol 178
Chapman, Percy 160
Chappell, Greg 300
Chappell, Ian 7, 298–9
Charlie Walker Trophy 174
Chatby Military and War Memorial Cemetery 55
Cheetham, Albert 147
Chegwyn, Jack 215
Chipperfield, Arthur 153, 159, 174, 179
Chitty, Bob 163
Christie, Bob 145
Churchill, Winston 19, 146, 191, 207, 266
Civil Defence Services vs British Army (1944) 246
Clarke, Gother Robert Carlisle 105–7
Clayton, J.H. 32
Coates, Albert 180
Coates, Joe 14
Coburg Cricket Club 93
Cochrane, C.B. 31
Coetsee, J.M. 244
Cole, L. 157–8
Collegians Football Club 93
Colley, David 297, 300
Collingwood Football Club 74

Collins, Fred 71–6
Collins, H.L. 'Herbie' 117–20, 128–30, 132–7
Collins, V.H. 107
Collins, William 73
Colombo 191, 275
Combined Services rugby team vs NSW Colts 221
commandos 228–30
Commonwealth Department of Air 162
Commonwealth Department of War Organisation 214
Commonwealth Prime Ministers' Conference 245
Commonwealth XI teams 178, 226, 283
Compton, Denis 258, 274–5, 285n
Conan Doyle, Sir Arthur 19
Connolly, Alan 300
conscription 5–6, 27
Constantine, Learie 254, 268–9
Contemporary International XI (1939) 138
Coogan, Jackie 195
Cosgrove, Peter 306
Cotter, Albert 'Tibby' 4, 30, 62n, 72, 83, 96–111, 113, 308
Cotter, John 74, 105
Cottesloe Cricket Club 148
The Courier-Mail 243
Coward, Noel 194, 196
Cowles, William 44
Cowley, Rex 104
Craddock, Robert 243
Crawford, Harry *see* Falleni, Eugenia (alias Harry Crawford)
cricket
  administrators as recruiters 143
  AIF touring team (1919–20) 112–38
  players/administration rift prior to Great War 29–31, 94, 97
  umbrella field 254
  during wartime 3, 27–9, 31–4, 113–14, 144, 146–8, 201, 255
Cricket at the Crossroads (Johnson) 219

Cricket Australia 7n, 307–8
Cricket Crisis: Bodyline and Other Lines (Fingleton) 216
Cricket Crossfire (Miller) 283
The Cricket Field 14
The Cricketer 162, 264
Cricketers' Club of NSW 284
Cristofani, Bob 267–8, 270–1, 284
Crossman, Kathleen 42
The Cumberland Argus and Fruitgrowers' Advocate 16
Cunningham, Ken 298
Curtin, John 146, 147–9, 194, 207, 245–6
Cussen, Justice 32
Cutler, Sir Roden 7

D-Day invasion, Normandy 253
The Daily Express 188
The Daily Herald 238–9
Daily News 189
The Daily Telegraph 166, 185–7, 213, 222, 229, 287
Dale, Peggy 251–2
Dalton, Eric 156
Darcy, Les 141
Dardanelles 305
Darling, Joe 30, 72, 97
Darling, Len 152, 165
Davidson, Alan 285
Davis, J.C. 3, 39, 118–19, 134–5, 137, 158
Davis, Joe 94
Davis, Richard Harding 19
de Lacy, Hec 212
Defending the Ashes (Wilmot) 265
Dell, Tony 7–8, 293–303
Denmark 259
Dewes, John 263
Dexter, Padre 58
Diamond, Austin 29, 46
DiMaggio, Joe 221–2
Distinguished Flying Cross 253, 257
District cricket, in the Second World War 144
Dixon, Charles 110–11
Docker, Cyril 38, 117, 128, 130, 136–7
D'Oliveira, Basil 299
Dominion Post 279n
Dominions XI 254, 268–9

Donnelly, Martin 268
Dooland, Bruce 228–39, 282, 309
Douglas, Sir Ade 107n
Douglas, Johnny 48, 101
Douglas, Osborne 107–8n
Drake-Brockman, Jean 252, 289
Dublin 161
Duff, Reg 30n
Dulwich College 258
Duncan, Ross 300
Dunkirk 190
Dusseldorf 205
Dwyer, Bill 233, 284
Dwyer, E.A. 'Chappie' 175, 209, 223, 235, 282–3, 288
Dyer, Jack 'Captain Blood' 156
Dymock, Geoff 300

East India Club 160
Eastbourne 252
Eastern Suburbs Cricket Club 13, 294
Easton, Frank 252
Eastwood, Ken 297
Eden Gardens 274
Edrich, Bill 167, 207, 236, 263, 285n, 299
Edrich, Geoff 167
Egypt 49, 54, 69, 101, 113
El Alamein 175, 262
Elliott, King 212
Ellis, Reg 268, 280, 285–6
Ellis, William Webb 58
Eltham, William Cooper 68
Eltham, William Keith 68–70
England *see* Great Britain
English class system 2, 185, 238, 258
Enoggera 295
Essex Super Six 142
Evans, Ted 13
Evatt, H.V. 144, 184n, 246, 269
Evening Despatch 183
The Evening News 97
Everett, Dudley 204

Fags for Fighters 212–13
Falleni, Eugenia (alias Harry Crawford) 106
Far East Fleet 191
Farewell to Cricket (Bradman) 213–14

Farhart, Patrick 306
Farnes, Ken 158
Farrar, Frank 80
Fell, Desmond 268
Fender, Percy 38
Ferguson, Sir Ronald Munro 130
Ferris, J.J. 'The Tricky' 11–20, 308
Ferris, Thomas 12
Fingleton, Jack 22, 62, 118, 157, 159, 187, 209, 211, 215–16, 219–20, 229, 283
First World War 3–4, 27–138, 200, 309
Fischer, Tim 6
Fishlock, Laurie 263
Fitzpatrick, Kate 198
Fizelle, Florence 44
Fizelle, Rah 44
Fleetwood-Smith, Les 'Chuck' 149, 154–5, 165–6, 211, 213, 294
Folkard, Bert 28n
Football Record 142
Forde, Frank 269
Foster, Frank 48
France 65–6, 69–71, 74, 125
Francis, Bruce 297
Fraser, Lieutenant 89
The Free Lance 18
Freeman, A.P. 237
French, Major-General John 20
Frith, David 100n, 153, 160, 169
Fromelles 61, 308
Fry, C.B. 12, 149, 153, 264
Fullilove, Michael 246n

Gaba Tepe 56n, 68
The Gabba 5, 53, 99, 179, 250, 297
Gallipoli
 Bill Trenerry at 127
 C.E.W. Bean at 57–9
 Charles Backman at 49–50
 Claude Tozer at 40
 Cricket Australia refuses permission to visit 308
 dead soldiers never found at 47
 Frank Lugton at 65–6
 impromptu cricket at 57–9, 61
 Jack Massie at 35–7

INDEX

J.C. Davis on 3
re-enactment of Bean
cricket photo 306–8
Stan McKenzie at 54–5
Tibby Cotter at 101
William Eltham at 68
Game, Sir Phillip 184n
Gandhi, Mahatma 196
Garnsey, George 30n, 279
Garrett, Tom 13, 83
gas attacks 126–7
Gasmata Harbour 149
Gatenby, Lawrence 70
Gaza 102
Geddes, Margaret 214
Geelong College 247
George V, King 91, 165
Ghezireh Sporting Club 113
Giffin, George 72
Gilchrist, Adam 306–7
Gillet, Private 50
Gilmour, Gary 297
Glazebrook, William 'Woz' 103
Glebe Cricket Club 97
Gleeson, John 298
Glenelg Cricket Club 145
Gloucester Castle (ship) 55
Gloucestershire County
Cricket Club 14–15
Glover, Cecil 200–1
Glover, Fred 200–2
Goddard, Paulette 196
Goldsbrough Mort & Co 42, 243, 286
Goodchap, Charles 'Chilla' 173
Gordon Cricket Club 42
Gover, Alf 263
Gowrie, Lord 213n
Grace, Charles Butler 59
Grace, Henry Edgar 61
Grace, W.G. 14, 52, 97
Grandstand (documentary) 307–8
Graveney, Tom 297
Great Britain (cricket team)
vs Australia (1886) 13
vs Australia (1887) 13
vs Australia (1889) 13–14
vs Australia (1903–04) 98
vs Australia (1905) 96
vs Australia (1907) 99
vs Australia (1911–12) 30, 100
vs Australia (1920-21) 43
vs Australia (1926) 136
vs Australia (1930) 174

vs Australia (1932-33) 62–4
vs Australia (1932–33) 156–7
vs Australia (1934) 165, 207
vs Australia (1934-35) 184–5
vs Australia (1936–37) 152–4
vs Australia (1937) 188–9
vs Australia (1938) 159, 165–6, 174, 247, 258
vs Australia (1948) 209–10, 223
vs Australia (1950–51) 225
vs Australia (1956) 236–7
vs Australia (1958–59) 239
vs Australia (1965–66) 5
vs Australia (1968) 7
vs Australia (1971) 7, 298–9
vs Australia (2017–18) 305
vs Australian Prime Minister's XI (2015) 302
vs New South Wales (1886) 13
vs South Africa (1891–92) 14
vs South Australia (1911–12) 48–9
vs South Australia (1933) 243–4
vs Tasmania (1912) 55
vs Victoria (1936–37) 152, 157–8
vs Western Australia (1935–36) 204
Great Britain (government) 16–17, 266
The Great Trek 16
The Great War *see* First World War
Gregory, Dave 83
Gregory, J.M. 'Jack' 62n, 117–18, 120–1, 124, 127–37, 280
Gregory, Ross 4, 150–5, 157–62, 179, 308
Gregory, Syd 31, 59, 83, 132
Grieve, John 88
Grieve, Robert Cuthbert 'Bob' 87–95, 151, 225
Griffith, Billy 263

Grimmett, Clarrie 159, 185, 215, 237
The Guardian 85
Gullett, H.S. 102
Gunn, George 48, 55

Haifa 248
Haigh, Gideon 100n, 227
Hamence, Ron 174n, 235
Hammond, Jeff 300
Hammond, Wally 153, 155, 157, 207, 236, 242, 263–4, 266–7, 288
Hardacre, James 169
Hardwick, Harold 141
Harris, Lord 129
Harvey, Merv 222–3n
Harvey, Mick 223n
Harvey, Neil 223n, 285n
Hassett, Lindsay
in Australian Services Team 261–2, 267–8, 271–2, 275–6, 280
becomes Test captain 286
captains Australia against West Indies (1952) 223
captains Australian Services Team 261–2
coaxes Cristofani back onto field 271
hands captaincy to Constantine 268
informed of Iverson's decision to quit 225
on Jack Iverson 226
plays in AIF XI against British Services (1941) 147
plays in New Zealand tour (1946) 235, 281
plays in Victory Tests 267
unflappability of 169
war service 247–9
Whitington writes biography of 289–90
Hawthorn-East Melbourne Cricket Club 76n, 165, 175
Hay 78–9
Hay Cricket Association 79, 83
Hazlitt, Gerry 28n
Heath, Henry 'Harry' 117, 136
Helmrich, Jack 201
Hendren, Patsy 38
Hendry, Hunter 'Stork' 133, 136, 202

The Herald 93, 188–9, 194–6, 278
Hill, Clem 28n, 30, 72, 87, 94–5, 100
Hiroshima 293
Hirst, George 128
HMAS *Perth* 170
HMS *Ithuriel* 252
Hobart Choral Society 68
Hobart City Council 70n
Hobart Orpheus Club 68
Hobbs, Jack 48, 55
Hodgetts, Harry 213
Hodgson, Aub 221
Holmes, Errol 263, 265
Holmes, Percy 128
Hopher, J.C. 84
Hopkins, A.J. Bert 30n
Hopman, Harry 212
Horan, Tom 110
Hordern, Herbert Vivian 'Ranji' 28n, 87
Horrocks, Bill 231–3
Hosking, John 256
Houston, Angus 302
How We Kept the Flag Flying (Macdonald) 20–1
Howard, Rupert 288
Hubble, Jimmy 294
Hughes, Billy 32, 216
Hughes, Ernest Selwyn 166
Hurst, Alan 300
Hutton, Len 165–6, 225, 242, 263–6

Ikin, Jack 236
Illingworth, Ray 7, 298–9
Imperial War Museum 169
Imtarfa Military Hospital 54
India
  Australian Services team tour (1945) 269–75, 280
  Richard Casey as Governor of Bengal 195–6
  vs Australia (1947–48) 236
  vs South Australia (1948) 288
International Cricket Council 178
International Defence Cricket Challenge 301–2
International Lawn Tennis Federation 178
Internationals–AIF match (1925) 93–4

Interstate Patriotic Competition (1941–42) 144
Invincibles squad (1948) 174n, 223
Invitation team vs Air Force teams (1944) 215
Iredale, Frank 35, 83, 100, 135
Irvine, W.M. 146
It Isn't Cricket (Barnes) 217
Iverson, Jack 223–7
Iwo Jima 272

Jacka, Albert 74
Jackson, Stanley 97
Jagel 259
Japan, in the Second World War 146, 148, 161, 168–73, 176–9, 190–1, 196, 201–2, 219, 221, 229, 232–4, 260
Japanese midget submarines 216
Jardine, Douglas 62, 156, 244
Jarrett, Pat 188, 193–5, 197, 198n
Jeanes, Bill 273
Jeffreys, John 205–6
Jellicoe, Sir John 38
Jenner, Terry 298–9
Jerilderie 137
Jessop, Gilbert 190n
Johnson, Bill 285n
Johnson, Ian 151, 206, 219–20, 225, 235, 262
Johnson, Keith 261, 272, 274, 282
Johnston, Bill 223
Jones, A.W. 31
Jones, Ernie 62n, 72, 87, 94
Jones, Sammy 13
Jose, Gilbert 150
Jose, Tony 150n
journalists, in South Africa 19–20

Keane, Vivian 110
Kelleway, Charlie 28n, 31, 38, 66, 83, 115, 117–19, 136–7
Kensington Cricket Club 174
Kent Cricket Club 183, 189, 284
Kerr, John 184n
Kerville, Ben 226

Khallassa 104
Kilner, Roy 128
King, Stuart 202–4
Kipling, Rudyard 19
Kippax, Alan 80, 133
Knott, Alan 299
Kokoda Track 309
Kortlang, Bert 109
Kumar Shri Duleepsinhji, Prince 270

Ladysmith, South Africa 20–1
Lae 221
Lae War Cemetery 204n
Lagnicourt 60
Lahore 270
Lampard, Albert 117
Lancashire Cricket Club 236–7
Lancashire League 283
Lang, Jack 184n
Langmore, Diane 194
Larwood, Harold 62, 138, 244
Lawry, Bill 7, 298
Laycock, Son & Co 244
Le Havre 161
Le Peuplier Military Cemetery 111
The Leader 66
Lebanon 145
Ledward, Jack 223
Leese, Oliver 196
Leeton 137
Lefroy Football Club 206
Leveson-Gower, H.G.D. 101–2
Libya 244
Lightening Bolt 2 Invictus convoy 302–3
Lillee, Dennis 100, 298–300
Lilley, Dick 52
Lindsay, Norman 185
Lindwall, Ray 221–2, 235, 262, 276, 279–80, 285n, 294
Lion Tile Company 214
Little, Elva 219n
Lockley Primary School 252
The London Reference 97
Lone Pine 36, 40
Long, Ted 117–18, 128
Lord's 127, 241, 246, 258, 264
Lossiemouth 160
Love, Hammie 117, 136, 138

INDEX

Loxton, Sam 151, 225, 300
Luckenwalde prison camp 255
Lugton, Frank 65–7
Lush, Ginty 157
Lyons, Jack 72, 109
Lyons, John 72

Macarthur, Douglas 216
Macarthur, John 58
Macarthur-Onslow, George Macleay 58, 307
Macartney, Charlie 28n, 35, 38, 74, 80–3, 110, 114–15, 117, 124
Macdonald, Donald 19–23
Mackay, Alan 142
Mackay, Sir Iven 35–6, 270
Mackay, Jim 30n
MacLaren, Archie 82, 131
Maclean, John 297
MacMillan, Percy 18
Macnaghten, Colonel 36
Macpherson, Deirdre 191–2
Maddison, Larry 262–3, 266, 275, 286
Madras 274
Mail Cup 145
Mailey, Arthur 18, 80, 83, 112–13, 133, 137, 148n, 166, 187, 202, 213, 229
Malaya 146, 172, 178, 191
Mallett, Ashley 7, 298
Malta 54, 66
Mandalay 196–7
Manila 161
Manjrekar, Vijay 283
Mann, Tufty 285n
The Marathon (ship) 37
Margaret, Princess 2, 209
Marien, Bill 271–2, 274
Marriott, Tim 303
Marshal, Alan 51–4
Maruyama, Hajime 168–9, 176–8
Marylebone Cricket Club (MCC) 30, 48, 114, 197
Massie, Bob 300
Massie, Hugh 34, 81–2, 132
Massie, John 39
Massie, Phyllis 39
Massie, Robert John Allwright 'Jack' 28n, 34–9, 46, 114, 124, 132
Masters of Cricket (Fingleton) 118
Matheson, Helen 289

Matthews, Alec 84
Matthews, T.J. 'Jimmy' 33, 38, 87, 115
Mauretania (ship) 248
Mayne, Edgar 28n, 110, 122–3, 130
McAlister, Peter 30, 71–3, 87, 94–5, 98
MCC *see* Marylebone Cricket Club (MCC)
McCabe, Stan 62, 153–4, 158, 165, 171, 200, 215, 248
McCleery, Mr (soldier) 111
McCool, Colin 227, 235–6, 262, 282
McCormick, Ernie 159, 258
McCoy's Reach 68
McDonald, Ted 62n, 136
McEvoy, Fred 100
MCG *see* Melbourne Cricket Ground
McGrath, Glenn 100, 307
McIntosh, H.D. 'Huge Deal' 134
McKenzie, George 56n
McKenzie, Graham 298
McKenzie, Harry 54–6
McKenzie, Stan 54–6
McKivat, Chris 98
McLachlan, Elma 267
McLaren, Jack 80
McLeod, Charles 72
McMahon, William 184n
McMillan, C.G. 31
McMillan, Leslie 231–2
McWilliams. Neville 171
Meek, Jock 259
Meillon, John 285
Melbourne Cricket Club 29–30, 32, 121, 142, 202, 225
Melbourne Cricket Ground 87, 121, 145, 182, 297
Melbourne Grammar School 142, 146
Melbourne Junior Cricket Association 147
Melbourne Metropolitan Fire Brigade 213
Melbourne University Cricket Club 202
Men and Women of Australia! Our Greatest Modern Speeches (Fullilove) 246n
Menzies, Robert 143, 213, 240

Merchant, Vijay 271, 275
The Mercury 68–9, 280
Merin Road 114
Messines 71, 88–90, 107, 126, 200
Meuleman, Ken 235, 285
Middle East 143, 224, 248, 250–1
Middleton, Syd 116–17
Midwinter, Billy 12n
Miles Standish training base 257
Military Cross 35n, 114, 127
Miller, Keith Ross
  on Cec Pepper 283–4
  on Graham Williams 240–2
  on Hassett's appointment as captain 261
  hostility towards Ian Johnson 219–20
  on Jack Iverson 226
  on Keith Carmody 285
  on Laurie Nash 159n
  literary collaboration with Whitington 287–8
  in New Zealand tour (1946) 235, 281
  plays in Australian Services Team 271, 273, 275–6, 279–80
  plays in Dominions XI at Lord's (1943) 254
  plays in RAAF XI at Lord's 206, 245
  plays in Victory Tests 264–9
  plays with RAAF XI at Lord's 207
  on pressure 1–2
  rift with Bradman 209–11, 261, 286–7
  on the Victory Tests 261
  war service 1–3, 227, 256–61
  works out Iverson's delivery 225
Mills, Roy 168–9, 175, 179
Milne Bay 203
Minnett, Roy 87
The Mirror of Australia 83
Mombasa 191
Monash, Sir John 124–5, 131
Monroe, Marilyn 222
Montgomery, Bernard 'Monty' 266
Morning Bulletin 60

Morotai 219, 233–4
Morris, Arthur 220–2, 225, 260, 262
Morshead, Leslie 147
Mort, Dorothy 42–6, 106n
Mort, Harold 42
Mort, Thomas Sutcliffe 42
Morton, Bob 232
Morton, Reg 273
The Morvada magazine 103
Mosman Cricket Club 200, 253, 261
motor rallies 142
Mountbatten, Lord Louis 195–6
Mouquet Farm 71
Moyes, A.G. 'Johnnie' 28n, 35, 39, 113–14, 214
Moyle, Ross 174–5
Muir, Bonnie 212
Munro, Barbara (née Peden) 181–2, 184, 188–90, 192–3, 197, 198n
Munro, Colin 190
Munro, Colin jnr 192, 198n
Murdoch, Billy 12n, 13, 14
Murdoch, Keith 188, 194–5
Murphy, William 145n
Murray, John 117, 130, 136
Murrumbidgee Cricket Council 86
My Spin on Cricket (Benaud) 237
Mystery Spinner (Haigh) 227

Nagel, Lisle 93
The Narandera Argus and Riverina Advertiser 100
Nash, Laurie 155–7, 159, 162–3
The Natal Mercury 18
National Library of Australia 215, 220, 286
national service 294–5
National Service 5–6
National Women's Press Club (US) 194
nationalism 27, 305
New Delhi 270
New Guinea 146, 162, 203, 220–1, 223–4, 227, 248, 250, 260, 272
New South Wales
 vs AIF touring team (1920) 132–4
 vs Great Britain (1886) 13
 vs Queensland (1909) 128

vs Queensland (1915) 80–3
vs Queensland (1920) 43
vs Queensland (1939–40) 250
vs South Africa (1911) 39
vs South Australia (1940–41) 230
vs South Australia (1945) 234–5
vs Victoria (1912) 80
vs Victoria (1926) 202
vs Victoria (1939) 259
vs Western Australia 109
New South Wales Colts 4, 80, 221, 297
New South Wales Cricket Association 14, 29–32, 39, 82–3, 105, 134, 144–5, 282
New South Wales Mounted Rifles 58
New South Wales Women's Cricket Association 184–5
New Zealand
 vs Australia (1913) 53–4
 vs Australia (1934) 182
 vs Australia (1946) 235, 281–2
 vs Australia (1973) 300
 vs Victoria (1914) 121
The News 243, 251
The News Chronicle 238
Newton, Bill 259–60
Noble, Monty 30n, 42, 72, 82–3, 87, 109, 132, 136
Norman Callaway Medal 86
Northcote Cricket Club 66
Nottinghamshire County Club 237–8
Nourse, Dudley 285n
Nui Dat 296
Numurkah 137

O'Brien, Leo 154
The Observer 268
O'Connell, Tom 233
O'Connor, Clifford 117
O'Connor, Jack 30n
O'Donnell, Ron 172
The Official History of Australia in the war of 1914–18 (Bean) 61, 90
O'Keeffe, Kerry 297–8
Okinawa 272
Old Trafford 267

Oldfield, Bert 63, 104, 113–14, 117–20, 128–9, 135–8, 160, 165–7, 247, 273, 276
Oliphant, Ernest 33
Olympic Games 78, 212
On Top Down Under (Robinson) 118, 247
Onlooker 131
Oosttaverne Line 89–90
Operation Playtpus 231–4
Opperman, Hubert 198n, 213
Orange Free State 16–17
O'Reilly, Bill 136, 154–5, 159, 167, 214–15, 250, 276, 279–80
Original AIF Team (1939) 138
O'Shea, Jack 264
Out of My Comfort Zone (Waugh) 306
The Oval 189

Packer, Sir Frank 136–7, 289
Packer, Kerry 136
Packer, R.C. 137
Paddington Cricket Club 52, 80
Palestine campaign (1917) 96
Palmer, A.R.P. 216
Pardon, Sydney 52
Park, Roy 28n, 32, 117, 121, 152
Parker, Ernest Frederick 'Ernie' 107–11
Parker, Harry 110
Parkes 249
Passchendaele 74, 105, 114
Paterson, Banjo 19
Patriotic Cricketers (Reece) 76
Pearce, George 129
Pearl Harbor 144, 148
Pearsall, Alan 206
Peden, Barbra *see* Munro, Barbara (née Peden)
Peden, Sir John 184n
Peden, Margaret 184, 188–90
Pellew, Clarence 'Nip' 117, 130, 132, 136
Penton, Brian 185–7
Pepper, Cecil 247, 249, 254, 265, 268, 271, 277–8, 281–4
Perth 276

INDEX

Perth High School 108
Petersham Cricket Club 250
Pettiford, Jack 268, 284
Philippines 272
Pieta Military Cemetery 54
Ploegsteert Wood 88–9
Poeppel, George 82n
Pollard, Dick 263
Polygon Wood 113–14
Ponsford, Bill 62, 152, 202, 260
Ponting, Ricky 307–8
Pope, George 263
Port Moresby 221, 224
Pozières 40, 60, 67, 128
The Preston Leader 67
Prime Minister's XI, vs Great Britain (2015) 302
Prince Alfred College 243
prisoners-of-war
  Barbara Munro founds APOWRA 192–3
  Ben Barnett gives evidence at War Crimes Tribunal 164, 176–8
  Burma–Thailand Railway 148, 164, 168–70, 172–3, 176–7
  German POWs prepare cricket grounds 264, 267
  Germany 190, 192, 206, 241, 244–5, 255
  Graham Williams helps Russian POW 286
  impact of experience on Ben Barnett 175
  impact of experience on Ern Toovey 179–80
  repatriation of from Europe 246
  Sandakan 148, 201–2
  Singapore 150, 173, 178, 191, 201
  torture and execution of Bill Newton 260
PTSD 300, 302–3
Puckapunyal 247
Puttick, Phyll 191–2

Queen Elizabeth (ship) 257
Queensland
  vs AIF touring team (1920) 131
  vs New South Wales (1909) 128
  vs New South Wales (1915) 80–3

vs New South Wales (1939–40) 250
vs South Australia (1950) 179
vs Victoria (1926) 202
vs Victoria (1945) 175
vs Victoria (1970) 297
vs Victoria (1971) 297–8
Queensland Colts 5, 297
Queensland Cricket Association 282
The Quiet Australian (Whitington) 289–90
Quinn, Bob 174
Quirk, Joyce 234

racism 268
Ramalli, Cec 172
Ranau 202
Ransford, Vernon 28n, 30
Ransom, Henry 219n
reconnaissance units 229–30
Recorder (cricket writer) 84
Red Cross 192, 264, 286
Reece, Craig 76
The Referee 3, 39, 53, 65, 81–2, 111, 115–16, 118, 129, 131, 134–5, 137, 158
referendum, on primary producers 158
Reichman, Max 150
Reid, William 205–6
Remembering Bradman (Geddes) 214
Returned Soldiers' Distress Fund 87
Rhodes, Wilfred 48, 128
Rhodesia, vs Australia (1957) 238
Rhusemoff, Vladimir 'Raz' 286
Richards, Barry 298
Richards, Lou 'Louie the Lip' 256
Richardson, Arthur 213n
Richardson, Vic 18, 157, 179, 244, 251, 270
Richmond Cricket Club 223
Ridings, Ken 204–5, 260
Ridings, Phil 204
Rigg, Keith 151, 157
Ring, Doug 222–3, 236
Ringwood, John 215
The Riverine Grazier 79–80
RMS *Oceania* 15
Roach, Mignon 208

Roach, William 206–8
Robertson, Allen 154
Robertson-Glasgow, R.C. 148n, 268
Robertson, Jack 263
Robertson, W.F. 89
Robins, G.R.V. (Richard) 214
Robins, R.W.V. (Walter) 207, 214, 263
Robinson, Ray 23, 118, 215, 247
Roosevelt, Eleanor 195
Roosevelt, Franklin D. 194
Roper, Mick 254, 262, 271–3, 286
The Ross Gregory Story (Frith) 153, 160
Rowe, Normie 6
Royal Air Force
  Personnel Dispatch, Bournemouth 160
  vs Australian Army (1941) 161
  vs RAAF team (1944) 207
Royal Australian Air Force
  20 Squadron 203
  39 Squadron 244
  99 Squadron 160
  617 Squadron 253
  Air Force Reserve 211, 254
  Charlie Walker joins 174
  Empire Air Training Scheme 206
  Frank Thorn joins 149
  Jarrett writes propaganda about 197
  match at Dulwich College 258
  Ross Gregory joins 160
  Services games at Lord's 206–7
  Victory Tests 264
  vs British Empire XI 241–2
  vs Warner's XI 245–6
Royal Naval College, Greenwich 191
Royal New Zealand Air Force 236n
Royal Perth Golf Club 143
rugby 27–9, 294
Rugby School 58
Runic (ship) 101
Russia, in the Second World War 255

Ryder, Jack 28n, 32, 130, 202, 209
Ryrie, Granville 58–9

Saggers, Ron 260, 285
Salvation Army 184
Samuel, John 238–9
Sandakan 148, 201–2
Saunders, Jack 72–3
Scannell, Tim 109
Schofield, George 247
Scotch College 164–5, 251
Scotland, vs Yorkshire (1952) 285
Scott, Jack 153, 157, 277–8, 282–4
Second World War 3–4, 141–290
secret missions 228–39
Selarang barracks 173
Selwyn-Smith, Hubert George 70–1
Service, Robert W. 85
Sharp, Jack 69
Shaw, Alfred 13
Shea, Paddy 122
Sheffield Shield
  AIF players return to 136
  Ben Barnett plays for Victoria 175
  Bruce Dooland plays for South Australia 234, 238
  Cec Pepper plays for NSW 250
  Dick Whitington plays for South Australia 251
  Frank Sides plays for Victoria 204n
  Graham Williams plays for South Australia 243
  Jack Iverson plays for Victoria 225–6
  Keith Miller plays for Victoria 284
  postponement of (1915) 31, 83
  Ross Gregory plays for Victoria 160
  Ross Stanford plays for South Australia 256
  Stuart King plays for Victoria 202
  suspension of (1941) 144
  Thorn dismisses Bradman (1939) 149

Tony Dell plays for Queensland 293, 297, 300
  Victoria wins (1914–15) 32–3
  Western Australia admitted to 284
Shell Green 57–8
shell shock 126, 128
'Shell Shock' (theatrical show) 303
Shore 41–2, 106, 127
Shropshire (ship) 49
Sides, Frank 204n
Sidon War Cemetery 146
Simpson, Reg 238
Singapore 146, 148, 150, 161, 167, 172–3, 178, 190–1, 200–1
Singapore Cricket Club 167, 178
The Singapore Free Press and Mercantile Advertiser 11, 190
Single, Clive 103
Singleton 295
Sismey, Mrs 276–7
Sismey, Stan 160, 205n, 207, 242, 252–4, 258, 261–3, 266–7, 272, 274, 276, 285
sledging 283
Slessor, Kenneth 147
Slim, William 196
Sloss, Bruce 125
Smart, Edward 269
Smith, Len 221
Smith, Mike 5
Smith, Syd 29, 31, 94, 134, 192
Smith's Weekly 104, 222
Snow, John 298–9
Something Uncommon in the Flight (Bonnell) 12
South Africa
  vs AIF touring team (1919–20) 129
  vs Australia (1910) 53
  vs Australia (1931–32) 156
  vs Australia (1932) 143
  vs Australia (1949) 209
  vs Australia (1951) 288
  vs Australia (1957) 238
  vs Australia (1966–67) 5
  vs Great Britain (1891–92) 14
  vs Tasmania (1931–32) 156

vs Western Australia (1932) 143
South African Cricket Association 28n
South African Light Horse 17
South African Soldiers' Association of Victoria 23
South Australia
  vs Australian Services Team (1945) 277–8, 286
  vs Great Britain (1933) 243–4
  vs India (1947) 288
  vs MCC (1911–12) 48–9
  vs New South Wales (1940–41) 230
  vs New South Wales (1945) 234–5
  vs Queensland (1950) 179
  vs Queensland (1971) 297–8
  vs Tasmania (1936) 253
  vs Victoria (1896) 15
  vs Victoria (1899) 72
  vs Victoria (1906–07) 73
  vs Victoria (1933) 243
South Australia Cricket Association 144, 174
South Australian Colts 243
South Australian Cricket Association 33–4, 251, 278, 282
South Melbourne vs Carlton (VFL grand final 1945) 163
Southall, Ivan 230–1
Southern Football Association 68
Southern Tasmania Cricket Association 68
Special Duties (Dambusters) squadron 253
Special Operations – Australia 230–1
Spofforth, Fred 'The Demon' 13, 87
sport, during wartime 27–9
The Sporting Globe 15, 115, 152, 156, 162, 188, 212, 226
Sporting Life 224
Springvale Cemetery 95
SS *Ceramic* 84
St George Rugby Club 222

INDEX

St Kilda Cricket Club 162n, 202
St Kilda Football Club 203, 256
St Peter's College 108
Stalag IX-B 245
Stalag IX-C 245
Stalag Luft III POW camp 206, 255
Stand Tall for PTS 302
Stanford, Ross 252–3, 286
Stapleton, T.E. 23
The Star 182–3
Stirling, William 117, 136
The Story of Anzac (Bean) 61
Stott, Don 231–2
The Strand 101
Street, Pip 216
Sturt Cricket Club 174
Suicide Club 77
The Sun 6, 187, 287
Sunda Strait 170
The Sunday Telegraph 148n, 210
Sunday Times 85
Surrey Cricket Club 52–3, 189
Sutcliffe, Herbert 128
Swan Hill Guardian and Lake Boga Advocate 60
Swanton, E.W. 267–8
Sydney Cricket Ground 182, 188, 288
Sydney Cricket Ground Trust 105
Sydney Grammar School 98
The Sydney Morning Herald 4–5, 18, 45, 59, 62, 81–2, 94, 105, 132–3, 192, 198, 271–2, 274, 278–9
The Sydney Sportsman 83–4, 103
The Sydney Sun 114, 135
Sydney University Cricket Club 34, 39–40
Sydney University Veterans 39
Syria 145

Tallon, Bill 250
Tallon, Don 163n, 165, 170, 175, 178, 235, 285n
Tartakover, Theo 78
Tasmania
  vs Great Britain (1912) 55
  vs South Africa (1931–32) 156

vs South Australia (1936) 253
vs Victoria (1931) 156
Taylor, Johnny 117, 136
Taylor, Percy 150, 155
Taylor, Ray 110
tennis 110
Tet Offensive 296
Thai-Burma Railway *see* Burma–Thailand Railway
Thebarton Oval 239
Thompson, Barbara 160
Thomson, Alan 'Froggy' 300
Thomson, Jeff 300–1
Thorn, Frank 149–50
Tibby Cotter Walkway 105–6
Tiger (O'Reilly) 214
The Times 38, 298
Timor 234, 272
Tobruk 145, 147
Tocumwal 137
Toovey, Ern 169–73, 179–80, 309
The Torch Bearer 41
Tozer, Claude 39–46, 106n, 114
Transvaal Republic 16–17
Trenerry, Bill 117, 127, 136
Trent Bridge 159
Triangular Tournament (1912) 30–1, 59
Tribe, George 175
Trimble, Sam 293, 299
Trott, Albert 12n
True Colours (Gilchrist) 306–7
Trumble, Hugh 23, 72
Trumble, Victor 30
Trumper, Victor 28n, 46, 51–2, 66, 83, 99, 101
Truscott, Keith 'Bluey' 257
Truth 278
TSS *Karoola* 40
Turner, Charlie 'Terror' 12–14, 18–20, 83
Tyldesley, Ernest 38
Tyldesley, Johnny 97–8

umbrella field 254
Underwood, Derek 299
United Australia Party 216
United States Army
  Fifth Air Force 145
  US Services team vs Australia (baseball) 222

United States Marine Corps 145
United States Navy, Third Fleet 272
University of Sydney 197
USS *Perch II* 231

Veivers, Tom 294
Verity, Hedley 153, 158
versatility, in athletes 141
VFA 203
VFL 121, 124–5, 137, 142, 163, 206, 257
Victoria
  vs AIF touring team (1920) 129
  vs Australian Services XI 278
  vs Great Britain (1936–37) 152, 157–8
  vs New South Wales (1912) 80
  vs New South Wales (1926) 202
  vs New South Wales (1939) 259
  vs New Zealand (1914) 121
  vs Queensland (1926) 202
  vs Queensland (1945) 175
  vs Queensland (1970) 297
  vs South Australia (1896) 15
  vs South Australia (1899) 72
  vs South Australia (1906–07) 73
  vs South Australia (1933) 243
  vs Tasmania (1931) 156
  vs Western Australia (1910) 109
  vs Western Australia (1934) 152
Victoria Barracks 84, 105, 215
Victoria Cross 74, 87, 90–3, 95, 172, 205–6, 260
Victorian Cricket Association 32–3, 73, 76n, 122, 166, 223, 260, 273
Victory Medal 85
Victory Tests 242, 245–6, 261, 263–9, 289–90
Vietnam War 3, 5–8, 293–303

Villers-Bretonneux 67, 78, 309
Voce, Bill 62
von Nida, Norman 217–19

WACA 143, 184
Waddy, E.F. Mick 30n
Wagner, Peg 257
Waite, Merv 174
Walker, Charlie 'Chilla' 165–6, 174, 179
Walker, George 179
Walker, Max 300
Wallace, Edgar 19
Wallace, Johnny 221
Waller, Hector 'Hard Over Hec' 170
Walters, Doug 4–8
Wandsworth Hospital 69
war correspondents 195, 265
War Graves Commission 85
Waradgery Cricket Club 79
Ward, Frank 159, 163n
Warlencourt British Cemetery 75
Warne, Shane 239
Warner, Pelham 'Plum' 23, 37–8, 129, 160, 206, 245–6, 261, 268
Washbrook, Cyril 225, 236, 263, 266–7
Watkins, John 5
Waugh, Steve 305–7
Waverley Cemetery 46, 83
Waverley Cricket Club 83
Webster, Jim 4–5
Weekes, Everton 285n
The Weekly Times 131, 142
Wesley College 88, 93, 95, 121, 151
Wesley Old Boys 157
Wessels, Kepler 12n
The West Australian 108, 110, 143, 183
West Indies
  vs Australia (1952) 223
  vs Australia (1954–55) 220, 235–6
West Perth Cricket Club 143

West Torrens District Cricket Club 48, 230, 239
Westerland 259
Western Australia
  admitted to Sheffield Shield (1947–48) 284
  vs Great Britain (1935–36) 204
  vs New South Wales (1909?) 109
  vs South Africa (1932) 143
  vs Victoria (1910) 109
  vs Victoria (1934) 152
Western Australia Cricket Association 148
Western Australian Cricket Association 285
Western Front, First World War 29n, 35n, 39–41, 60, 67, 70, 77, 84, 107, 114, 309
Western Mail 17
Western Suburbs Cricket Club 252
White, Crawford 238
Whitington, Alison Margaret 252
Whitington, Richard 'Dick' Smallpeice 136, 247, 251, 261–3, 268, 270, 272, 280, 282–3, 287–90
Whitty, Bill 28n
Wilding, Tony 108, 110–11
Wilkins, Phil 277, 285
Willes, Christiana 198
Williams, Graham 241–5, 264, 267–8, 286, 309
Williams, P.L. 'Percy' 151–2
Williams, Spencer 243
Willis, Carl 'Smiler' 38, 117, 121–7, 130, 132, 137
Willis, Rupert 121
Wilmot, Chester 265–6
Wilmot, R.W.E. 'Bung' 265
Windsor-Clive, Archer 34
Winneke, Sir Henry 164
The Winner 92, 98, 122–3, 125–6

Winning, Charlie 117
Wisden Cricketers' Almanack 15, 52, 207, 237, 261, 268–9, 293
women at war 181–99
Women's Army 181
Women's Army Training School 195
Women's Auxiliary Australian Air Force 195
Women's College, University of Sydney 197
women's cricket 182–9, 197–9
Women's Cricket Association 189
Women's Royal Naval Service 190–2
Wood, Fred 98
Wood, Percival Barnes 'Barney' 141–3, 145–6
Woodcock, Ashley 298
Woodcock, John 298
Woodfull, Bill 63, 154, 202
Woods, Sammy 12n
Woolley, Frank 48
Workman, Jim 266
World War I *see* First World War
World War II *see* Second World War
Worrell, Frank 285n
Wren, John 73–4, 76
Wright, Doug 225, 263, 285n
Wyatt, Bob 244–5
Wytschaete-Messines ridge 88

Xavier College 202

YMCA 190
The Yorkshire Post 125
Ypres 88, 113–14
Ypres (Menin Gate) Memorial 71, 76n
YWCA 190

Z Special Unit 229–34

www.ingramcontent.com/pod-product-compliance
Lightning Source LLC
Chambersburg PA
CBHW071954290426
44109CB00018B/2018